The Roots of Rock
from Cardiff to Mississippi
and back

The Roots of Rock
from Cardiff to Mississippi and back

Peter Finch

Seren is the book imprint of
Poetry Wales Press Ltd.
57 Nolton Street, Bridgend, Wales, CF31 3AE
www.serenbooks.com
facebook.com/SerenBooks
twitter@SerenBooks

The right of Peter Finch to be identified as
the author of this work has been asserted in accordance
with the Copyright, Designs and Patents Act, 1988.

ISBN: 978-178172-266-4
ebook: 978-1-78172-273-2
Kindle: 978-1-78172-292-3

A CIP record for this title is available from the British Library.

The publisher acknowledges the financial assistance of the Welsh Books Council.

Printed by TJ International, Cornwell.

Contents

to water • Cold Mountain • boiled peanuts • Brevard • The Steep
Canyon Rangers • Steve Martin • *Foggy Mountain Breakdown*

Cemetery • the George Jones memorial • Boudleaux and Felice Bryant's last resting place • Tammy Wynette • Eddy Arnold • William Owen Bradley • Castell Gwynn, the Tennessee Castell Coch and its builder Mike Freeman

Introduction

The ends of my fingers are coming off. The tips crack. The friction ridges of the epidermis fragment and the skin starts to bleed. This is an allergic reaction and, of all things for a writer, it's to ink. Specifically it's to laser-printed documents and to newsprint. That black smear that can cover your hands when you read. In the Victorian era broadsheet news was hot ironed downstairs before delivery up. To remove the paper's creases I'd always imagined. But no. It was actually to dry and seal the ink.

I'm supposed to wear rubber gloves when I handle print but it can be so distracting. Sitting there like Donald Duck with yellow kitchen gloves holding the paper's edge. I do it. Then I don't. I forget myself. I read the *Western Mail* again, like a native, skin to print. My fingers blacken. The itch and scratch restart. I wash it off and apply one of the many creams my hopeful dermatologist has prescribed for me. But it is generally too late. Buggered again.

In the background I've got Jeff Beck playing. No longer fashionable but to my ears still absolutely on the spot. He's reviving rock and roll with great swooping guitar licks. What is this music? Where did it come from? How did it take over the world?

Back in the days when I was an aspiring guitarist I owned a copy of the late Bert Weedon's seminal guide, *Play In A Day*. Everyone owned a copy of this. I'd have it open in front of me as I attempted to strum. C, D and then the truly awful F. It was all such a painful process. The strings made the ends of my fingers ache. I read that over time the tips would thicken, like trumpet players' lips. This couldn't come soon enough. I wanted to do this guitar stuff and do it with ease. I persevered.

I'd heard The Outlaws' *Ambush* and the twang of The Shadows' *Apache*. I wanted some of that. Bert Weedon, it turned out, had actually recorded the original account of Jerry Lordan's world-stopper.

Everyone I knew, however, preferred the one The Shadows had done. Play them back-to-back today, fifty years on, and they still sound good. Yet something still remains uncool about the Weedon take. Weedon the youth worker, full of non-stop smiles. Marvin, king of The Shadows, greased back hair, craggy jaw and a vaguely underfed look.

Things are all relative, of course. Smooth, black-rim bespectacled Marvin was hardly what you could describe as a non-conformist. He wore a suit on stage and shined his shoes. But compared to session musician Herbert Weedon he was nothing short of James Dean.

The guitar and I didn't go far. I took up listening instead. On my racks I've got a copy of *Apache Mania*[1]. It's a CD that contains twenty-two versions of the great guitar instrumental sequenced one after the other. The Ventures, The Surfaris, The Jordans, The Spacemen, Les Guitares Du Diable, The Jet Blacks, The Cousins, The Shadows and then Bert himself. They all take the tune through its twangy paces. Listening to it in a single sitting is a Zen experience. You are intrigued, engaged, impressed, lost, bored, and then finally engaged again as *Apache* reasserts its crisply British sound.

The odd thing is that it is the French who have compiled and pressed this CD. Obscure guitar instrumentals of the 1960s are a Gallic obsession. In the UK we've long moved on from such things. Other than at The Shadows Club in Penarth, that is. But going there is another story[2].

With my damaged fingertips enmeshed with plaster and thick with Liquid Bandage I'm on a journey and *The Roots Of Rock From Cardiff To Mississippi And Back* tracks where it goes. It follows the music back to the American Southern States, driving in a great ellipse. It bowls through Tennessee, Mississippi, Alabama, and Georgia. It drives across the Appalachian Carolinas, both of them, and then returns to the heartland state of Tennessee that seems to go on in straight historical lines forever.

I'm tracing an obsession.

I want to find out where the material I listened to as a young man and which became the backdrop to my life came from. I want to discover where it lived. How it was. How it is. How it got there. I want to find out on the ground how the blues, hillbilly, old time dance music, bluegrass, Hank Williams country and western, rockabilly, Nashville slick and straight ahead *Rocket 88* rock and roll came about. I want to discover what drove the folk song fanatic Cecil Sharp to roam the Appalachians in search of British roots. I want to discover why it was so important that the Lomaxes, Alan and John, father and son, set out across America armed with a primitive recorder to capture the country's primitive music before it vanished. What were the components of all these musics? How did they cross the Atlantic? What parts came from England, Scotland, Ireland and Wales? Most importantly I want to discover how the magic all this became made the transition back to rain drenched Wales. How did it flow across the Bay of Tigers to manifest itself in the bright blue drape jackets of Valleys' born Teddy Boys? How did it appear amid the banjos plucked in folk clubs in pub back rooms on the Welsh capital's Broadway and Charles Street? How did it rock in the dance halls of Sophia Gardens, Cowbridge Road and Death Junction? And, in particular, how did it inform the taste of more than one Welsh generation? Mike Harries, Man, The Sons of Adam, Amen Corner, The Sun Also Rises, Edward H, Meic Stevens, The Manic Street Preachers, Cate Le Bon, Richard James, Georgia Ruth, Gruff Rhys, Trampolene, Baby Queens, Climbing Trees, and Euros Childs.

Roots. Where are they and how do they grow?

The Roots Of Rock From Cardiff To Mississippi And Back is a record of finding out. It's an expansion of the music, a delving into it and beyond it, at tangents to it, underneath it and on top.

I don't much like researching at libraries where time slows down and the world without music in my ears can be so cold. I'm not keen, either, in dragging data up in great Wiki sweeps, informational dross accumulating against my keyboard, holding me down in a clunk of ordered and numbing stats. Data: it's simultaneously the stuff and the bane of life. Fly with it and you'll crash because you're too heavy. Ignore it and you won't take off at all. But use it when you must.

I prefer to walk, that's when the eyes and the brain are most attuned. I take photographs constantly – as aide memoir, as illustration, to capture detail, to collect bits of a place's soul. I make notes. They arrive when it's raining and the pen ink smears on the notebook's pulp.

I record them speaking into my iPhone, can't decipher when I listen later, for the drumming of the air.

The Roots Of Rock is a travel book because it recounts a journey. And it is also not one, simply because it spends much space and time not actually going anywhere at all. It is full of diversions and recollections and the recounted voices and sounds of others. There are guides, opinions, casual conversations, overheards, read abouts, listened tos. Stuff recalled and forgotten stuff remembered after all.

The book starts in South Wales, in the place I come from. The Cardiff delta. The flood plain made by the three city rivers – the Ely, the Taff, the Rumney – aided ably by the Roath Brook, the Nant, and that long lost waterway, the Tan. Cardiff is not the centre of the music universe by any means but it has had its moments. Bill Haley came here in 1957 and played the Cardiff Capitol. Lynyrd Skynyrd did the same thing in 1975. John Lee Hooker was here in 1964 at a surf club on the Wentloog flatlands. Jerry Lee played Sophia Gardens in 1962. Dion wandered to the Capitol in 1964. Chuck Berry duck walked there a year later. Johnny Cash visited in 1966. Elvis never. How and why? I want to know.

The book flies the Atlantic again and again to hire cars and to drive and drive and drive. It traverses a great arc, full of plains and wooded hills. Here there are conifers, high harmonies, fields of rolling corn and rocking rhythms, flatlands bustling with the white tails of cotton, shacks and dust, bent strings, steels, overalls, Stetsons. Where you from, Honey? Cardiff, huh? Never heard of that place.

The Roots of Rock hears the music, considers its history, and sees how the disparate bits fit together. And if you keep listening for long enough, then you'll discover that they do, indeed, fit. From Cardiff to Mississippi, from the Bay to the Delta. Ain't nothin' shakin' sang Eddie Fontaine in 1958. How wrong he turned out to be.

1 • Howlin' Wolf In City Road

I've come up through the light drizzle on my blue Raleigh. I've turned the sit up and beg handlebars upside down to give the bike a vaguely contemporary, cruiser look. I'm convinced even if my peers are not. It's 1964 and such things can prey on the mind. Stay cool. Cord jacket, hush puppies, tight straight trousers, slim jim tie. Parka, fishtail, Italian insignia on the shoulder, fur trim round the hood if you can afford one. I can't. I've an old mac, belt, double-breasted, just like my father wore. I go up Albany, swing the corner into City Road. This is the land of car showrooms, places where you can get your radio fixed, and shops stacked high with used furniture[3]. There it is, my destination, Freeman's Records, full of light. There are racks holding twelve-inch covers tacked to the wall. They have listening booths. There's a woman lacquered blonde hair behind the counter. Red nails. White cardigan. Fag in hand. You could do that then.

The past is populated by smokers. In the sixties half the world streamed smoke behind them as they walked. They carried lighters in their pockets and they had that smell about them. The one you can only sense when you don't partake yourself. Balkan Sobranie, Kensitas, Senior Service, Park Drive, Woodbine, Embassy, Gold Leaf, Players Navy Cut. Their voices were etched by hacking and their fingertips were stained nicotine brown.

If that time was this time then we'd deconstruct that list of brands to trace their maritime beginnings. We'd check the tobacco for additives, density, moisture content and country of origin. We'd go out and visit the plantations. We'd review the tobacco workers' hourly rates and conditions of employ. We'd write up the fate of the mills that provided the papers and the saltpetre manufacturers whose product kept the cigarettes smoulderingly on fire. We'd investigate the tricks of the marketing men. And we'd close down those suburban corner stores that would sell you a single cigarette drawn from a packet of twenty, at an inflated price naturally, age no barrier. But back then no one cared.

Today, amid the fear that smoke drift can infect us and within five years turn our lung linings to stone, we have regulated the cigarette almost out of existence. It's heading for the same heap that holds flick-knives, DDT, asbestos, Codeine in bottles of a 100, helmetless cyclists, and contact adhesive that actually works.

These things, they are the preserve of the poor, the knuckle tattooed and hoop ear-ringed, the unredeemable ancients in bright white Asda trainers and half-mast terylene pants. We rush from them. Unless we are newly young, of course, and filled with cheap vodka, hedonistically spinning, lit fags in hand, down the night-time streets of our towns.

I'm young. In my early 60s incarnation. I have ten Consulate Menthol Fresh hidden where no one can find them, in a bag under the hedge. Cool as a mountain stream. The only brand I can cope with that doesn't make me retch. All the long-trousered boys smoke. You just have to keep up. This is a world full of big dresses, tight slacks, beehives, combs and the tail end of rock and roll. A place that'll soon be spinning with change. But not yet.

I cycle down the road that in time will become the most multi-racial in the whole of the Welsh capital, a place of itinerants and immigrants and constant shift. City Road, the thoroughfare that runs right on into the city. Home of the Park Conservative Club where men in sheepskin coats leave their string-back gloves on the counter and women with necklaces laden with charms sit on high stools. They tap their packs of Bensons with the ends of their golden lighters. City Road, land of dreams.

Freeman's Records is opposite. My bike I park in a heap against the wall. I leave it unlocked. I've never had it stolen. These are the early sixties and the world here is a different place. In the shop they know me. I'm a regular. I buy a single every week. It's about all I can afford.

It's autumn and the Tories have lost the election by a margin as thin as Alec Douglas-Home's hair. In my blossoming youth I've just discovered how socialism really works. Forget equality, that's full of smoke, if what you need isn't out there then offer money to make it so. Do that and the world will jump. Do I want Pat Boone, Mark Wynter or Craig Douglas, anodyne domineers of the British hit parade? I don't. I'm after recordings by the Wolf. I want *I Ain't Superstitious* backed with *Just Like I Treat You*. I want the Chess original.

The Wolf, how can anyone be called that? In reality he's Chester Arthur Burnett and he's been powering out guitar-led, roaring blues now for at least twenty years. I discovered him when Manfred Mann, who recorded his *Smokestack Lightning*, came to Cardiff to perform it at Sophia Garden's now long gone Pavilion. "Smokestack lightning, shinin' just like gold, don't you hear me cryin'? Stop your train. Let her go for a ride". So hip it shimmered although in reality I didn't understand a word. I wasn't inside the pavilion, either. I just couldn't afford the ticket. I was in the fresh air between the rear wall and the river where I thrilled to every note.

Manfred Mann might have been high in the British hit parade and a band which for a time were the smartest new thing on the block but they were in Cardiff as support act. They were warm up for a resilient Bill Haley, still touring, still rattle and rolling, still on stage trying to make his kiss curl work. Mann just walked on and blew him away.

The Wolf's original, recorded back in 1956, had come out over here on the Pye International label and I'd already bought my copy. I'd got his amazing *Down In The Bottom* too, cut in the distant past of 1961 when the world's highlights were Petula Clark, The Temperance Seven and The String Alongs. You paid your money and two days later the Wolf arrived. The shop assistant smiled at me indulgently. "Do you really like these songs?" You could tell from her tone that she didn't. The Wolf wasn't one of us. The sound he made was anarchic, barbarous, and electrifying, right to the core. Unreal. Unsafe. I nodded my head.

Chester Burnett, born 1910, West Point, Mississippi. Died at Hines, Illinois, 1976. Gravestone at Oak Ridge Cemetery, paid for by Eric

Clapton. But at the time I'm writing about he was still very much alive. His blues were of the city where amplification was the norm. He had his own six string Fender which he wore high above his belly and on which he'd thrash out chords. It was the nimble Hubert Sumlin who gave us those memorable soaring runs.

There were two Wolfs. The first was the electrifying shouter who roared out *Spoonful, Tail Dragger, Red Rooster* and *Going Down Slow,* staples of what was to become the British Blues. This was the singer who came here in October 1964 as part of the American Folk Blues Festival tour. In the company of the now forgotten Sugar Pie Desanto, the bowler-hatted Sony Boy Williamson and the jug blowing Hammie Nixon and his partner, blind guitar wizard Sleepy John Estes, he brought the real blues to the British stage. I witnessed all this at Bristol's Colston Hall. Wolf, the mighty Wolf, the 300-pound rival to Muddy as the leader of the blues, he stole the show. His best was on an album called *Howlin' Wolf* which had a picture of a rocking chair on the cover. We all owned copies.

The second was the earlier Wolf, the one whose rough-edged 1950s work was, now he'd found 60s fame, indiscriminately shoved out by the record companies as if it were the latest thing. The Wolf's origins, like that of so many rediscovered blues men, lay in a place where recording techniques were rather more primitive and where the things we'd all come to love – Jeff Beck rippling stretched-string leads, electric bass and a drum-driven beat – had yet to form.

In the matter of the blues time blurred as its passage became unavoidably compressed. I had the idea that everything I was listening to came from years ago. The records mostly sounded as if they'd been recorded vaguely under water. The fact the Wolf himself was there on the dusty Bristol stage fresh from laying down tracks for Marshall Chess back home in Chicago made no difference at all.

In Cardiff we had the blues in our blood. No idea just what it was but it was there rushing round our bodies all the same. The love of it hadn't come from Tommy Steele, even if he had recorded a song called *Singing The Blues*. It hadn't come from Cardiff's Shirley Bassey who sang *Blues In the Night* in the style of Dinah Shore. Nor, for that matter, had it come from the very British named-named Gale Warning and

The Weathermen. They'd made an unaccountably awful big band cover of *Heartbreak Hotel* in the style Barbara Windsor might have managed if she'd been a singer at the time. There had been loads of this kind of thing coming out of my grandfather's great wooden steam radio during my formative years. It was situated in our Ty Draw Place upstairs communal lounge. I would glue myself to it when I was allowed. I listened to Don Lang and Tony Crombie and even, for God's sake, to Lita Rosa. I suffered any amount of early rock around the block, stay awhile crocodile and beat beat that drum boogie woogie. Big Ben Boogie. Dixie Boogie. Left Hand Boogie. Even Bygraves Boogie. Honestly. We love to rock. We do. We love to Boogie. The blues, they haven't arrived quite yet.

Actually I didn't know what they were, the blues, but that didn't prevent me from having an opinion. Just like the twist in 1962. I didn't know what that was either but I won the school twist contest nonetheless. The judges, a bunch of twist fanatics if I ever saw one, sat in a line – Mr Thomas History, Miss Gregory English and the thin-faced ever so distant headmaster, Mogg Morgan. With apposite style on came Joey Dee and The Starliters' *Peppermint Twist*, part one naturally.

Felicity Jenkins and I swung at it, arms and legs flailing in a rhythm-driven free form. I ducked and dived. Shuddered and shimmied. Since I'd never actually seen anyone twisting made it all up as I went. Felicity followed my every step. By the time we'd rolled right through *Peppermint Twist* (Part 2) followed by a raft of distinctly non-twist numbers from people like Victor Sylvester, Ray Ellington and Beryl Bryden, we reached the second twist record on which the school had somehow laid its hands. This was *Mama's Doing The Twist* by old-style big band blues singer, Linda Hopkins. How something as obscure as this had ended up on the Cae'r Castell Secondary Modern record player I'll never know. But it had and it was good. Hopkins knew how to rock. Felicity and I excelled ourselves. We weaved, we wound, we swirled, we shook.

Everyone else on the floor was eliminated apart from us. I'd abandoned my jacket and in some sort of prefiguring of the future 40 years distant my shirt was flying outside my trousers in a ballooning swirl. We did a victory stalking shiver right round the dance floor to wild cheers from our assembled classmates. We were the only ones left. We'd won, God we had. What had I ever won before? A book token for a shilling for attendance at Sunday school in 1954. The prize this time was a headmaster delivered handshake, a bottle of Coca-Cola each, and recognition throughout the school that someone there from Cardiff's eastern suburbs knew how to bop.

But the blues, which is what all this is really about, what were they? Something that black men could play but white men could not. That was what the world was given to understand. Out there in the music papers argument raged. How can anyone from south London make genuine blues music? The blues are only possible if you are born in Mississippi. John Lee Hooker he can do it, he's a sharecropper's son from Coahoma County. Long John Baldry must be faking it. He comes from East Haddon, Northampton. I waded in. I sent letters to *The Music Echo, Disc, NME, Melody Maker* and the Teenage Post section of the *South Wales Echo*. I knew what the blues were, didn't I? "The blues have jazz," I wrote to *Melody Maker*. They picked that as their star letter, festooned it with pictures of the Wolf and Sonny Boy and awarded me a lp token. Delighted I exchanged that for a rare Hooker album recorded by Atco, New York and issued here on London Atlantic. John Lee was on the cover looking suitably moody. The real stuff. Baldry took exception and wrote back to the *Melody Maker* saying how could he know what the blues were as he'd only been singing them for a dozen years. He would bow, he said in a fit of vitriol, to the views of those who clearly knew more about the music than he. The maelstrom of what the blues were. The debate rolled and rocked.

The music press turned out to be a great proving ground. Rarely a week went by without a Finch letter appearing somewhere. I learned to court controversy. In life it doesn't all have to be real. Expound opinions that you don't necessarily agree with. Make it up. What's happening to that great rhythm and blues singer Ray Charles? With *I Can't Stop Loving You* he's lost his genius touch. I think it's about time *Juke Box Jury* had panellists who either liked pop music or knew something about it – get rid of the no hopers they use now. It's the loud music that makes girls scream not the singers – it's nothing to do with sex. The only authentic R&B groups in Britain come from London. Irish show bands are rubbish and they all have silly names. Jet Harris should play things that have melodies like he used to. Studio gimmicks will be the death of beat music. Brenda Lee has hits because of her girl next door appeal. I won tickets to go see her with that piece of perceptive musical analysis. A free seat and a bag of popcorn. Brenda Lee backed by Sounds Incorporated on stage at the Cardiff Capital. Support came from Tony Sheridan, Mike Berry, and those housewife-friendly smiling kings of analgesic pop, The Bachelors. Amazingly The Bachelors turned out to be not bad at all.

I was usually paid in record tokens, my early remuneration as a professional writer. At 6/8d a time these were just enough to buy a 45. This was the vinyl seven-inch single, an iconic piece of plastic first marketed by RCA as a replacement for the shellac ten-inch in 1949. They were thinner and easier to hold and considerably more durable. They might not have spun round as fast but their fidelity was good. The sound would be just like the real thing. They stormed the world. Bill Haley, Elvis and a few of their rock and roll fellow travellers were there at the time of transition. For a very short period you could go into record stores and be offered the same song in either shellac or vinyl format. Which you bought depended on what sort of gramophone you owned.

As these discs couldn't hold much more than five minutes of music songs did not last that long. The radio loved them. Short, sharp, get in and out in as fast as you can. According to Billboard the average length of a song in the 50s and at the start of the 60s was 2'20". Irresistible hooks in the first twenty seconds ensured the listener's attention. *Tutti Frutti, Heartbreak Hotel, Ready Teddy, Well Alright* – these wonders were all almost over before they'd begun. It took until 1964 when The Animals released their organ-led recording of *House of the Rising Sun* for songs with room to manoeuvre to become the norm. *House of the Rising Sun* lasted an amazing 4'31". Bob Dylan took this trend to its logical conclusion with his *Sad Eyed Lady of the Lowlands* which took up an entire twelve-inch vinyl side of 1966's *Blonde on Blonde*. This masterpiece didn't get played that much on drive time radio but who cared. Arlo Guthrie went further the following year with *Alice's Restaurant*, a talking blues which at 18' 34" lasted almost as long as a Welsh vicar's sermon. But the real blues, the genuine stuff, the abrasive, badly-recorded stomps and squeaky hollers recorded in the back woods of the southern American States, they had no truck with any of this innovation. With the blues nothing ever lasted longer than 3 minutes. They were simple, they were primitive, and they were repetitive. They got inside your skin.

The blues seeped slowly into Britain. From my outpost on the northern end of City Road I ordered Sonny Boy, Jimmy Reed, and Little Walter. Downtown amid the 12" vinyl racks at that centre of classical excellence, City Radio, albums with the world *blues* in their titles had started to arrive. *Ray Charles in Rhythm & Blues Greats* on Oriole, *The Blues Vols One* and *Two* on Pye International, *Livin' With the Blues* on Realm Jazz, *The World's Foremost Blues Singer Memphis Slim* on Fidelio High-Fidelity and *Blues In the Night* from Hal Cornbread Singer. Some of this material was actually okay. Most of it featured singers with Christian names I hadn't ever come across. In my school people were called things like Trevor, Martin, Terrence and Ronald. At Cae'r Castell Secondary Mod there was no one called Bo, Pee Wee, Sunnyland, Peppermint, or even Big Joe. The nearest we had to a blues nom de plume was the sports master and Harlequins rugby player who went under the name Cowboy Davies.

In the City Radio racks, at sale price, I discovered Brother John Sellers, Willie Wright and Big Bill Broonzy. The first two, despite having albums out with the word *blues* in their titles, were pretty poor. Big Bill, on the other hand, turned out to be something else. The album I found came from the series of Library of Congress recordings he'd made in 1957. Big Bill, the country backwoodsman, solo voice and guitar, rambling, tambling, pure blues where you could hear every word. In the listening booth at the store's rear I sat on the high stool and leant against the plywood partition. I was entranced. For once the assistant was kind. I was allowed to listen to every track.

Big Bill, who was born Lee Conley Bradley in Lake Dick, Arkansas in 1903, had risen to success among black Americans as a fully-fledged, combo-fronting rhythm and blues shouter. During the 1930s, first for

Paramount and later for Bluebird and to the accompaniment of piano, saxophone and drums Broonzy knocked out dance music and rocking blues in the black clubs of New York and Chicago. Robert Hammond thought him good enough to have him substitute for the recently deceased Robert Johnson at the seminal 1938 *Spirituals to Swing* concert at Carnegie Hall. This was an early and, as it turned out, highly successful attempt to bring black American music over to white audiences. Broonzy, asked to take the role of a Mississippi backwoodsman played the part to perfection. One man one guitar. *Louise Louise, Done Got Wise, In The Evening When The Sun Goes Down* – rhythm and blues classics delivered as 12-bar folk. He went down a storm.

Spotting a good market when he saw one Big Bill gave up his Chicago sophistication, donned a pair of bibbed denim overalls and became just what white audiences wanted to see – a traditional black country blues singer. On the back of the European folk revival he was brought to Britain in the early 1950s by promoter Chris Barber. Big Bill the genuine article. One man and one guitar. The blues ain't nothing but. He died of lung cancer in 1958. By the time I got to his records he was history.

Big Bill opened my ears to tales of the American South– floods, railroads, whiskey, misery and women. His mamas would rock. They had great big legs and they caught southbound trains. They were called Willie Mae and Louise and Alberta. They never did Big Bill right and they always ended up gone. How could I relate to this? None of the women I fancied had any fat on them, this being shortage-ridden early post-War Britain. None of them rocked for that matter, not that I was really quite sure just what that meant. And mama, well she was usually back home making us meatless dumplings for dinner.

The blues were full of things we didn't have around here. Mojos, Little John the Conquerors, black cat bones, crawdads, cotton pickers, and hollerin' in time to swinging hammers. Big Bill made it all float over a fluidly played acoustic guitar. Compared to the amplified twang of Duane Eddy Big Bill's acoustic mastery was a revelation. This man didn't just play tunes or strum a rhythm he did the whole composite thing. His up-tempo instrumental boogie wobble tagged onto the end of the classic *Joe Turner Blues* was about the best bit of guitar work I'd heard. Until I came across Davy Graham's *Angi*, that is, but that's for later.

This music had roots, that was for sure. And they were not mine, at least I didn't think they were. Somehow or other this music had evolved from sources that did not include insurance salesmen with home counties accents, the Royal Family, Churchill, Nye Bevan, Owain Glyndwr, the Light Programme, valley's choirs, Welsh coal mines, endless drizzle and pale bitter beer.

In Womanby Street, that most ancient of Cardiff streets, stood a bulwark of old fashioned value – a safe, sure, rule-following place where they wouldn't let you in unless you were both a member and wearing a jacket and tie. This was the British Legion Club. The Royal British Legion, founded in 1921, organiser of the annual poppy appeal, and a bastion for ex-servicemen and women of which in the city at this time there were a goodly number. The Legion's premises were large and leaky and they cost a lot to keep up. To balance the books they rented out space. In 1964 their largest room, which had a small stage at one end, had been leased by the Middle Eight Jazz Club. This was a home for sensible mainstream local jazz with fans who smoked pipes and wore sleeveless knitted jumpers. Music came from the residents, The Tim Watcher Jump Band. They featured trumpet, clarinet, two saxes and one trombone. There was nothing electric and there were certainly no guitars.

Revolution came when the Middle Eight, as part of its policy to bring in guest jazzers to the city, booked the diamond earring wearing boogie pianist from New Orleans, Champion Jack Dupree. Dupree's background was as exotic as they come. He was an ex-boxer who had a father from the Belgian Congo and mother who was a Cherokee Indian. He'd honed his blues piano in Chicago in the company of Leroy Carr and Scrapper Blackwell. He'd found Europe congenial and had settled in Switzerland. On this side of the Atlantic we liked his music and we paid more than they did back home. At the Middle Eight he was introduced as a jazz pianist but the hip among us knew that actually he was a black American blues singer from Louisiana. The pipe-smokers were joined by great crowds of dope-using youths wearing parkas and Mod jackets. "There are some of you here smoking

Mary Jane," announced the club's MC in a strained voice. "You'll have to stop that or we'll be all asked to leave." The audience cheered.

Champion Jack came on and went straight into a sequence of rocking piano blues delivered with verve and considerable style. *Junker's Blues, Shake Baby Shake, Mean Old Frisco, Rock the Boogie Woogie*, and *How Long, How Long*. As long as it takes, I guess. People bought him pints and he stacked them along the top of his piano. The joint was rocking, certainly was.

At ten o'clock, for reasons of which no one is quite sure, a blazer wearing Legion official came on stage just as Champion Jack was pulling his ever-rolling set to a tumultuous climax. "You'll have to stop," he proclaimed. "Our licence doesn't allow for this." He waved vaguely in the direction of the rocking Champion Jack. The pianist was giving off a wide white-toothed smile and rippling his dexterous hands from one end of the keyboard to the other. "Mama don't allow," sang Jack, boogie woogie foot stomp, smile, "no piano playing round here." We were all on our feet. There was loads of applause. These blues, even delivered on an old fashioned piano, weren't they terrific. Then the lights went out. The Middle Eight Jazz club moved across the city to what was to become the Moon Club not long after that.

Down on the flatlands, the levels, where if South Wales had a delta then this would be it, a surf club in a crumbling warehouse on the outskirts of Newport was hosting a Waikiki waxing your surfboard Beach Boys recycled rock and roll night. Surf music, an early Beatle-era American import designed to lift the endless Welsh greyness and replace it with big smiling joy was high in the charts. Some of us in town had been seen wearing brightly coloured shirts. There was a move in the sealess suburbs to have surfboards leaning casually against garden sheds and the Morris Minor Estate, doubling as a surfer's woodie[4], had become highly desirable. I was at the Newport club expecting to hear the local bands bashing out slightly off key versions of *Surfing USA, Surfing Safari*, and *Surf City*. Instead, amazingly, what the Hawaiian-shirt wearing resident band played was electric guitar led rhythm and blues.

It was a cramped place with everyone standing shoulder to shoulder. Most of the audience were smoking and half of them were tensed up tight on bombers. On came the special guest. A thin, handsome-faced, suit-wearing black man with close-cropped hair and a guitar slung around his neck. He plugged in and began to beat out a rhythm. I'd heard this stuff before, on record, the Animals did it and so did Canned Heat. Electrifying, exhilarating material. Blues wrapped in a primitive sheet but with power underneath. "I love the way you walk. I like the way you switch. You my babe, I got my eyes on you. You got Dimples on your jaw". John Lee Hooker.

The crowd surged forward almost jostling our man off the tiny stage. Amid a sea of coloured parrots and pictures of pineapples the mike swung away from Hooker's mouth. He flicked it back with a confident gesture, pointing first at it and then at himself. I'm in charge. Boom Boom. He was.

In a sense Hooker, primitive though his music often sounded to our beat music ears, was the link. He merged the faux country blues of Big Bill Broonzy with the full-blooded electric band sound of Chicago R&B as exemplified to perfection by Wolf and Muddy. With its walking bass his guitar work held echoes of not only the boogie pianists but the finger work and chords of Robert Johnson, Blind Lemon Jefferson and Charley Patton. The age of scratchy recordings, muffled guitar and screeching harmonica was that much nearer with Hooker.

But in the context I was hearing him – band-fronting, hollering, guitar wielding – Hooker came over as a blues machine of rocking sophistication. *Boogie Chillen* never sounded so good as it did then with the South Wales crowd milling around it. Hooker was to inspire a whole way of playing the electric blues. One where the twelve bars of the blues actually often got by on less than a dozen, where rhythms stopped and started at will, lead runs flicked and flipped as their creator chose and one where accompanying musicians had considerable trouble following the master's line.

Boogie Chillen, his first hit from way back in 1948 would follow me around for the rest of my music listening life. From that original high-voiced solo version recorded for Modern where Hooker beats out an irregular but completely compelling rhythm; through the mass-market 1952 version recorded for Chess as *Walking The Boogie* and featuring an over-dubbed speeded-up guitar part pasted back into the middle; to the thoroughly thumping and greatly extended version recorded as *Boogie Chillen No 2* with a rocking Canned Heat in 1971.

"I was laying down one night and I heard mama and poppa talking. I heard poppa tell mama, let that boy boogie woogie. It's in him and it's got to come out. I felt so good. I felt so good. I wanna do the boogie woogie," sang Hooker. I felt like that too.

Hooker's SouthWales appearance seems to have vanished from race memory and hasn't contributed much to our collective consciousness. Hooker sang in Wales? He did. What worked here in the place where the industrial valleys tipped themselves into sea wasn't so much Jimmy Reed and John Lee Hooker but Elvis and Jerry Lee. Long after the rest of the western world had turned away from rock and roll the SouthWelsh teds were still bopping. But I'm getting ahead of things.

I got back home from Newport and put *The Blues Vol One*, my much-cherished compilation on Pye International onto the Dansette. And there it was – somewhere between Little Walter's *My Babe* and Muddy Waters' *Hoochie Coochie* – Hooker's *Walkin' The Boogie* complete with that high speed guitar part which made my teeth rattle. Bliss.

2 • Back In The 1950s UK

There's a photo of me in one of the family albums taken in 1961. I'm sitting in an armchair with my hair brylcreamed back like Cliff Richard's. Although you can't see it I have that mark of the real cool cat, a steel comb, in my back pocket. I'm at Ralph Thomas's house in the heart of Roath. Ralph's parents are fervent Plymouth Brethren. They have little truck with fashionable hair. They clap in rhythm and they gospel chant. Most days they attend services. Round here in East Cardiff you just can't get enough of the Lord. On Sundays praising Him is all Ralph does.

In an arc around me are displayed LP sleeves from the 1950s. Pat Boone's *Hymns We Love*, Bobby Darin's *The Bobby Darin Story*, then *Pat Boone Sings*. Just out of shot, stacked against his parents' shiny walnut radiogram, are orchestral discs by Mantovani and Cyril Stapleton, Sing Alongs with Max Bygraves and sweet and heavenly dancing with Guy Lombardo. On the covers everyone smiles. The world here is in glorious High Fidelity. The oily face of Lombardo, dinner jacket, black bow tie, his hand wielding an overlong baton, leers out of his album's Capitol cover. Ralph's parents were hot on this tosh.

"What on earth is high fidelity," I'd asked Ralph? "No idea," he'd replied.

We'd taken the shot on Ralph's Brownie Box camera. Photographs in those days were rare things. This picture of ours with the album sleeves was an attempt to have some of music's inherent hipness rub off on newly teenage us. The 1950s, the decade of balloon skirts, swirling petticoats, Blue Nun and austerity, has just drawn to a close. The new world is arriving fast. Moon rockets, teenagers, the hit parade.

Rock and roll in its Bill Haley manifestation has rocked the joint since 1955. Now change was imminent. We all felt we were on the edge of something. You could feel it in the air. We wanted to be there when it happened.

Nobody I knew could afford LPs. Ralph and I poured over the ones his parents owned as if they were alien artefacts just arrived from Mars. We held them out and marvelled at how narrow the tracks were. We made the light from the front room window bounce off their sexy black microgrooves. One day soon we too would own wonders like these. Did we then play the ones we held in our hands and be overcome by Pat Boone's diction or Cyril Stapleton's saccharine swing? We did not.

"We'll wear the stylus out," said Ralph. "My father checks these things and he'll know if it's been used." 1950s radiogram owners watched their styli like hawks. Sapphire wore down. Diamonds were forever. It was always a great occasion when one was replaced. Sapphire were affordable. Diamond cost the earth. Suddenly your entire record collection took on a renewed sonic life as the bright new chiselled point slipped its micro way along the grooves.

"So what are they like then, these albums," I asked. All I'd heard to date were singles, hit singles or attempts at that, emanating from my parent's radio. *Shake Rattle and Roll. Behind the Green Door. Last Train to San Fernando.* "What they mainly do," Ralph informed me knowingly, "is to make versions of other people's hits. You get Elvis singing the songs of Little Richard and then Marty Wilde doing Elvis. And then Pat Boone doing everyone." "Are they any good," I asked. No. Ralph was a font of wisdom. His taste was the best there was.

Back in the 1950s the album had not been around for long. It had only been invented in 1948. Before that the world of recorded music consisted of stacks of fragile shellacs whizzing round and falling down the auto-changer with an air displacing thwack every two minutes or so. The 78 might have served as the essential format for the rock and roll revolution but it was really far too brittle for daily use. If you dropped it or stood on it then you were stuffed. I can remember when this happened with my Aunty Joan's copy of Frankie Lane's *Jezebel*. All I did was put it down on the bed and accidentally sit on it. Five useless pieces. She went up the wall.

Not that I owned a record player on which I might have spun my aunt's 78. My mother didn't believe in music. In the *Daily Sketch* she'd seen photographs of Elvis gyrating and on the Home Service heard about rock and roll being truly the devil's music. She introduced a total ban on anything resembling it in our house. In my case if it was in him then it certainly would not be allowed to come out. "Why can't you like Bing Crosby?" She'd demanded this of me on a day when I'd been discovered using the bathroom as an echo chamber and singing *Be-Bop-a-Lula* into the cupola of the toilet. Bing? Who is he? *White Christmas.* God.

From a used goods store in Canton I'd bought a pre-war gramophone. "We buy, sell and exchange almost anything in the second-hand world" it said in the window. They hadn't wanted much for it. No one is playing these big records anymore, they complained. I took the wind-up monster home and set about adjusting its speed control. It took a lot of experimentation, chewing gum, and the use of one of my father's hammers but I got there. More weight on the flywheel meant a turntable spinning at a slower speed. Mine ended up going round at something like 52.

I rigged up a great cone made from newspaper and attached this with cellotape to a biro from which I'd removed the ink tube. There was a sewing needle through the top. I fixed one end of the cone to the wall with a drawing pin and had the other dance among the microgrooves on the first real 7 inch single I ever owned. *Where Have All the Flowers Gone* by the bright and fresh-faced American college boys, The Kingston Trio. *O Ken Karanga,* on the flip, was the test track. I wound up the gramophone and let it spin. I put the needle in place and, after a deal of crackle, out of the paper cone came the tinny and slightly high pitched sound of the Kingston Trio. O ken Karanga, o ken karangoa, yea, yea. O ba ro bo, o ken Karanga. It's no wonder I ended up as a sound poet. But there they were. In my room. Singing African material that not even they understood. Brilliant.

I turned the record over and got the start of *Where Have All The Flowers Gone.* It was only the start because the sewing needle had now begun to remove black vinyl in curling slivers. I watched in disbelief as my first and brand new 7-inch was turned into a table mat before my eyes.

Things did get better. Rock and roll ban or no rock and roll ban I was eventually given the money to buy a real record player. I chose a Dansette. This was for my birthday. Or perhaps it was reward for helping my father build yet another of his hardboard on wooden frame constructions, this one the airing cupboard in the bathroom. These things were all over the house. Hardboard was the medium of the decade. We owned hardboard shelves, hardboard tables, hardboard bedside lamps, hardboard door fronts, hardboard pelmets and hardboard bath surrounds. Every single one was painted regulation cream.

The Dansette had a red Formica lid which lifted to reveal a stylus bearing playing arm and an electric deck complete with auto-changer and speed control. I could rack up eight 7-inch hits in a pile and have them spin one after another or I could select a single record and have it play over and over again. The Venture's *Walk Don't Run* once and then the Venture's *Walk Don't Run* for the tenth time. This was what young people did. The age of the bedsit had begun.

Before rock and roll came along the music market had been dominated by the middle-aged. Who else had the money? In the years before the war when more homes had pianos than gramophones it was sheet music that shifted. You could hear Caruso singing his latest on the radio and then get the self-same song knocked out on a jingling piano by Aunty Bess that evening at the Old Bull and Bush. Recordings were specialist items. Even as late as 1960 Ralph Thomas's parents were very much the exception. Owning a collection of albums and a gramophone on which to play them was rare. My mother had no interest in such devices. "Why would we want a gramophone," she said. "It would only get in the way".

The roots of the new incoming rock music were not as distant from listeners as they are today. My grandfather would have been around when he first gramophone records went on sale. My aunts would have been able to attend concerts given by Duke Ellington and Louis Armstrong had they wanted to. They could even have gone to Paris in 1949 to thrill to the songs of Lead Belly. Not that I have any evidence that they did. New was new but nothing was that old.

How did rock and roll start? With Jackie Brenston and His Delta Cats' recording of *Rocket 88* is the one you read in the official histories. That was made in 1951. Brenston was an alias of Ike Turner although we didn't know that then. Or know anything at all, actually. *Rocket 88* would only emerge to British ears fifty years later. It featured in the great rush of copyright-free material[5] put out in the 2000s to squeeze just a little bit more profit out of the rusty stuff that had excited us all so long ago. *Rocket 88* became the star of any number of roots of rock and roll compilations: *The Music That Inspired Elvis, The Greatest Rock and Roll Album Ever, Rock and Roll – Where It All began.* Playing it today *Rocket 88* still rocks and sounds amazingly advanced for something from so long ago as the dark, shortage-filled year of 1951.

Rocket 88 could well be a lode. But so too could Ella Fitzgerald doing *Rock It For Me* back in 1937 or the Andrews Sisters giving it one with *Boogie Woogie Bugle Boy* in 1940. "Rock" goes back to the practise among blacks of giving all kinds of new names to the activity of getting it on. "My man rocks me (with one steady roll)" sang Trixie Smith in 1922. "Rock Me" sang Sister Rosetta Tharpe in 1938. Neither lady was referring to jigging round on the dance floor.

The music is a combination of sassy black attitude, blues song styling, rip it up boogie piano playing, and upbeat white country and western. To that has been added staccato drumming in the style of Gene Krupa who featured so brilliantly on the recordings of swing band leader Benny Goodman. It took time to gestate and decades to form. Somewhere between the birth of recorded sound and the emergence of Wild Bill Moore, Wynonie Harris, Louis Jordan, Arthur Big Boy Crudup, and others in the 40s what became known as rock and roll started to come together.

Elvis didn't go into the studio until 1954. Bill Haley and Fats Domino both made records with a rock and roll edge before 1949. Early in the 50s in Britain there was skiffle. This was one of the few things we produced that actually raised the bar. This was Lonnie Donegan's seminal *Rock Island Line*.

Skiffle was like punk. You needed no particular musical ability to play it. Instruments could be found out the back – combs and paper, kazoos, washboards, basses made by running a piece of string from the top of a broom to the edge of a wooden tea chest. Your skiffle group would be better if it also had a guitar in the line-up but the ability to thrash only a few simple chords was all that was required. Donegan's record, an up tempo version of an old Lead Belly song from the 1930s, was a revelation. With its echo and its feet shifting rise in tempo it became a great hit, first here and later around the world. Donegan had recorded it as a sort of side project, part of his residence with Chris Barber's Jazz Band. In 1954 with Barber on bass and Beryl Bryden on washboard he cut *Rock Island Line* and *John Henry* for Decca. The legend goes that he was paid a mere £3 for the session and that's all he ever earned even though the record went on to be a million seller. He did one wangle, however, and got himself listed as the song's composer although clearly he was no such thing. This brought him in a steady income stream over the years as copyright holder. And considering how good the record was back then and how fresh it still sounds today who would deny him that.

Skiffle swept the airways. The Vipers, Chas McDevitt, Johnny Duncan. At first the groups were seen simply as providers of skiffle breaks included in the performance repertoires of trad jazz bands but they soon outgrew such restrictions. Ralph and I decided to start our own. All we need is a tea chest, I told him. But in resourceless 50s Britain such things were hard to find. Once we'd got ours, located out the back of Thomas & Evans the grocers, and contrived to obtain a broom and some string the craze had passed. There we were out my back garden, no guitar, a pretty ineffective bass and a dustbin lid instead of a washboard trying to make our way through *Cumberland Gap* while the rest of the world had discovered rock. Sometimes you are at the cutting edge. Other times you are not.

The British turning point was the emergence from the 2i's coffee bar in London of full-fledged British rock and roll maestro Tommy Steele. Hard to credit it now. His early records have not aged well. They rock but they leak. They hold the line, just, but do little for the soul. At the time, however, it was a very different matter. Tommy Steele and The Steelemen's first record, *Rock With The Caveman*, came out in 1956. He followed on with a stream of mainly cover versions of

American originals, giving them his distinctive Bermondsey stamp. *Elevator Rock, Singing the Blues, Knee Deep In the Blues.* Teenagers loved him. It said so in the Daily Express.

Steele started out in life as Tommy Hicks but changed his name make himself more marketable to his newly emerging audience. Power, Fury, Wilde. These were the names of the age. Steele was managed by Larry Parnes who saw him as the British answer to Elvis, although it didn't turn out like that.

Tommy Steele records flooded the airwaves. Outraged vicars around the country saw his work, as well as that of his mentor Elvis Presley, as a threat to public morals. Records were publically destroyed. Being 78s that was easy. You just stood in a small town square with a banner behind you and smashed the things on the ground.

Not that this stopped his popularity. Steele was our man. He was for a year anyway. After that Tommy and rock parted company. He went on to fame and fortune as a cockney stage and musical star. There'd be the British king of rock roll on stage singing about bulls, butter, flowers and half a sixpence. What could you do?

At this distance Britain seems such a pale, 30-watt place. The streets were poorly lit. There were no motorways. Television had a single flickering 405-line black and white channel. Where you had them carpets never went to the edge of the room. The music industry was a two dimensional unionised place with agreements set in *I'm Alright Jack* stone.

The musicians unions ensured that live musicians and, in particular, live British musicians would never lose out to visiting Americans. For every Buddy Holly and The Crickets performing this side of the pond America had to accept The Ted Heath Orchestra swinging their way through the Appalachians or else no deal.

What actually happened was the stars came but left their tight-knit bands behind. Little Richard had to rock with session Brits rolling behind him. Jerry Lee, Chuck Berry and Brenda Lee the same. Did we care? Not a bit. The fact that rock, genuine rock, had reached these shores was enough.

Hearing the new music was another matter. The BBC with its policy of British music first did the emerging teenage world no favours. The Home Service pretended rock and roll didn't exist. The Light Programme would dabble, now and again. But largely it remained Ambrose and his Orchestra and Billy Cotton's *Wakey Wakey* sweetly bouncing across the airwaves.

If you wanted to keep up with genuine rock then you needed access to a decent radio and could put the time in listening the wavery crackles and pops of Radio Luxembourg. Luxembourg was free-enterprise's answer to the restrictive state broadcaster that was the BBC. Lux played rock, in fact by the time I got round to listening to it in the early sixties it played little else.

The station had been established as long ago as 1933 but had come into its own post war as a commercial opportunity for advertisers willing to plug their products relentlessly between the discs. We got adverts for cigarettes, for faith healers and, most memorably, for Horace Bachelor's football pools scam, his infra draw method of getting rich quick. This gave his Bristol suburb address, Keynsham spelt K E Y N S H A M, country-wide fame. Keynsham, Memphis, Presley and Bachelor – they were all the same.

Radio Luxembourg broadcast almost exclusively in the evenings when the night skies helped propagate its transmissions. Music was largely derived from records, spun and introduced by the first DJs I'd ever heard. Keith Fordyce, David Jacobs, Pete Murray, Alan Freeman, Brian Matthew. The sound came and went, whooshing into inaudible fog and then swaying back[6]. It brought with it elicit pleasure – unadulterated rock.

And when Luxembourg failed me, as it did from time to time by giving air space to Hughie Green and his *Double Your Money* or to Billy Graham and his evangelical Christianity then there was always AFN. American Forces Network broadcast loud and strong out of Germany could always be relied upon for good music. Jazz, US teenage pop, rock.

The radio I used belonged to my aunt. So when she wanted to use it then I couldn't. New records came out all the time. How could anyone ever afford to keep up? The answer for some was Woolworths. At Woolworths there was a different world. Each stores' record department would present a lavish display of the entire hit parade all on offer at budget prices and all recorded by people you'd never heard of. You will not be able to tell the difference was the claim. But in reality you could. The label was Embassy. Buy it, spin it, love it but never tell anyone you had. The Embassy label was in the heartland of the unhip.

The Embassy label was owned by Oriole and would put out its fake rock discs at a furious rate. It had the entire hit parade to cope with. Songs were recorded with little time to spare, four per three-hour session, usually on a Thursday which would allow for production to deliver new discs to the shops by Monday. Embassy used a roster of professional session musicians and singers who, in turn, deployed a wide range of pseudonyms. *Perfidia* was made by Steve Stannard and his group. *Are You Lonesome Tonight* by Rikki Henderson. *Beatnik Fly* by The Gordon Franks Sextet. *Handy Man* by Johnny Worth. The label's most recorded singer was Ray Pilgrim who covered almost 150 British hits in his time.

When you bought an Embassy single you got two songs for your money, often by two different artists, one hit each side. B-sides here didn't exist. Great value though they were these things were not it. If you listened you could hear that the excitement missing. This was rock and roll somehow pasteurised, flattened, made clean and crisp. Made British in fact.

In Ralph's parents' broad collection there wasn't a single item on the Embassy label. I might have been willing to give the idea of cut price rock and roll houseroom but not Ralph's folk. Stay genuine. It's good advice.

3 • Bill Haley Reaches Cardiff General

In the UK on his first European tour Bill Haley finally reached Cardiff on the 21st February 1957. He arrived hot foot from his show the previous night at the Liverpool Odeon. He came by train. The *South Wales Echo* ran the story. The Cats Are getting Hep. Haley pandemonium. Teenagers go wild. "I'm coming back," says Haley. And he'd only just arrived.

These were old fashioned days. Haley and His Comets, only two of whom had actually played on his world-wide smash *Rock Around The Clock*, had crossed the Atlantic the traditional way. They'd done it with full entourage and crates of ale aboard a luxury liner The Queen Elizabeth. QE1, the first – port out starboard home, giant funnels, dinner suits. "We're rockin' through the ocean and rollin' through the waves," Haley reported back to UK tour sponsors the *Daily Mirror*. The world was dancing to his beat.

The song that had done it for him was the ubiquitous *Rock Around the Clock*, a teenage anthem that sounds today like chanting men from a trad band trying to be hip. But back then the song was right on the nation's button. It had a honking sax solo and a wild electric guitar break. It had lyrics you could remember and an infectious beat. It was rhythmic, irreverent, and it got under your skin. Against a backdrop of Perry Como, David Whitfield and Vera Lynn how could the emerging first teenage generation not like it? It stormed the land.

Rock Around The Clock had been issued originally as the B-side of a much earlier Haley attempt at music world domination: *Thirteen Women (and only one man in town)*. *Thirteen Women* was a song owned by Haley's music publisher Jimmy Myers, a man determined to cash in wherever he could. It had been recorded in 1954 as Haley's follow up to the world's first charting rock and roll record – his *Crazy Man, Crazy*. It wasn't until the song was used the following year under the opening credits of the film Blackboard Jungle that people began to buy it in large quantities. *Rock Around the Clock* was reissued as an A-side and spent the next two years charting the world over.

Born in Highland Park, Michigan in 1925 Haley was the most unlikely of pop stars. As a country singer with one dead eye he'd worked the scene for at least a decade before The Comets came along. He began after the war as a solo act known as the Rambling Yodeller. His first band was The Range Drifters which morphed in 1948 into The Four Aces of Western Swing. The Four Aces made records but nothing hit. As the fifties dawned and *Rocket 88* was out there showing the world how it would eventually be, Haley changed his band's name to The Saddlemen. The Saddlemen were an improvement but only just. In 1951 they made their own white men's version of *Rocket 88* and the year after cut *Rock The Joint*. It was a start but it wasn't quite enough. In 1953, swapping their cowboy boots and western shirts for Italian suits, the band was enlarged and renamed The Comets. Haley and his Comets. This time Haley caught the spirit of the age. *Crazy Man, Crazy*. They lit up the sky.

Looking at Haley now from the distance of more than five decades he appears fat-faced and salesman slick. You could imagine him pushing insurance or double glazing, knocking on doors, doing his best to get invited in. In reality he was a dance caller rather than a pop star. He stood there in front of the microphone and encouraged the audience to get up and move. Country singers had been doing this sort of thing for decades. All Haley had done was to change the beat. Song collector Alan Lomax described Haley and his Comets as "a white hill-billy combination doing its best to imitate the barrel-house blues popular among Negros about 20 years ago[7]" which, through the telescope of time, sounds pretty accurate. In the famous photograph of him taken by the *South Wales Echo* he hangs from a carriage window on Cardiff General Station. Beyond, out of shot, are hordes of screaming teenage girls. Thrilled by the music, by the rebellion it amounted to, by the excitement of the occasion, by being there in the presence of a real world-wide star. It couldn't have been be the sexiness of the man, could it?

In keeping with the style of his transatlantic liner arrival Haley and his entourage had gone round the UK by train. In the 1950s Beeching had yet to ruin the railways and you could get virtually anywhere you wanted by steam. From Southampton to London the train had been dubbed 'The Rock and Roll Special' and the Haley carriage had been joined by eight others, all full of screeching teenage fans. That was on February 5th. By the time he got to Cardiff it was the 21st and things had cranked up several notches. Rock and roll meant pandemonium, screaming and crying, waving your arms around. Did then, still does now. Crowds of fans surged and swarmed.

The concert series – 23 dates in all taking in everywhere from Croydon to Cheltenham – had been promoted by Lew and Leslie Grade. It used cinemas as venues and had a full printed programme that even detailed the set lists. *Razzle Dazzle, Rip It Up, Rudy's Rock, See You Later Alligator, The Saints Rock and Roll.* On the bill with Haley were a number of old-style warm up acts. In their wisdom the Grade's had stuck to what they knew. Teenage fans, Teddy Boys and school kids excitably buying tickets with their pocket money had to endure a first half of Vic Lewis and His Orchestra playing tightly-arranged big band jazz – *Canadian Sunset, What A Difference A Day Makes, In The Mood.* Vocalists included Kenneth Earle and a straight-laced Malcolm Vaughan. Not what the new audience had paid to hear.

Haley's concert included all the hits. It also featured the show-biz antics of double-bass twirling, musicians in tartan jackets doing the splits, Haley rocking like a ring master and a band of Comets rolling in rehearsed chaos. This was music as entertainment, full on.

At the Capitol there had been two sell out shows and queues snaking down Queen Street for at least a quarter of a mile. I didn't go. I was ten at the time and this sort of thing was out of my league. But its backwash did reach me. I tried to fashion a kiss curl on my forehead using extra dollops of Brylcreem. Didn't really work, I'm glad to report.

Yet was this the revolution? Certainly the adults around me thought so but to my ears the whole Haley thing didn't sound quite right. Put a 78 of *Rock Around the Clock* onto the gramophone and did the walls shake? Not really. There were stories in the *South Wales Echo* about teds jiving in the aisles at cinema showings of the film *Rock Around the Clock* and about cinema balconies being closed for fear of collapse. Ralph and I sneaked out and saw it one afternoon at Queen Street's Olympia. No one jived when I was there which was what we'd come to see, I guess. I suggested to Ralph that maybe, just to keep the revolution going, we should get up and bop about a bit but he said he'd rather not. We ate our ice creams. We watched Bill in grainy B-movie black and white rock his stuff. We went home and we moved on. *R-O-C-K Rock* was on the way to being forgotten.

Haley hung on for a while as the scene around overtook him. He made albums of instrumentals, of songs containing the names of girls and of other people's hits. Nothing stuck. He then disappeared back into the vastness of America and returned to his country music roots. He had no more hits. Lost and disillusioned he tried his luck in Mexico before turning determinedly to drink and the inevitable depression. He died in Harlingen, Texas, in 1981, a forgotten man. As Tom Russell has it "talking to the windows and the walls[8]", too drunk to sing. Many of the famous don't last. The road is long and hard. The money never seems to help at all.

How has his music stood the test of time? Not well. What was once the centre of the music universe, embodying its glorious future now sounds amateurishly thin. Like the Beverley Sisters. Like the Big Ben Banjo Band. Yet it does have its surreal qualities. I've just bought myself a double-CD containing 60 versions of *Rock Around The Clock*. Only a psychogeographer would get pleasure out of things like this. On the set are 30 cuts of the song by Haley himself followed by 30 more from the likes of Freddy Cannon, Chubby Checker, The Platters, John Lennon and The Sex Pistols. I'd like to say that listening is like an extended meditation but it's not. You get bored, you get excited, Bill rocks off yet again, you want the thing to finish, you want it to never end.

Elvis and Bill Haley were once on the same bill. Haley was the star and Presley the warm up. That was in Brooklyn, Ohio in late 1955. Hard to credit looking back. From 1956 on there was no stopping the

King. The two were as alike as water and wine. Haley was an upright and unthreatening band leader who also sang, the sober face of teenage pop. He promoted the idea that listening to rock and roll would keep potential delinquents off the streets. They'd be home listening to his music rather than out there smashing phone booths and ripping up cinema seats. Elvis was the complete antithesis. He had the looks, the moves, the voice. He'd stand there, skew hipped, guitar at the ready, a simmering threat to civilized order. Ride with him and you'd win the world. That's certainly what we all did.

Rock and roll was the life for me, for the next five years at least. It started in 1957 when I realised that Haley, rock and roll giant that the *South Wales Echo* declared he was, might not be quite the ground-breaking hero I needed. Were my mates idolising him, buying his 78s, combing their hair like he did? Nope. Most of them were forming football teams, getting their boots muddy, buying baseball bats and whacking balls miles and miles up the endless grass of the Rec at Roath Park. You could only make it in this world if you could dribble a ball effortlessly or hit one, straight off. Knock it right out of everyone's reach. Two paths. One to choose.

I could hit a baseball and I could run faster than a penny rocket, but to the eternal shame of my Cardiff City following father I couldn't kick a football to save myself. In life soccer was somehow a dominant force. What could I do? I chose rock.

None of this happened overnight. The transformation was slow. But it was sure. Somewhere between 1957 and 1961 the idea slowly solidified that music rather than sport might just be the most important thing in the world. Round at Ralph's we spun Elvis records, the few he had. *Heartbreak Hotel, Hard Headed Woman, Jailhouse Rock*. Hard headed, thorn in the side of man – the Biblical sounding Elvis turning us all on. These were RCA 45s with triangular centres which could be pushed out to facilitate juke box play. A couple of Ralph's had been pushed out already in the spirit of teenage experiment and, since we had no juke box, had been stuck back in with the aid of Elastoplast. In 1958 cellotape was as rare as hen's teeth. When things broke and cow gum wouldn't solve the problem then thick, sticky, pink fabric plasters were the fall back. Thus fixed *Dixieland Rock* spun and bumped.

Rock and roll between 1956 and the early sixties gripped the British nation. No matter how many *Little White Bulls* and *Cherry Pinks* Denmark Street[9] rolled out the future of music was in the hands of rocking Americans. Little Richard, Chuck Berry, Eddie Cochran, Jerry Lee Lewis, Duane Eddy, Gene Vincent, The Everly Brothers. There was an inevitability about this. Supported by its world-beating economy America had become the world's ideal and the consuming world's prime source of consumable goods. Backed by military might and promoted first by Hollywood and now by its revolutionary new teenage music American was something we all wished we were.

Not everyone agreed. The view, as expressed by my Polish uncle was that Elvis Presley was okay but the rest of the American rockers just screeched. There wasn't a real singer among them. He'd know, I suppose, my uncle, with his background of vodka drinking, white eagles and opera houses on every corner.

Down on Queen Street, the yet to be pedestrianized Cardiff city centre main drag, the teds gathered. The Teddy Boy was a very British phenomenon. While a fair number of the lads decking themselves in fake Edwardian costume, crepe soled shoes and string ties came from the capital most came down on the steam trains from the South Wales coal mining valleys. They came just to be seen strutting their stuff.

To a man they were fans of the King. They carried flick knives and knuckle dusters. They'd spend time at Cardiff's cinemas watching the era's string of low budget rock and roll exploitation flicks – *Don't Knock The Rock, Rock Rock Rock, Rock Around The Clock*. Tanked up with cheap beer on payday they'd throw fire extinguishers and fight among themselves in the aisles. They all wore drainpipe trousers. In an era of shortages and darkness they had style in spades.

All attempts I might have made to follow suit were naturally blocked. Teddy Boys were an anathema, an insult to common decency, a thing well beyond the pale. They lasted for what was not much more than a blink of the eye although their legacy hung on. On Valley day Thursdays as late as 1970 the odd blue drape jacketed throwback still wearing lime green socks and sporting a greased quiff and D.A.[10] could be seen swaggering among the parka-wearing proto hippies outside Boots. Dinosaurs.

But in the fifties they were where it was at.

American rock and roll surged. The British answer was imitative flattery and a whole raft of British rock and rollers emerged. In reality they were pale pretenders, lacking the heartbeat and coming from a completely different tradition. In the UK there was no black music to turn white, no history of guitar-toting travellers, no cowboys, no honking sax players, no Spanish Harlem, no Mississippi, no Tennessee. We had Bermondsey. We had Aberystwyth. We had the ukulele. Our wellspring was George Formby or if it wasn't him then it was Max Bygraves.

Nonetheless our aspiring rockers flooded the airwaves. They had no battles with musician's unions to win, no wide Atlantic to cross and they'd perform their repertoire cut price. Marty Wilde, Duffy Power, Billy Fury, Tony Crombie, Wee Willie Harris, Don Lang, Dickie Pride, Vince Taylor, Terry Dene and Jim Dale were our guys. The bands they fronted were called things like Lord Rockingham's XI, The Rockets, and The Frantic Five. We also had Cliff Richard who everybody not on the button muddled with the black rock dynamo Little Richard. Harry he'd been christened but that had been changed to Cliff because the name sounded sort of hard.

Middle of the road, Christian, unoriginal, sweet beyond, and utterly passé though Cliff may be to many ears today back in 1958 things were different. With *Move It* he'd cut the first genuinely original rock and roll record outside the United States. His backing band at the time were the Drifters (later and with a different personnel to be reborn as The Shadows). Then lead guitarist Ian Samwell had written *Move It* on the way to the studio intending it to be the B-side for Cliff's cut of *Schoolboy Crush*, a song they'd lifted from American Bobby Helms. When producer Jack Good heard the song, as happens often in music legend, he recognised a winner and had the A and the B sides reversed. The record became a huge hit and Cliff never looked back. Unlike Haley, whose 50s recordings sound unrockingly wooden, *Move It* still sounds fresh and exciting today.

With a few exceptions most everything else British from the period is now utterly forgotten. What we did was to make cover versions of American originals. Terry Wayne did *Matchbox* imitating Carl Perkins.

Marty Wilde covered Jody Reynolds' *Endless Sleep*. Jim Dale recorded Johnny Madara's *Be My Girl*. Ken Mackintosh imitated Duane Eddy's *Raunchy*. When Ray Peterson's *Tell Laura I Love Her* arrived both John Leyton and Ricky Valance covered that. In the lower reaches of the charts you could regularly see rival versions battling it out for the place at the top. Craig Douglas vs. Dion and The Belmonts. Marty Wilde vs. Ritchie Valens, Jody Reynolds, Phil Phillips, Bobby Vee, Bill Monroe, Freddy Cannon, and Dion once again. Often, to our chagrin, the winner ended up being our flaky and imitative own.

In a sense the whole of British pop and rock before The Beatles was a version of the Embassy Records experience. Hear the hard rocking original and knock out a pale copy as fast as you could. Smile, sell, and rake in the cash.

My rock and roll life consisted of listening to this dross until I began work in the drizzly days of 1963. Money arriving in my hands then, the trickle that it was, meant that I could actually show my face at the record store and be greeted with a smile. I'd buy. They got to know that I would.

But by this time rock and roll had stood back. The beat world was now upon us. The British beat and rhythm and blues boom was foaming up. In amongst the tracks I followed were any number of retreads of early rock and roll originals. These were beat group guitar-led copies of the thundering first outings from years before. The Rolling Stones doing Bo Diddley's *Mona*. The Beatles singing Chuck Berry's *Sweet Little Sixteen*. The Searchers playing *Stand By Me* and *Love Potion Number 9*. Everybody seemed to be doing *Johnny B Goode* or things that sounded just like it. On cue Chuck Berry was released from prison and recorded *Nadine*. High powered rock and for my money the best thing he's ever done. Little Richard came back from the religious brink and gave us the pile driving *Bama Lama Bama Loo*. The world was still rocking.

For me the answer to discovering rock and roll's great history came in the form of Trevor Williams. Trevor, a slightly tubby lad about town, came from the deep blind reaches of the coal mining valleys. He worked as a fellow clerk in Glamorgan County Hall, my first serious employer. He showed me the ropes. Trevor's two obsessions were women and rock and roll. Rock and roll he placed first.

The highlight of 1964 was Granada TV's broadcast of *The Little Richard Spectacular*, a rare music TV concert featuring the man Trevor reckoned to be rock and roll's overlord backed by both the Shirelles and Sounds Incorporated. The show was to go out in May and Trevor was enormously excited. "I'm going to make an LP of it,§" he announced. He'd borrowed a big reel-to-reel Grundig tape recorder and intended to stand right next to his household TV, his mother and father banished to their small kitchen, and record the whole event with a hand-held microphone.

The show turned out to be as spectacular as Trevor said it would be. Richard was adrenaline-charged. Sounds Incorporated with their line of sax players were totally convincing. It was a broadcast first meeting of Beat music with founding rock and roll. It was a triumph. Trevor had captured it all and was excited beyond. Disappointment set in when he went round to see the company who had agreed to turn the tape into a one-off vinyl album. "They said the quality was too poor," he reported later in a resigned voice. The tape speed was too slow and there was too much extraneous noise from the mic. You could hear the traffic outside apparently. Bugger.

In order to help expand my personal knowledge of rock and roll's great history Trevor would regularly loan me stacks of his seven-inch singles. He had a whole house full. I'd take them home, play and explore, and make copies of the best using my recently purchased from Dixon's PrinzSound[11] Compact Cassette System. Join the future, the advertising had said, compact, versatile, lightweight, low noise, hi fidelity. Buy one, you won't regret it. Hum.

What were they, these wonders? Jerry Lee Lewis' *Don't Be Cruel*, and *Rocking Pneumonia*, Eddie Fontaine's *Ain't Nothing Shaking*, Link Wray's *Rumble*, Eddie Cochran's *Cut Across Shorty,* and *Three Steps To Heaven*, Sandy Nelson's *Let There Be Drums,* The Everly Brothers' *Lucille*, Conway Twitty's *Halfway to Heaven*, The Coasters' *Peanut Butter*, Elvis's *Trouble*, Ernie Fields' rocking rehash, *In The Mood*. Chuck Berry's *School Days*, Fats Domino's *Don't Blame It On Me*, Little Richard's *Chicken Little Baby*, Johnny and The Hurricanes' *Sand Storm*, Freddie Cannon's *Tallahassee Lassie*, Larry Williams' *Short Fat Fannie*. All

American. And then one genuine-sounding British contribution: Johnny Kidd's *Shaking All Over.*

These records were astonishing. How could the BBC have not broadcast them? How could I have not come across any before? *Bloodnok's Rock and Roll Call*[12], The Goons send up of the genre, endlessly popular with the nation's broadcaster, had a lot to answer for.

4 • The Down and Out Blues

It's 1964 and there's definitely something going on out there in rock and roll land. The bands have stopped looking to Chuck and Bo. They've cut back on *Hey Bo Diddley* retakes and left *Sweet Little Sixteen* alone. Instead they are delving deeper into black America. In the dark core records are being made by Muddy Waters, Sonny Boy Williamson, Jimmy Reed and John Lee Hooker. The blues are on the rise. Names like Lightning, Howlin', Little, Slim, Big, and Mighty are pouring from the journalists' pens. In their reporting I can detect a subdued but distinct edge of glee. Rock and roll, that dead end where real musicians never went, is at last losing sway. Bobby, Billy, Jerry and Johnny have ceased to be the threat they once were. Arriving in their place is something far more primitive. It's a music with a great and still largely undiscovered history. This is no frivolous Tin Pan Alley upstart. This, my friends, is rock and roll's ancestor and, it seems, its nemesis: the blues.

In some quarters the blues have been around for a long time. In America, where they come from, they've been an Afro-American indispensable for decades. They've filled the dance halls, the bars and the clubs, the corner shop jukes, the back country stoops, the fields and the crossroads. They are black America's vibrant national music.

White audiences by contrast have suffered anodyne waterings almost since recording began. Peggy Lee did the version of *Basin Street Blues* we all listened to. Dean Martin softly massaged *Singing The Blues*. Frank took *Blues In The Night* to the road's middle. We even had Cyril Stapleton waltzing through *Swinging Shepherd Blues*. To cap it all pipe-smoking Bing Crosby was the man Hollywood had chosen to star in the film they'd made about the success of black music – *Birth of the*

Blues. Golf clubs. Cardigans and soft shoes. Characters called Limpy, Ruby and Suds. Peg Leg Howell hadn't stood a chance.

The blues that were now arriving were of a different order from those jazzy things that had gone before. They were black and they were pretty primeval. They were filled with dark pain. They were straight from America's African heart. Victor Sylvester would not recreate *Speckled Red* in strict tempo for the Light Programme. Mantovani would not be heard knocking them out on a wet Sunday afternoon. Our roots were different. We had to evolve a different way of relating to this music.

Elements of the blues had been seen here before. Skiffle had its origins in the jug band music of the American south. Added to that were strains of traditional English folk song, a great slab of cockney humour, mountain music and then that all important slice of back country blues. Skiffle's heroes were Woody Guthrie, Josh White, Lead Belly and Big Bill Broonzy. The last two singers had the blues right at their core.

The jazz bands of the early fifties – Ken Colyer and Chris Barber in particular – liked to show that they'd moved on from the swing movement and heavily featured New Orleans Dixie in their repertoires. Colyer replicated the sound of Bunk Johnson and George Lewis. Barber revived the earlier period of King Oliver, Louis Armstrong, and Sydney Bechet. Both bands interlaced their music with their own take on the blues.

For a while in the mid-fifties this was the music to make. But as with all booms bust was not long in coming. Barely had Stan Freburg time to record his *Rock Island Line* take-off than Bill Haley had arrived with his knock you out substitute. The airwaves were suddenly swamped with shouted swing jive rock and roll. Trad jazz was out. Skiffle was dead.

However, as far as the blues in Britain were concerned, popular interest in the songs of Leadbelly had been pivotal. Fanatical entrepreneurs, Chris Barber and Alexis Korner among them, had taken to inviting genuine black American blues singers over here to do the rounds. Big Bill came, so too did Odetta, Josh White, Memphis Slim, Sister Rosetta Tharpe and Muddy Waters. To small and sometimes startled audiences they played what they knew best. A blue seep into British music had begun.

At the church jumble where I get most of my stuff I'm riffling through the records. The table is swamped with shellac 78s as the nation unloads as part of the vinyl revolution. This is the time to pick up discarded Elvis on blue HMV or fat ten inch copies of John Burnette doing *The Train Kept a Rolling* but I don't want the past. I am here for the future. What I get my hands on is a slightly warped copy of Alexis Korner and Blues Incorporated's *R&B From The Marquee*, issued on Decca's Ace of Clubs. I've no idea who Korner is, nor the Marquee for that matter. I'm slightly puzzled by the downmarket Ace of Clubs branding. Ace of Clubs? That sounds like something my parents would like. But the thing does have the magic word *blues* in its title and, as a bonus, it's cheap. I take it home.

Back in my room the record spins and I hear it, electric blues, harmonicas, drums. It still sounds a little like a trad jazz band does before the trumpets come in but with track titles like *How Long How Long* and *Hoochie Coochie* who cares? The guitar might be merely functional but the harmonica soars. Cyril Davies it says in the liner notes. Who is this guy?

Davies, it turns out, was one of the lost white hopes of British Blues. He was a south London panel beater with a short fuse who'd come up through the skiffle movement playing banjo and had turned to the harmonica after hearing blues legend Little Walter. He'd done his time with Alexis Korner's Blues Incorporated and then formed his own band, The All-Stars. His recording of *Country Line Special* made late in 1962 was one of the all-time greatest of harmonica rockers. I bought it unheard entirely on the back of what I'd uncovered on the Marquee record. Davies, the blues purist, made the train roar through my living room, as much as my underpowered Dansette record player would allow it to anyway. He cut another four tracks for Pye's new RnB label and then died. Officially endocarditis although drink had to be in the mix somewhere.

I spent hours in the bathroom with a Horner SuperVamper trying to imitate him. I could get the rhythm but somehow lacked the stamina to keep it going for more than thirty seconds. Cyril Davies could blow for hours. The bathroom added echo. My own piece of black Chicago in Roath. "Why can't you play like that Larry Adler," my father asked. "He does tunes. All you do is make a noise."

Out in the Cardiff coffee bars the blues were the hot subject. The guys with the fur-lined parkas and the girls in hoop earrings all knew what they were. They came in on Luxembourg amid the waves of fade and crackle. They were delivered by The Rolling Stones, The Pretty Things, The Yardbirds, Manfred Mann, and The Kinks. More importantly, and much more locally, they were delivered by Bernie McCarthy standing there, blue as hell, the front man for The Sons of Adam.

My friend Clive had just arrived fresh from his stint at selling *Sanity* to the bomb-loving hoards rolling down Saturday's Queen Street. CND was big and if you were young you joined. Under his arm he had The Downliners Sect's first album. This was R&B at full tilt by a bunch of casually-dressed white lads from Twickenham. They had long hair and their main man wore a deerstalker hat. They did the usual Jimmy Reed Coasters Bo Diddley catalogue but with a significant amount of added energy. These were the blues on speed, although speed wasn't called that yet. They had a large female following. "This is what we should do. Form a band. Get on board." Clive had always harboured guitarist pretentions although I'd never heard him play.

It seemed a good idea. I'd be front man with maracas, harmonica, kazoo and Jew's harp. Geoff, who had access to his brother's drum kit, would do percussion. Jan, who'd never picked up an instrument in his life, would play bass. And Mike, the only person we knew who could actually play and furthermore owned an amp, would lead on lead. We all loved the blues. We said we did. So that's what we'd play. Clive had already styled his hair after his hero, Keith Relf from The Yardbirds. Relf with his mellow blond bob and eternally cool gaze was how most of us would look if we could.

Most important was to get a name. We needed something that was as distressed and distraught, that reflected where the music came from. We needed to signal howling, moaning, roaring and harmonica wailing. And, significantly, we needed to be different. No all-star incorporated set crew quartet quintet ensemble marching mariachi for us.

We finished our Russian Teas. The Down and Out Blueswailers it was. Not a bad name. Check it out on Google – the only one listed is us.

The following day we had the band promotion photograph taken. One single black and white shot. In it we stand in Clive's back garden done up in Mod gear, caps, pointed boots, tight jeans. Me wearing shades, Jan holding an acoustic guitar with no strings as if it were an electric bass. He has it upside down like Paul McCartney. Geoff had brought drum sticks but they are not evident in the photo. I'm holding a single large and very round maraca and pretending to blow into a harmonica. With the cap, shades and hands surrounding my mouth you can't tell it's me at all. The only person looking real is Mike who holds his genuine electric guitar as if he is about to play. His left hand fingers E7, a chord at the heart of the blues.

We printed a few dozen and sold them to our followers. Somehow or other we'd acquired a fan base without ever having played a note. Down at the Kardomah where women were hip the girls flocked. They'd have us sign the front in biro and glow a little in the glory.

Actually making music was another matter. Apart from one hopeless attempt at street busking we didn't do much. Our practice sessions were in Geoff's loft above his father's garage. Here a room had been sound-proofed with egg boxes by his drummer elder brother. Ken played with The Sect Maniacs who were fronted at that time by the only one we knew ever to get anywhere musically, Andy Fairweather Low. Geoff would sit behind the drums while the rest of us discussed what to play. Mike wanted to do Chuck Berry, mainly because he could rip off a Berry lick without much effort. The rest of us preferred something bluer. I got out my copy of John Lee Hooker's *Don't Turn Me From Your Door* album and played his *Misbelieving Baby*, an introspective guitar mumble with, even for Hooker, little sign of structure. Hooker free forming on a blue electric guitar. I thought it was amazing. "I can't play that," said Mike, shaking his head. "There's nothing I can copy. No chords. No rhythm. No tune. This band is not for me." And with that he got up and left, taking his precious guitar and even more precious amplifier with him. The rest of us just sat there in an atmosphere of acoustic hopelessness. The Blueswailers were stuffed.

On the radio everyone, blues or not, was incorporating the harmonica in their recordings. Paul Jones was out in wailing front with the Manfreds. Ray Davies with The Kinks. John Lennon blew a bit on his band's first hit. Pye had released what has to be the blues greatest harmonica recording, *Help Me*, a wailing version of *Green Onions* with added lyrics by Sonny Boy Williamson II. The Dance Orchestras were heard featuring straight up and down Horner chromatic players in suits doing soft-edged versions of *How Long How Long*. Even Frank Sinatra, spurred by the 60s musical revolution, was adding bluesy harp to his singles.

The down and out blues, sound of the sixties, were taking over the world.

5 • Trying To Play A Stringed Instrument

Playing music is a gift. I'd read that somewhere. Kids I knew would be proficient on the piano, almost without effort. They'd be taught by tutors who'd cost the earth. They'd be able to plonk versions of *Chopsticks* with ease and to the delight of any family member within earshot. They'd do it daily and there would be joy in their households. The rest of us thought it made them sound retarded.

I never went for music lessons, naturally. Didn't ask. Quavers and keys and those funny briefcases in which you kept sheet music were not to be for me. But when I got older I found enthusiasm for music among my fellows to be the common denominator. It was certainly the best subject to use as an introduction when talking to women. I had to do something. Faking it, like the wide boys who went round with guitars they never took out of their cases, was not in my nature. I went to Cranes music shop at the bottom of St Mary Street and asked what was the cheapest instrument they had. Jew's harp. I bought one, took it home and managed to split my lip within minutes. How did these things that looked like silver potato peelers sound? I had no idea.

On the liner notes of one of my Sonny Terry and Brownie McGhee albums there was reference to Terry having recorded a set of Jew's harp blues. I tracked it down. Folkways, US import only. *Sonny Terry's New Sound: Jawharp in Blues and Folk Music*. Recorded by the Smithsonian Centre for Folklife and Cultural Heritage in 1961. Jew transformed into Jaw – politically correct ahead of its time. Ten quid. I couldn't afford it. In fact I wouldn't get to hear it for forty years. But its very existence was enormously encouraging.

Sonny Terry was a piping, jiggery harmonica player in the do-it-yourself folk tradition. He was about as far from Muddy's harpist, Little Walter, as you could get. Chicago-sounding amplified harp was not for him. But he could play like a devil. The fact that he'd apparently done the same thing with a jaw's harp sent me back practising.

Eventually, breaking quite a few of the L-shaped tongues, the source of the instrument's sound, I got the hang of it. While thumbing the silver tongue you pressed the metal against your teeth and, keeping your lips still, moved your cheeks as a sort of note changing chamber. If you simultaneously breathed in and out across the vibrating blade then the sound thrummed. It was quite compelling. I turned my jaw's harp into a fashion accessory, stringing it round my neck on a leather thong and wearing it into town. Finch the folk blues man was what I'd hoped people would think. Pretentious twat was what they actually did.

Jaws harps, however, where not where it was at. Neither were the sliding whistles, kazoos, ocarinas and penny whistles I'd also bought. The ocarina was especially naff. Mine was a red-painted plaster of Paris affair that I'd inadvertently broken and had repaired with Evo Stik. Carrying it around made me look as if I'd just won a prize on the duck shoot in the fun fair at Barry Island. When people asked what it was I'd be obliged to blow into it. It's weedy tooting sounded more Walt Disney than Bo Diddley. I had to do better.

Better eventually arrived in the form of a Horner Echo Super Vamper in C bought at full price from Cranes. This was the model the blues men used, I was assured. One line of holes to blow into rather than two. The harp (as harmonicas were called in the blue vernacular) was an immediate success. It was no effort to carry about. I made a sort of cloth pouch thing to hang it from my belt. Just being seen turning it over with your fingers while sipping the inevitable Russian tea was amazingly hip.

I taught myself to play, learned how to bend the tongue into the comb so the breath went in and out through a single reed, became adept at bending notes. Tunes I didn't do. But blues I certainly did. You could freeform here so long as the structure around you was in full support. Like Cyril Davies I wanted to be a train. I listened to Jack

Bruce doing *Train Time* for The Graham Bond Organisation and then Sonny Terry doing *Lonesome Train*. There were trains everywhere, hundreds of blues songs mentioned them, and a good many featured harmonicas. This train that train slow train lost train found train fast train blue train.

The secret was in the breathing – you had to do it both in and out in order to keep any kind of rhythm going. Trains took effort. Stopping half way through to cough just wasn't allowed. I discovered that harmonicas were easier to play if you dipped them into a pint of beer before you started. I also discovered that they went out of tune pretty fast. Sonny Boy Williamson II, the one with the bowler hat who'd come to London and made a series of albums with The Yardbirds, was rumoured to simply crush his failing harps with his shoe. I kept mine in the hope that overnight as they dried they'd perhaps return to tune but they never did.

Boldness was the way. The majority of groups playing the dance hall circuit had yet to acquire harmonica players. I'd introduce myself in the break and ask if they'd do a sort of slow 12-bar blues shuffle in C and allow me to put some harmonica on top. The answer was inevitably yes and we'd get yet another version of *Pete's Blues*, my one or two note wailing white boy number that if heard today would sound mightily unadventurous but back then was ahead of the curve.

Eventually the rhythm and blues boom rocked right through South Wales and almost every band acquired a blues harmonica player of their own. There was no space for me. Where next? Down the record stores the hipsters were buying Cisco Houston, Rambling Jack Elliott, Woody Guthrie and the new face on the block, Bob Dylan. These guys played guitars and often had harmonicas strapped up in front of them in a harness. One man bands. The folk boom was in full swing.

In the Cardiff Folk Song Club, held every Thursday in a rented room upstairs at the Estonian Club, the old guard, who had held sway since the club had been formed by Roy Harris in 1960, were being infiltrated. Standing there, eyes shut, one finger in your ear and the other in your wide leather belt was how most traditional folksingers approached their art. But it was going out of fashion. Trad singers often followed the line set by one of their greatest – Ewan MacColl – and there was a sense among them that the folk world was changing and in ways they did not welcome. Their repertoire of Irish, Scottish and English material had no place for guitars and imported blue harmonicas. Bob Dylan with his reworkings of Americana was not their hero. Quite the reverse.

The shake down had come at MacColl's the Singer's Club in London in 1962 where the early Dylan had guested and exposed that circumscribed world to the future – "and it was a future that had no room for an anachronism like MacColl[13]". MacColl believed that folk singers should only ever sing songs that came from the tradition of the country they were born in. This would avoid, as he put it, "blokes from Walthamstow pretending to be from China or the Mississippi"[14] It was a policy that he and his followers stuck to with rigidity. Clearly Bob Dylan with his penchant for mixing everything from Negro blues to Irish ballads did not fit.

I'd sit in the corner nursing a bottle of Newcastle Brown and soak it all up. What we usually got was a parade of singers in the MacColl, AL Lloyd, Dominic Behan mould – sea shanties, collier's rants, wild mountain thyme, Northumberland fiddle tunes, whack fol de diddle, oh the north wind blows. Occasionally someone would turn up with an autoharp or a dulcimer – instruments that looked right up my street as it seemed to take hardly any effort to play them. There'd be a hint of Appalachia but applied with such clear intellectual vigour that even that usually lively music came over as dry and historical. The folk world was icily intellectual. I began to wonder why I came. Shouldn't I be enjoying this?

Ed Kelly, the man who later rose to local fame as the owner of Kelly's Records, the peerless used record stall in Cardiff Market, was a club regular. He was a traditionalist in the style of Ewan MacColl. Hand cupping ear, no backing, went on for hours. But he was the friendliest of men. "If you ever want to join in on that one of mine with that harmonica of yours then feel free," he said to me. When Penguin published a paperback of Australian Ballads[15] Ed bought a copy and worked his way right through. In traditionalist style he applied the words to whatever tune he had in his head at the time. He sang with book in hand. This was something of which MacColl would certainly have approved. So long as Ed pretended that had Australian roots.

As the months went by there was a hint of change. This was the revolutionary sixties after all. Singers with guitars became more prevalent. The kind of traditional music that had been promoted by Pete Seeger, Burl Ives and The Weavers for years began to be heard in SouthWales more regularly. Occasionally we'd get a hint of the new wave. Bob Dylan had taken the world by storm and locals keen on riding his coat tails would show, singing *God on Our Side* and *North Country Blues*. Everyone wore caps like he did. Now and then I'd get up and on harmonica join in.

I was gaining in confidence. After all I'd hitch-hiked to London and in the record yourself for a half a crown booth on Paddington Station had made a recording of a harmonica train blues. You got three minutes alone and then a five inch one-sided disc containing a low-fi version of whatever it was you'd done would appear from a slot on the front. Neil Young has recorded a whole contemporary album using one of these machines[16]. I blew, roared, wailed and thundered. I stamped my feet and knocked on the booth's side to add rhythm. Half way through Geoff opened the door and yelled "Hoy". When you listen to the record, which, at this distance in time and played on present day competent equipment, appears to be something from the crackle and hiss-filled dawn of phonography, it sounds terrifically authentic. A Great Western *Country Line Special* done in a single take. As Allen Ginsberg was later to espouse, the best way with most things.

But mouth harps could only take you so far. I wanted to go further. And to do that I needed a guitar. I located one in the Polish fighter pilot's[17] second-hand shop half way along City Road. Spanish acoustic, nylon strings, only slightly warped fret board. Best I could afford. I changed the strings for steel ones, bought a capo (every acoustic player I'd seen had one of these and made a great play of changing them mid performance) and a fabric case.

Singer songwriters were on the rise. Both Phil Ochs and Tom Paxton had played at the Cardiff Students Union. Elektra had released the *Singer Songwriter Project* featuring Bruce Murdoch, Dick Farina, Dave Cohen and Patrick Sky. Tom Rush had brought out his first album. On the covers these guys were usually depicted looking pensive, standing in railroad yards, rolling cigarettes, sitting on their guitar cases, staring into the distance. They'd be dressed in check shirts and would wear narrow cord jeans. Almost all of them rambled although, to a man, none of them knew where they were bound.

I bought myself a harmonica harness and a kazoo and strapped the thing onto my chest. Dylan did this and, on TV, so did Donovan. I put bottle caps on my shoes. Corona lemonade bottle caps, I recall, held on with rubber bands. I wanted to be a one man band. Trouble was I could barely strum a chord. The fretboard was bent, the strings stood high. I did my best. I listened to Dylan doing *In My Time of Dyin'* from his first album. On this he was reported to have used his girlfriend Suze Rotolo's lipstick holder to block and slide the chords. Suze Rotolo, the woman on the cover of *Freewheelin'*, the person almost every woman I knew wanted to be.

I tried a knife, a bottle, a metal comb. It all sounded dreadful. You need a special tuning, Pete Morgan told me. Then it'll work. Pete was a poet and Robert Johnson fanatic who would later become a cornerstone of the second aeon traveling circus. Special? I could hardly manage normal.

The message was plain. Get out there and watch other guitarists, see how they do it. Watch their fingers on the fretboards, check out how they finger pick, how they pluck, how they strum. I did. Went to London and found my way to Les Cousins to hear Bert Jansch. He played his version of Davy Graham's *Angi*. With a huge variation in degrees of competence almost every acoustic guitarist in those days did. This is a piece of guitar instrumental wonder where, as Bert Jansch's biographer, Colin Harper, has it, Graham had created a baroque bass line and then moved it slightly. To the uninitiated it looked and sounded as Bach must have to his predecessors. Written and recorded by Graham in 1962 it had appeared first on an obscure EP, *3/4 AD* , made with Alexis Korner. By 1965 the tune had spread far and wide. There were versions out there by Bert Jansch, Paul Simon, John Renbourn, and Gordon Giltrap. And later on by Chicken Shack and Chumbawamba.

At the Cardiff Folk Song Club I sat and watched Graham Hemmingway[18] flick his fingers through a local version. I was in awe.

I could never do this. Me, with my incompetent *Midnight Special* chord thrashings, bottle tops on feet rattling, kazoo tunelessly tooting, harmonica ignored or forgotten. I got myself down to the Greyhound in Bridge Street. This was an historic Cardiff tavern. According to local historian Brian Lee the Greyhound had been frequented in the mid nineteenth century by "those who went down to the sea in ships… and all the well-known faces of the town could be found in the back parlour.[19]" But by the time I arrived its best days had clearly passed. The Greyhound was a scrumpy pub. Two front bars, down and outs to the left, regular drinkers to the right. Hard, actually, to tell the difference. The bar had two pumps – beer or cider. There were no further choices. Everything was a shilling a pint. Out back you could get scrumpy leavened with added blackcurrant, thruppence extra. Only the properly-waged went for that. Being an aspiring member of the beat generation and certainly a singer-songwriter wannabe I always drank with the less well off.

I was in there on my own, which I suppose was a brave thing. The locals, somnambulantly slumped across tables or propped in a miasma of alcohol in the corners, generally took no notice. But on this occasion they did. I guess it was the guitar and the superstructure holding my harmonica and kazoo that I'd put on. "Can you play something," a bloke in a long rotten overcoat asked. It was more a demand than a request. I got the guitar out, fumbled a tuning and tried the first few bars of *Midnight Special* as learned from a Jesse Fuller album. He played it with gusto. My version was with gall stones and grovelling, a stumbling, tuneless mumble. "Do Nellie Dean," someone else shouted. I couldn't. Didn't. The drinkers surrounded me, menacingly. "You're useless," one of them decided, waving a half empty pint glass. "You should piss off, you bloody student". Students were what they hated. The landlord leant across the bar. "Best be gone, son," he advised. I left.

That was it. My career as a singer over. The guitar went back into its case. It came out again briefly a few years later, to have a chord or two strummed on it as part of the poetry and music band, the second aeon travelling circus, but mostly I was now writer rather than musician. Speaker not singer. Songwriting done, I was a poet instead.

6 • How The Blues Made It To The UK

I'm sitting at home listening to The Rolling Stones. *5 x 5*. The best EP of the decade so far, by a million miles. These guys with long hair and attitude have chased the blues right back to source. They've crossed the Atlantic, gone up to Chicago and bearded Willie Dixon in his den. They've recreated the blues at the place where it all started: 2120 South Michigan Avenue, studios of Phil and Leonard Chess. This is the spot where Chuck and Bo and Howlin' Wolf, Buddy Guy, Little Walter and Muddy Waters hold court. Nobody but those signed to the label ever record here, that's the house rule. But for the Stones Chess broke it. Muddy helped unload the equipment. Chuck Berry and Buddy Guy came by to watch. Willie Dixon did his best to sell them songs. Andrew Loog Oldham, Stones manager, was the ostensible producer but it was the Chess studio engineer Ron Malo who did the biz. The result was the most satisfying set of white boy r&b tracks UK Decca had yet to put out.

The music papers were ecstatic. In anticipation first and then, once the EP had hit the shops, over the tracks themselves. This was the real stuff. Everyone said it was. The 5x5 sessions – which were far more extensive than the five tracks officially released in the UK, and to this day contain tracks that are still in the can – were a mixture of r&b, Mod-generation soul, and Chicago mainstream electric blues. The Valentino's Bobby Womack song, *It's All Over Now*, The Drifters' *Under the Boardwalk*, Dale Hawkins' *Suzie Q*, Wilson Pickett's *If You Need Me*. The selection was neatly leavened with more traditional sounding numbers such as Big Bill Broonzy's *Tell Me Baby*, Howlin' Wolf's *Down In The Bottom*, and Muddy Waters' *I Can't Be Satisfied*. The stand out was the Stone's own composition, credited to Nanker Phlege, and titled after the address of the studios themselves, *2120 South Michigan Avenue*[20]. This was a guitar and harmonica jam of the kind I'd been trying to emulate for months. Three minutes thirty-nine seconds of echo chamber harmonica, riffed guitar and Booker T-styled organ interplay. This was the real blues.

Only it wasn't. How could we find out what was? The popular music press didn't know (and to this day still doesn't – sending re-released John Lee Hooker best-ofs out to wet-eared young reviewers who declared him to be the soul of authentic country blues. Hooker had never been that. With his thrummed electric guitar he was where the blues were heading not where they'd been). At the record shops it was all Josh White and Brownie McGhee, and Brother John Sellers. In the discos it was Manfred Mann and The Pretty Things. On the radio I heard Blackburn chart-toppers The Four Pennies singing a soft-edged version of Lead Belly's *In The Pines*. They'd called it *Black Girl* and the Light Programme Saturday Club DJ spinning it said it was the most authentic Deep South country blues he'd ever heard.

Slowly though, the truth arrived. The names of hitherto unheard bluesmen began to be quoted by the cognoscenti. Bukka White. Son House. Charley Patton. Mississippi John Hurt. Skip James. Robert Johnson. These guys had not recorded for Chess or Checker, had not made it onto the bills of the annual UK touring American Folk Blues Festival, were not available in the racks down at City Radio, not yet. They were not played on the radio, not on my radio, not on the fuzzy warble of Radio Luxemburg, not on upbeat Hamburg-based AFN, and not on anything broadcast by those guardians of our intellect, the BBC. We had to wait for DJ Mike Raven, the Sounds of the Seventies, and the morphing of Manfred Mann front man Paul Jones from performer to radio record-spinner for that.

Many of these singers were, by now, dead. Little wonder their latest recordings had not appeared in the racks downtown. But the record industry, on the rise, probably for the last time in its history, wasn't slow to capitalise. Genuine material from the blues' great pre-war history started to appear. Albums collecting music from the dawn of recording were issued. They featured singers moaning and crying into great acoustic microphones. The blues as masterpiece, laid down in a single take.

As hiss-removing digital technology, and indeed digital technology itself, had yet to be invented we listened to the real McCoy through a veil of pop, smudge, crackle, click click, hiss and fog. Gus Cannon, Blind Lemon Jefferson, Blind Blake, The Mississippi Sheiks. As far removed from The Rolling Stones as Beethoven. Roll over Beethoven, Tell Tchaikovsky, Chuck Berry. Ah, you already have.

The blues have a reputation for being sung by the less well off from the black American south. By farm workers wearing patched overalls. By cotton pickers just in from labouring in the Mississippi fields. These guys would sit in the corner, straw in mouth, strumming their bought from Chicago by mail order guitars. They'd growl out their songs. If you believe the myths then you'll understand that this acoustic and, by now, pretty ancient music had made its way slowly north to Detroit and to Chicago. There astute African-Americans adopted it, added electricity and drums to give it power, and played it for money in bars. The field clothes had been replaced by suits with wide lapels. The music had moved on.

This music had drawn its strength from the chants and work hollers of African slaves. Its players used instruments that perhaps resembled those found in Africa but not quite. Banjos, guitars. The diddley bow[21]. The Jew's harp. Kazoos. Harmonicas. Bottles and jugs you blew into. They were brand new in the early years of the twentieth century. But there persisted allusions to a long and unsophisticated past that went back decades before the start of recording. Jug band music. Men with stringed instruments hollering into the distance. There was a certainty that the rural South had been the core. Sitting in my front room I heard the great and the musically good on the radio talking this history up. The certainty took hold. Had to be. It was from here that the blues had come.

The hard evidence, however, doesn't quite support this theory. Bandleader WC Handy, composer of *St Louis Blues* and a blues founding father[22] with a whole park named after him in Memphis, allegedly took a rail journey across the South sometime in 1903. When his train stopped in tiny Tutweiler, Tallahatchie County, Mississippi, he overheard a ragged "lean, loose-jointed Negro plunking a guitar". As the man played he "pressed a knife on the strings of the guitar in a manner popularised by Hawaiian guitarists who used steel bars." He sang a line which he repeated three times. 'Going where the Southern cross the dog'. Handy thought it was the weirdest music he'd ever come across. It stuck in his mind and he eventually incorporated the sounds into music of his own. Handy's *Yellow Dog Blues*, *The Memphis Blues*, and *St Louis Blues* which held echoes of the sounds he'd heard were all published in 1914. This was before the advent of widely available recordings when sheet music still ruled the day. Was this the genesis of the blues? But then Handy was most likely merely copyrighting versions of the music being played around him.

I listened to the first blues recording or, at least, to the piece of music that stakes the claim, and I found that it has only the faintest resemblance to the blues that were to come. Handy's *Memphis Blues* recorded on acoustic equipment in a single take by the Victor Military Band sounded for all the world like German marching music, or rough jazz with a distinct lack of jive. No guitars, no singers, no folk blues moaning, no bending notes. I'd expected the first blues to be something like Robert Johnson with even more hiss and crackle overlaying his sighing slide but that's not what I got.

At the start of the twentieth century in the Southern States blacks listened to ragtime. They danced to the hits of the day. They liked the idea of being entertained not by a hick sitting in the corner but rather a fully turned out and well-presented band, no stringed instruments, and if possible with a female lead. These women crooners, done up in sequined dresses, long gloves, lots of sparkling jewellery and with feather boas draped around their necks were what pulled in the listeners. Torch singers like Bessie Smith, Victoria Spivey, Ma Rainey, Ethel Waters, Sippie Wallace, and Ida Cox emerged as the black stars of the day. The blues queens. Where recorded blues really began.

When Handy got together with music publisher Perry Bradford to convince record companies that there was a market for the new emerging blues music there was little enthusiasm. However the General Phonograph Company was eventually convinced to put out black vaudeville singer Mamie Smith doing *Crazy Blues*. This was the first of what were to become known as race records, discs aimed solely at the black market. Whites wouldn't be interested, certainly not. The song was a giant hit. It sounds today like early jazz and still not a lot like the music that was to come. But it was the blues. That was 1920 and for the rest of the decade the form held sway. The blues queens were on top, the female vaudeville blues singers, the first to moan, holler and yell in rhythm, the first to get 12 bars down as the dominant style. They were not badly-dressed black men up from the plantation with battered guitars round their necks. That material, the real down home country blues of Bukka White, Charley Patton, and Son House, would take a few more years to arrive.

The pre-war folk blues that white audiences from the sixties on have revered as the mother lode didn't really start until the mid-nineteen-twenties. That was when singers like Blind Lemon Jefferson, Charley Patton, and Blind Willie McTell were recorded by record company executives eager to extend their reach. They were solo singers, one man one guitar, telling life like it was. Not that Blind Lemon and his fellow travellers were in any way backwoods country boys. By contrast they were the epitome of style and sophistication. Check the surviving photographs of him, Blind Blake and the singer later to take all the glory, Robert Johnson. All wear suits and look as if they are dressed for a wedding. Blind Lemon sports a white shirt[23]. Blind Blake is in black bow-tied evening dress. Robert Johnson sports a brimmed fedora, a wide lapelled pin stripe suit, tab collared shirt and clipped tie. These guys had not just walked in from the fields.

But there was a taste out there among audiences for material they could directly relate to. The solo singer accompanying himself on guitar with maybe someone there in the background blowing a harmonica became progressively more popular. And as this music drifted up to the northern cities it acquired slightly more sophisticated trappings. Pianos were added. The guitar and piano duo that cost a whole lot less than a band of the size required to back one of the blues queens became increasingly prevalent. Tampa Red and Georgia Tom. Scrapper Blackwell and Leroy Carr. Lonnie Johnson emerged as the blues singer with the best voice this side of Rudy Vallée. Big Bill Broonzy made his name as a blue shouter fronting a small instrumental combo. There were plenty of male folk blues stylists too. Imitation country folk riding in the wake of Charley Patton. But few of them sold many records. Most of them would have to wait for fame until a white audience rediscovered them as genuine originals.

As the blues settled in the cities they became transformed. Boogie-woogie pianists joined with amplified guitar players. Saxophones were added. Country origins were forgotten. The black big swing bands of leaders like Count Basie and Jay McShann all incorporated blues shouting into their repertoires. By the time the war came the blues had moved itself almost full circle – from the sophisticated dance rhythms of the blues queens through the elemental solo work of the country blues howlers and back to the smoke-filled clubs of the cities where singers who were the epitome of style held sway. This was jazzy, up-tempo, good-time music known as jump blues. In the immediate pre and post-World War II period this was where blues music was: Louis Jordan, Big Joe Turner, Roy Milton, Wynonie Harris.

White youth, white American youth that is, turned what they heard into rock and roll. Elvis, a self-confessed country boy, got hold of the stomping blues music of Big Mama Thornton and Arthur Big Boy Crudup, added western style, red neck attitude, and made it even bigger. *Hound Dog, My Baby Left Me, That's Alright Mama.* A decade on this material would form the heart of many a blues band's repertoire.

In Chicago and Detroit, cities where the cold winter winds would blow, black Afro-American blues singers began to use solid electric guitars. Blues music with solo breaks and power chords in place of finger picking and strumming became the norm. The style had regional centres – Memphis, Dallas, New Orleans. Men from a tradition of shouting, unamplified, over the crowd roar at house rent parties, juke joints and bars found their voices would go much further if they used the newly available electric microphones. Valve-driven amps took to the stage. Big Joe Williams, the country singer with the loudest and as a consequence the coarsest of voices, was eclipsed.

Just who it was who first put an electric pick-up onto their blues guitar could well be up for disagreement. Smokey Hogg, Lightnin' Hopkins, Lonnie Johnson and Slim Harpo are all early exponents. But, in an amazing bout of unanimity for the blues world, most agree that the legendary T-Bone Walker, born in Linden, Texas, way back in 1910, had to be a forerunner. He was a friend of early electric jazz guitarist Charlie Christian, and began to use the same equipment in the mid-1930s. Christian wanted to make his guitar sound like a saxophone and indulged in single-string lead runs rather than allowing his playing to languish in the rhythm section. The approach had an undoubted influence on T-Bone. His first electric guitar single, *Mean Old World* made for Capitol in 1942, is full of jangly lead, a forerunner of what was to come.

The backing bands at this time avoided percussion and used stand-up double basses amplified through microphones. But drums and solid electric bass guitars were not long in following. In Chicago the new style of full-on electric blues, often with distorted electric solos and power chords, caught the imagination. The pioneers were the heroes of the British sixties blues boom: Muddy Waters, John Lee Hooker, Howlin' Wolf and Jimmy Reed. Johnny Shines missed fame by a whisker. Elmore James, master of the super slide, came in fast behind.

We're in the late forties and early fifties now and Muddy is outside a diner somewhere listening to his first solo record, *I Can't Be Satisfied*, playing on the radio. This had been recorded for Leonard and Phil Chess's new Aristocrat label. The brothers hadn't managed to give their artist his own copy. Nor pay him very much either. It was Muddy's first hit, proof too that the electric blues were a booming thing. Soon they'd change the name of their record label to something a bit more memorable: Chess. Muddy's first Chess label single was the brooding, solo guitar accompanied *Rollin Stone*. After that the world changed gear.

The boom became a flood. Buddy Guy, Chuck Berry, Bo Diddley, Albert King, BB King, Otis Rush, Freddie King, Magic Slim and a good many other who were to become blues household names launched their recording careers. The records they made, often for small and transient labels, and almost always for no real money to speak of, became the foundation on which the emerging whiteboy r&b explosion would be based.

Back where I lived whiteboys were still largely pretending they were versions of Cliff Richard or Max Bygraves. These were days before internet, before TV music channels, before readily accessible music radio and before world markets took their incipient hold. Romantically, early electric blues discs made their way to Britain in the luggage of sailors. There were the occasional specialist shops such as Doug Dobell's in London's Charing Cross Road where imported blues records could be had. But generally the material was as rare as men on Mars. In the UK we were slow to get on board.

It all came in a rush once the real Sixties had dawned. I say real. For 1961 and 1962 things carried on pretty much as they had in the dying years of the decade before. There were more hopeless British rock and roll acts. The twist, really an opportunity to retread rock, was the dance craze. Top of the charts were guitar instrumentals from bands like The Ventures and The Shadows. Peter Jay and The Jaywalkers rocked up the classics. Offenbach, Tchaikovsky and Beethoven, through the distorting mirror of Jay and his fellow travellers, were hits all over again.

If you were there, like I was, then it was your formative youth. But in reality it was a time of musical back peddling, of weak repetition and the fading power of rock and roll. On TV Alma Cogan was presented as the most desirable and cutting edge of singers. Big Fifties hooped dresses, sequins, hair in a lacquered pile, lavish smiles. Laugh in the voice. Appeal to youth pretty much zero. The world rolled on in the charge of the elderly.

But in Liverpool and London, Belfast and Newcastle, kids with guitars had got their hands on early discs put out by Chess. Chuck and Bo and John Lee, the Wolf and Sonny Boy. The foundation of the future.

It took a pair of Europeans to capitalise on this. German jazz promoter Horst Lippmann with his partner Fritz Rau had formed the Lippman + Rau concert agency in the shortage-filled nineteen fifties. Prompted by German jazz publicist Joachim-Ernst Berendt they came up with the idea of bringing to the stages of Europe not jazz trumpeters nor white rock and rollers but genuine black down home American blues singers. Folk Blues Tours, they'd call them. It was a revolutionary concept. But then again this was the start of a revolutionary decade. With typical German thoroughness Lippmann decided that rather than fish around in the Chicago phone book for a Mr Wolf he would contact the Chess label's main record producer directly. This was the man at the centre of the electric blues, Willie Dixon. The great American Folk Blues Festival tours of Germany, France and Britain were born.

The tours, run annually right through the sixties and with a sort of coda in 1985, were a huge success. They blended the obvious (Sonny Boy Williamson, Howlin' Wolf) with the down home (Sleepy John Estes, Son House, Bukka White) and then added a sampling from the new generation blues hitmakers (Sugar Pie Desanto, Buddy Guy, Otis Rush). The result was a night of full on blues excitement, blues thrills and blues discovery. It was for me and it was for those thousands of other young sharps who'd just discovered the music. Blues boomed.

Bristol, which was where I first encountered the Folk Blues Tours, was another country. Before the building of the first Seven Bridge it was well across the sea-filled Estuary. But in 1964 it didn't feel like that at all. I'd got to Brunel's city on the train through the tunnel, poems in my pocket, notebook in my hands, without sight of water. At Colston Hall I'd witnessed the black stars of the third great American Folk Blues Festival tour slamming out drunken electric blues and unhinged country stomps in a way that made me wonder why the whole world wasn't whooping with excitement like I was. Hubert Sumlin sliding perfect licks behind Howlin' Wolf's primitive blues roar, Hammie Nixon downing a pint of gin on stage as support for Sleepy John Estes'Tennessee foot stomp and Sonny Boy Williamson in a bowler hat blowing the harmonica with his nose. At the centre of this joyous, shambolic manifestation of revitalised negritude was both Chess and Lippman's main man, the rotund song writer, double bass player and Chess record producer Willie Dixon.

Dixon's centrality at this time was vital. He knew everyone, had all the right contacts and understood perfectly how to fix a deal. He knew just what was hot. He was Chess session bassist on almost everything. He song wrote, he managed, he talent scouted, he was the perfect foil for Leonard Chess, an all-round achiever and with the outsized personality to match. A list of some of his hits includes *Hoochie Coochie Man, I Just Want to Make Love to You, Little Red Rooster, My Babe,*

Spoonful, and *You Can't Judge a Book by the Cover.* You might have thought some of these had ancient back history, were slave tunes, were African dances revitalised, were sung by itinerant miners, by plantation workers, by country boys sitting in shacks or strumming in the corner of the local juke. Not so. They flowed, professionally, from the pen of a single man. It was Dixon who would successfully sue Led Zeppelin for lifting his lyrics for their *Whole Lotta Love.* And it was Dixon who fought tirelessly for the rights of black blues artists in their battles for royalties from their non-paying labels. But right now he was on stage in the middle of it all, a giant of a man, well over six feet and topping seventeen stone. He took one solo, *Big Legged Woman*, delivered with style and steam. I wondered just why it was he'd stayed so long in the background and hadn't done more as himself. But such people, the circuit boards through which everything flows, are essential for the world to work.

Later, outside the Colston Hall's stage door I'd spotted Dixon, cigar waving, taking the air and shakily told him how great I though the was and would he like some of my songs. I had dozens, woke up this morning poetry, stuffed into my pockets, my creative gems. He took them without a glance and folded them into his own pockets among the bits of sterling he hadn't really got a handle on, and went back inside. "You write to me," I yelled after him. But I never heard a word.

In 1964 at Granada TV, the most exciting TV broadcaster Britain had at the time, producers decided that the blues were now the cutting edge. A set of black American singers were touring the country and were due to play at Manchester's Free Trade Hall that month. Advantage would be taken. Someone hit on the idea that since the blues was filled with songs about freight trains why not film the thing on the not yet privatised LMS? A disused railway station at Wilberham Road was co-opted, and done up with louvre doors and tumbleweeds in some stage manager's idea of what the South was like. Actually it looked more like something out of the wild west. For the occasion the station was renamed Chorltonville. Bring the blues to mind? Nope. But then that's how it all was in the about to swing sixties. People chancing their arms.

The resulting show, *Blues and Gospel Train*, presented some of the most sophisticated and exciting performers the blues had, hung about with aching British platitude and wincingly awful stage sets. Sister Rosetta Tharpe was delivered to the station by horse and cart. She had high heels, a fair-haired wig and a great white overcoat of the kind my grandmother wore. She also had a killer flat-bodied electric guitar. As the Manchester weather turned from wind to wind plus light rain and then wind plus driving storm the great gospel singer powered into *Didn't It Rain* giving many a British guitar wizard something new to aspire to when it came to rocking solos. Muddy Waters walked up the tracks, suitcase in hand, long coat, trilby hat. He mounted the platform using a jerry-rigged set of steps and picked up his guitar from amid a heap of boxes next to a black man swaying himself through the cold north western British evening in what the producers imagined would be a Southern States rocking chair. He did *You Can't Lose What You Ain't Never Had* including full bottle neck slides to rivet the 200-strong audience of assorted Mods and hangers-on brought in from Central Manchester.

The programme may have been riddled with cliché but it did present the blues, the real thing, to a much wider audience than had the Colston Hall. No Willie Dixon but Sonny Terry and Brownie McGhee, Rev Gary Davis, Cousin Joe along with Muddy's half-brother pianist Otis Spann instead. Down in sunny Cardiff I and my fellow youths watched this late night extravaganza in wonder and imagined we'd witnessed the blues at source.

But could we do it? Could we make this music? Alexis Korner, the godfather of British blues, had certainly thought so. And Chris Barber, the legendary fifties trombone player and blues promoter had no doubts. But the critics were gathering. The blues were a black Afro-American form (although that term had yet to enter currency). They were the sole preserve of those who'd suffered. Been downtrodden, put upon, hurt. *Can Blue Men Sing The Whites?*, was a question The Bonzo Dog Doo Dah Band were to pose in 1968. The answer in 1964 was not now, not yet, not quite. But soon.

7 • Getting To The USA

How does anyone ever manage to do this? The obstacles are huge, the cost is enormous, and the distance impossible. For several generations of British youth America was the dream you read about, you listened to, and you experienced, filtered by Hollywood, on the silver screen. To travel there was a fantasy. It could only be managed by those very few who lived the high life and who ran the world. It was a country that everyone I knew aspired to be part of but to which not one had been.

The British may well lay claim to have founded America but by the 50s we were forgotten men. We lived in a pale forgotten country where we sang forgotten songs. In musical terms we were not partners in one common adventure but imitators and poor ones at that. Our greatest success during the period was to send skiffle back to where it came from in a shameless coals to Newcastle operation. Could we make it new, as Ezra Pound wanted us to? We could not.

But the twentieth, if nothing else, was a century of unrelenting change. In 1962 when The Beatles first got their guitars into London's Abbey Road studios the die was cast. Music on our side of the pond went from pale imitation to world leader in about twelve months flat. Months that were trackable. From the release of *Please Please Me* in January 1963 to the band's position as American chart dominators by January 1964.

A little later Freddie Laker launched the world's first budget airline, Laker Airways, and offered flights to the wonders of America for £32.50. Access across the Atlantic for all had begun.

The British invasion in the wake of all this success came and went.

The flood of home-grown UK bands was led by The Beatles and including just about everyone of worth from the singer of *Windmills of Your Mind*, Noel Harrison, to Billy J Kramer and The Dakotas, Wayne Fontana and The Mindbenders, Peter and Gordon, Chad and Jeremy, Herman's Hermits and Freddie and The Dreamers. They all made it to strut their stuff across America's vast hinterlands. Some using Laker's cheapo aeroplanes although most taking label-paid-for business class scheduled seats. Taking a British version of American music back to America and making such a success of it was an unexpected twist to music history. But not for The Down and Out Blueswailers. For us the whole deal still seemed to be impossible.

Maybe music wasn't to be the door opener. Poets went there on tour. I'd read about this. Dylan Thomas doing the rounds of the US literary societies. Kingsley Amis as a visiting professor at Princeton. Ted Hughes in Massachusetts. From Wales Nigel Jenkins had travelled to work on circuses in the mid-West. John Idris Jones, the publisher of my first hard-backed book, had gone to America for a year and come back speaking with a Yankee accent. This all seemed incredibly romantic and desirably bohemian. But with no money how did you begin?

You start with a single invitation and then you build up from that. This was the advice of Tony Curtis, editor, poet, golfer and eventually Wales's first Professor of Poetry. Tony had done the thing at least six times, touring the great academic institutions, reading at colleges where only stellar high fliers had been before. "Get in touch and ask them," he said. I could write a few letters, I supposed, and hope that knowledge of who I was would not be too difficult for Americans to find. I'd run a magazine which had sold there, after all. And my archive was by this time safe in the State University of New York at Buffalo.

A dealer had come round when I was down on my luck and offered me what was then a considerable sum of money to sell him my papers – the manuscripts and correspondence I'd accumulated running the literary journal *second aeon*[24], my correspondence with Charles Bukowski and William Wantling, Allen Ginsberg and Louis, his poet father, my fights with the Kerouac archivists, my dealings with great European concretists, with the Japanese and the Yugoslav

Signalists, with RS Thomas and with Kingsley Amis, with Peter Porter, Peter Redgrove and Bob Cobbing. My whole raft of documentation of the poetry wars at London's Poetry Society. My exchanges with the Cleveland poets da levy, Kent Taylor, and Tom Kryss, with Doug Blazek, Gary Snyder, William Burroughs, Cid Corman, Robert Bly, Carol Berge, and Larry Eigner, tapes of me reading things on the BBC, my attempts to include science fiction writers such as James Blish and Poul Anderson, and to get poetry from the Doors' Jim Morrison, and my endless cat and mouse skirmishes with the Welsh Arts Council over money and just how do you spell the name of Prinknash Abbey's concrete monk, Dom Sylvester Houedard.

All these joys and gems now sat in filing boxes in Buffalo's great stacks. Today they've been processed thoroughly and shifted to the Fales Library in Washington Square, New York where they occupy 14 boxes, take up 6.75 linear feet[25] and can be searched online. But somehow, back then, I failed to capitalise on all this. I did write a letter or two suggesting that I might be a desirable person to invite. Why not have me over there to read? To deliver the British goods. These requests were letters, mark, not emails. This meant airmail costs, onion skin paper, loads of typing, plus at least a six day time lag before any answer could get back.

I had much silence and the occasional thank you but not at this time and then, out of the mists, one invitation from somewhere in the west offering me a solo reading for the local literary dinner club. We'd like to see you Welsh poets here in our State, it ran. We'll look after you well. The invitation offered a fee of $200, overnight accommodation at the home of the secretary and a meal. We like warmth and comfort, the invitation said. But travel expenses remained unmentioned. How could I manage those?

It was only later that I learned that the real trick was to get onto the circuit where travel costs would be covered by our leading international disseminator of UK artistic goods, the British Council. They were forever organising tours that would truly represent the diversity and originality of British culture and show it to the world. I was young and Welsh and with a poetry stage presence that attracted hundreds. The perfect choice. Trouble was it was mostly me that believed all that.

Those with their hands on the sources of finance preferred to send out folk dancers from Blaenau Festiniog and balaclava knitters from the Mawddach Estuary. Greater colour.

It took until 2003 for my first US trip to happen. In the intervening years between desire and realisation, the many decades between the revolutionary sixties and the recycling nineties, I'd contented myself with visiting the rest of the world. Readings happened in places as far apart as Bulawayo and Budapest, Frankfurt and St Petersburg, Belgrade and Dublin. Plenty of centres beyond the reaches of flying boats but nothing in that citadel of the free, where the buffalo roam and there's dancing in the street, America.

My glorious new millennium invitation was to visit upstate New York. It was sent by American-Welsh poet David Lloyd. The annual meeting of the North American Welsh Association for the Study of Welsh Culture and History, a grand academic gathering of the lost tribes and the ex-pats was to take place at Syracuse, NY. NAWASWCH, as the association was acronymically known, sounded a bit like a brand of toilet cleaner but was in fact a well-organised society with a wide membership and a record for drawing lines across the oceans. It wasn't only the Scots and the Irish who founded America. It has to be said, however, that identifying famous Welsh Americans beyond Jerry Lee Lewis and Bob Hope has always been difficult.

Syracuse, a northern city famous for salt, chemicals and the manufacture of traffic signals, is up near the Canadian border, between the Great Lakes and the Finger Lakes, in a place where the winters are cold and the country ends, but still wholeheartedly in tooth, accent and claw, America.

We went there by train. Well, no. But that's the sort of thing psycho-geographer Will Self declared he'd done when he set out to walk to America. He meant he'd walk to the airport rather than take the bus. We flew to New York and then got the Amtrak north. The old fashioned way. I'd hoped from Grand Central Station (where Elizabeth Smart had sat down and wept), the one in all the movies. But that place, although still architecturally wondrous, had been reduced to the operation of suburban services. Long distance, and most of America is long distance after all, ran from the savagely underwhelming Penn Station in midtown Manhattan. We caught a cab. Psychogeography notwithstanding I wasn't about to walk into the city from Newark airport out in the Soprano heartlands of New Jersey.

The train north was nothing like I'd imagined it would be. It was hard to look out of the narrow carriage windows but when I could there was not much more to see than trees. A little like a sleeper journey I'd taken in Russia from Moscow to St Petersburg, a green corridor with nothing to see but conifer. In Russia I'd imagined they set this up deliberately to shield their fair and bountiful lands from prying eyes. But surely that wouldn't apply in America? There was a break at Albany where we all got off, movie style with no discernible raised platform anywhere, to walk about a bit while the driver took a break. I looked out towards the ever present forest hoping for a glimpse of bears or men with feathers in their hair but nothing stirred.

We rattled on in the direction of Canada. We sat in cavernous low-lit compartments, lounging about with fellow passengers who mostly seemed down on their luck: glum faces, luggage held together with straps, a few reading their Bibles for comfort. God in America is much nearer the surface that he is back home. Somewhere beyond Schenectady a white haired, moustachioed traveller in a dark overcoat asked me where I was from. "Cardiff. You know where that is?" "Yep, Shirley Bassey. Coal. I know about Wales". I smiled. That was pretty much the last time such knowledge was evident. Most of America, it turned out, knew little beyond their own borders. Many had never left the state they lived in. My new companion worked in insurance, he said, "Selling, you know, door to door, it's hard work. Ain't these Amtrak trains just great? I use them all the time". He got off at Utica. Utica, the Phoenicians' first African colony. For a country pointing at the future the United States is full of the past. Every place you ever knew back again. Amsterdam, Rotterdam, Troy, Rome, Shenandoah, Galway, Waterloo, Berlin, Persia, Homer, Attica. The old world hanging on.

Syracuse was as full of wind, as I imagined Chicago would be. A city built on the junction of the Erie Canal and its branches. Right where Ninety intersects the Eighty-first. Right where the Onondaga

Indian reservation was full of swamp. A settler called Bogardus drained a lot of it. James Geddes built the corduroy road[26]. The Onondaga Nation moved out to a new reservation to the south. Full of wrecked clapboard housing with the insulation coming out when I visited. Trade seemed to be reselling cigarettes in bulk. Many inhabitants appeared drunk. There was forestry, naturally, and there was also a lot of rain.

The conference was being held at the University. The city has two, both grounded in God. The Wesleyans founded Syracuse University which in later years had distanced itself. Le Moyne, started by the Jesuits, stayed true. We were headed there. But first stop, naturally, was a blues club. For the Welsh in North America what else?

We rolled into the Dinosaur, a barbeque and booze Harley Davidson celebration on West Willow Street. The road outside was thick with bikes while indoors the good ol' boys wore leathers, pony tails and had tattoos across their knuckles. In the corner Sue Foley's[27] band were belting electric good-time blues, *Roll With Me Henry*, Fender Telecaster lead, drums and bass. This was drinking music, like the blues always were.

We had a few, so did the members of the Welsh poetry and music band travelling with us. This was an early Nigel Jenkins on harmonica configuration that featured John Barnie and Iwan Llwyd on guitars with Twm Morys on harp and keyboards. The band was known as Y Bechgen Drwg, the bad boys. To look the part they wore long coats, cowboy boots and black Stetsons picked up in New York on the way up.

The Dinosaur was an excellent introduction. Real blues, well, reprocessed and mostly rewritten material slightly pasteurised, harmonica dropped, guitar peddles added, and cranked out by a white female Canadian. But still the blues and twenty-first century blues at that. Here we were, the bad ol' Welsh boys, bringing the whole mess of it back.

The reality was that in its heartland none of this authenticity stuff that I'd been brought up on actually meant much at all. The real blues – just what did that term mean? We might know that the music had originated in some particular place, at some specified time. We might own recordings, if any had been made. We had also listened to them, cleaned up, de-popped, crackles removed, in as near to authentic reality as our digital HiFi science would allow. We would have sat there, in our clean front rooms, with our big speakers producing versions of how Blind Gary Davis had actually sung. All the croaks and groans of his voice would appear in ultimate clarity. We'd hear the sound of his fingers sliding along his fretboard and the strings of his guitar chiming out. But the real experience was the one he'd had, back then, playing in the dusty jukes and the dirty joints, among the rural poor, thrumming and thumping to his fellows as the night drew long and the whiskey went down. Those blues could never have been the same as the ones heard in the terraces of Aberystwyth, Abertawe and Abergavenny.

Up at Le Moyne the largely white middle-class academics nodded to the youthful rhythm being banged out by four distinctly non-teenage Welshmen. The blues up from Llanystumdwy. The blues sung in Welsh. The blues used as a backdrop for poetry. Via the Syracuse Dinosaur and more beers than they should have. The blues gone full circle.

In New York itself, the city where anything can happen, the blues were not on the streets. 9/11 had happened less than eighteen months back. Ground Zero was a raked hole surrounded by fencing. Unexpected silence amid organised chaos. There were flags everywhere. Flying from every pole, draped from every building, in every window, on every car. America telling itself it was still America. There was ash still drifted in shop windows and tributes to the loved and the lost and the heroic fire crews affixed to hoarding walls. Candles, names, drawings, tributes, photos, letters to the lost and to the still missing. New York, a fragile, damaged place.

Down in Battery Park Wynton Marsalis was giving a benefit concert. *The Majesty of the Blues*. Marsalis gone back to his New Orleans roots, dismissing the avant garde forever. "He could have been the heir to Miles, that boy," said the guy next to me on the crushed grass. "Only he kept looking back not forward." On stage Wynton sounded like Ellington's first main man, Cootie Williams. He stood there effortlessly pushing out those blue notes that just don't exist elsewhere.

On Bleecker I look for the intersection with MacDougal. I have my photo taken below the street sign, newly purchased Horner Super Vamper in hand. Harmonicas, the track and trail and time wasting ruination of my life. Fred Neil's *Standing on the Corner of Bleecker & MacDougal* ringing in my ears. Around me are all the legendary venues of the Greenwich Village folk revival of the early sixties – Gerde's Folk City, Café Wha, The Bottom Line, Café Au Go Go, The Bitter End, The Fat Black Pussycat, The Gaslight Café. Here the young Bob Dylan, corduroy cap and open shirt, first played. Another strand of America that would take over the world. For a time this place was the epicentre. Joan Baez, Carolyn Hester, Judy Collins, Dave van Ronk, Tom Paxton, Phil Ochs, Patrick Sky, Dick Farina, Eric Anderson, Fred Neil.

These were *folk* singers, whatever that term precisely meant. They revived hillbilly music, turned Americana into a staple, added touches of country, slices of bluegrass and jug band music, reprocessed tunes lifted from the traditions of Ireland, Scotland, England and Wales. And what did they underpin a whole mess of it with? The blues. Van Ronk pioneering *House of the Rising Sun*, Fred Neil added boogie woogie rhythms to things that half sounded like work songs and half things of his own creation. And Dylan himself, stomping and wailing, sliding steel on his acoustic guitar, his high nasal singing on *Fixin' To Die, Talking New York, See That My Grave is Kept Clean*. A yell of Afro-American darkness.

Dylan added harmonica to everything and clearly got away with it. And it was no good claiming, as some critics did, that he couldn't really play. His first professional recording, i.e. one where money changed hands, was backing Harry Belafonte with mouth organ on the great man's version of *Midnight Special*. But this wasn't the sort of sound I'd heard from Sonny Terry or Little Walter or Sonny Boy Williamson. The strands of American music were many. They started so far apart and then they ran together.

New York, capital of the world, showcased all of them. But mostly they did not originate in this place. Almost everything I admired about the singer-songwriters, for example – their love of blues licks, their re-treading of bluegrass rhythms, their extension of country music's penchant for confession, the way they were simultaneously new and old, their American heart – all these things originated in places west of where New York was. The nineteenth century Manifest Destiny of the United States, to move ever west and engulf the world, seemed to be a twentieth century accomplishment.

8 • Bluegrass Number One

Blue grass, the stuff that grows, is a real secret. It rarely exists in Britain. In Kentucky it grows two feet tall and then blossoms. It's the blossoms that are blue. Kentucky calls itself the bluegrass state, named after the grass. Bluegrass music came later. Its origins go back to the Ulster Scots, the southern Irish and the Christian English who had left their poor homelands for a fate in the new world. They'd run from famine, the desperation of debt and from religious persecution. They had reached the coal-filled heights of the American Appalachians and made the place their own.

They brought their music with them. Fiddle tunes, dance music, ballads, tales of love and loss, murder and death. Up there in the tree-thick hills was a time of endless manual work and unremitting faith. The music that evolved was a mix of older traditions – the ballad, the reel, the jig – with the sounds that the Afro-American brought, what would evolve into the blues. Most importantly the former slaves also brought with them another lead instrument to rival the fiddle. This was one that ended up delivering bluegrass's ubiquitous and defining sound – the banjo.

These stately, history-drenched origins are hard to hold in mind in the sticky, Dulux-glossed bar of the as yet unrefurbished Mackintosh Institute in Cardiff. Here the Boomswingers Bluegrass Club are putting on a well-amplified South Wales country rock four piece. The lead guitar has his long blonde hair hanging across his face like an alt country Texan on stage in Austin. He's backed by two other guitars and a man on drums. The audience is almost exclusively middle-aged and everyone is drinking pints. Here the years have worn us thin but we're not giving up. Blokes in old-fashioned denim have their thinning hair back in pony tails. The women have small tattoos on their calves, harps, dragons, a snake, a star. One in the corner has on cowboy boots. The man collecting cash at the door wears a country and western shirt embroidered with roses and a boot lace tie.

The music is bright and loud, The Byrds *Sweetheart of the Rodeo* pushed forward thirty years, western twang merging with indie rock. I don't recognise a single number. There's no history, nothing to latch on to bar the sound itself. The audience stare, tap their beer mats casually, shuffle back and forth to the bar for more drinks. It's before the ban and half the audience have roll ups going. On stage there are troubles with the power supply. Lights flicker, amps fail. The microphones shriek with feedback then refuse to work. An overweight technician in baggy jeans and a check shirt crawls about with a reel of insulation tape and a screwdriver. There are crackles and electric bangs then slices of returning sound before silence pervades once more. The audience smoke, smoulder and continue to drink. Then the sound comes back in a great rush: full blood electric Americana. Despite the mix failing with the singer's voice lost down there below the thundering lead like a man trying to make himself heard above the roar of a locomotive this is an enjoyable sound. I, too, fill it out with another pint of bitter. Great. But there's no banjo and it's not bluegrass.

Ethnomusicologists have tracked the banjo's origins back to African instruments, such as the kora, which have dried gourds as their bodies and sticks as their necks. Three strings run across them. These things went to America with the slave trade. Tuning pegs were added and the new bajar or banjar, as it came to be called[28], began to evolve towards its present shape. It was an instrument where the strings could both drone and be plucked. It was a Negro device and, in terms of the developing blues music, an immediate precursor to the all-conquering guitar.

The banjo was taken onto the American minstrel stage first by Uncle Tom blacks and then by whites black-faced. Back then, among the races, it was a very different world. The banjo was hauled around the country by itinerant musicians, plucked and strummed, danced to, sung over. But gradually the guitar with its greater musical range began to replace it. By the time the blues had got into the hands of Mississippi Delta singers in the 1920s, the banjo had been almost totally eclipsed. It hung on among rural musicians, in jug bands where it was played alongside accordions and harmonicas, and in Dixie jazz bands where it was a staple of the rhythm section. Magically, it then resurfaced in mid–fifties Britain in the heart of the skiffle movement.

A decade earlier the banjo had also become the defining music maker of the emerging bluegrass sound. Bluegrass, when I first heard it, on a cassette compilation called *Twenty-Five Greatest Bluegrass Hits*, sounded like an echo out of the deep American past. This was an ancient music, I thought, just like I'd imagined the blues to have been. Because of basic recording conditions the music sounded primitive. It was rough and full of fade and fuzz. It was a music, I imagined, that had antecedents that went back to that first Pilgrim Fathers landing and a history as long as that of the United States itself. Not long by European standards but long enough. There was something about its simplicity. These were songs sung in English but in a strange wayward version with vowels that bent and turned. The guitars, the banjos, the fiddles, the stand–up basses and, if you listened long enough for them, the mandolins, played in rhythms I was almost familiar with. They sounded like folk songs, like dance music, tunes you jigged to, ones where you swirled your partner round by the arm, where you stamped your feet in time like Geordie clog dancers, Scots sword leapers, Munster Riverdance foot stompers.

On this tape that scrolled slowly from reel to reel deep inside the cassette player of my black-topped, yellow Ford Capri were bands and musicians I'd never heard of. Johnny Duncan, The Stanley Brothers, Bill Monroe and His Blue Grass Boys, The Coon Creek Girls, Reno & Smiley, Jimmie Skinner, Jimmy Martin and The Sunny Mountain Boys, Don Reno and The Tennessee Cut Ups, The Osborne Brothers, and Earl Flatt and Lester Scruggs. The Flatt & Scruggs item held no singing. It was all banjo, racing, roaring banjo. Somewhere I'd heard this kind of thing before.

It came back to me. This was the music that rattled behind Granny Clampett as she filled her Beverley Hills bath with fish and burned furniture in the fireplace of the living room. It was the music that accompanied the endless car chases in the TV series *The Dukes of Hazzard*. And most importantly it was the eerie backwoods thrum that totally spooked the hunters in John Boorman's 1972 northern Georgia wilderness pic, *Deliverance*.

Flatt & Scruggs were a pair right at the roots of this music. They'd started off in Bill Monroe's band. Monroe was a high-voiced mandolin player in a big Stetson. If the start of bluegrass can be attributed to a single man then it has to be Bill Monroe. It was he who developed the string band sound, adding new and dynamic banjo players, innovative and melodic fiddle players and fronting the whole ensemble with his own loud and dancingly incisive mandolin. It was Bill, too, who had written and recorded *Blue Moon of Kentucky* way before Elvis did. And there it was on my cassette compilation, strolling out of my motor's rear-shelf speakers. A ballad in waltz time sung in a high tenor and nothing like the rock and roll version that was to come.

I suppose, though, that what really struck me about bluegrass and adhered me like thick brown old-fashioned contact adhesive to its folk on overdrive sound were the voices. The voices in harmony. The high and soaring vocals that could cut through smog, slice lines in the ceiling and raise the hairs right up on the back of my neck. Bluegrass's lonesome high keening. There was something in it that echoed back to the music of Ireland, something vaguely church-like, a harmonic interplay that just lifted anyone within range right up. The Everly Brothers had it in a sort of sanitised form. On *Crying In the Rain, Walk Right Back, When Will I Be Loved*, and, when I tracked it, the best song they ever recorded, *Kentucky*. The Everlys' close harmony was quite capable of high keening although their pop-minded producers usually held them back. On their 1958 album, *Songs Our Daddy Taught Us*, however, that pop hand had been lifted and the boys had been allowed to sing the stuff of the places they'd come from.

Kentucky was where they'd been born, that bluegrass state, where Karl Davis had written his eponymous ballad back in 1941. After he'd released it first as Karl & Harty, both The Blue Sky Boys (the cleverly named Bill and Earl Bolick, one of the most popular family duos of the period) and The Louvin Brothers put out versions. But it wasn't until The Everlys recorded the song that its true under your skin melody and so close harmonies became apparent. There it was. Slowed bluegrass. Achingly so. And I'd had it back home on my teenage Dansette record player all the time.

Kentucky, West Virginia, North Carolina, the high east of Tennessee, bits of Ohio, the top of Alabama and the northern rise of Georgia. These were the bluegrass states. They were full of mountains, the Appalachians. The author Bill Bryson had walked along them. I'd read his book. Almost as hard to say and spell as Mississippi, the Adirondacks or even Arkansas. "Why do you call it Arkansaw?" I asked one middle-aged American on my US rambles. "Sure as hell I don't know," he'd replied. Little in the world is ever quite how it first seems.

Bluegrass music was a case in point. It was nothing like as ancient as I'd imagined. There was no great prehistory of the music stretching back through the American decades before the advent of recorded sound. In fact most of the early music of the Appalachians, the material that had been cut at the dawn of recording was of a type now called old time music, mountain music, hillbilly – the true songs our daddy taught us. It was sung with a single lead voice and complemented by stringed instruments. Acoustic. Fiddle, old-style five-stringed banjo, occasionally that newly arrived instrument of the devil, the scourge of youth, even hillbilly mountain youth, the guitar. Stand-up bass was used, now and again. There were rare instances of harmonica. But there was no dobro, not yet, nor mandolins.

The songs were sentimental and often religious. They dealt with love, home and the family, the Lord and how he would save the world. They were joyous, sometimes, but they were usually sad. They were mostly sung by men. Many had adopted Jimmie Rodgers' yodel and added it to almost everything they did.

Hillbilly bands performed at home but mainly they sang as part of the medicine shows that toured the district flogging fake stomach cures and potions that would fix almost anything. They sang on the radio, they appeared between the films at cinemas, they sang on street corners. They dressed flamboyantly, often running up band uniforms, all turning out with the same wide-brimmed hat, or dressing themselves in exaggerated farm clothing, bright blue overalls, red check shirts, yellow straw hats. They incorporated humour into their acts and, as they rattled through renditions of *Barbara Allen* and *The Hangman Song*, the audience knew that following the downbeat would come a smile.

This was the world into which bluegrass music was born. The Everlys' daddy would have barely known the new music. But his sons, they played guitars, they knew how to harmonise, they could cut the air with their voices and make hair stand on end.

In 2000 film makers the Coen Brothers released their best film to date, *O Brother, Where Art Thou?*, a tale purporting to be based on Homer's Odyssey but actually no such thing. The film went back to an earlier American age, a favourite technique of the Coens. This time it was to depression era South, a place of Klan lynchings, baggy suits, travelling salesmen, holy revivals, dust and music. This music, produced by Americana genius T Bone Burnett, started with work hollers, progressed to old time mountain singing and then ended dynamically and dramatically with bluegrass.

The film grossed seventy-one million dollars and the soundtrack album went platinum. Non-singing star George Clooney got his face everywhere and the music itself made bluegrass a global sensation. Bob Dylan might have recorded a flat and pained version of *Man of Constant Sorrow* on his first album back in 1962 but it was The Soggy Bottom Boys (in imitation of Earl Flatt and Lester Scruggs' Foggy Mountain Boys) who took the song around the world.

The film also made a star of the surviving member of The Stanley Brothers, Ralph. The Stanley Brothers were a bluegrass duo from Virginia whose recordings with The Clinch Mountain Boys post-war had outsold Eddy Arnold. They were, however, hardly world pop stars. Carter Stanley had died in 1966 and Ralph had spent some years in the wilderness before reforming The Clinch Mountain Boys and going on the bluegrass circuit once again. His appearance in the Coen Brothers' film heroically delivering the ancient mountain dirge *O Death* as an accompaniment to a choreographed Klan rally, all white pointed robes and flaming torches, made him a new millennium star. Ralph Stanley, ancient as an oak, Stetson and guitar, became famous world-wide.

I'm on the 19 in my rented red Oldsmobile, a great red beast of a car with automatic gears, rolling down the highway like a swimming pool on wheels. On the radio is the country slide of some southern station broadcasting out of Carolina and selling God strongly between songs. In a sense this is how I'd always imagined it. Country roads winding through the Appalachian pines. A music I'm unfamiliar with singing of divorce, alcohol, loss and pain. The music rolling out of the car radio. Sun through the windshield. Not a cloud in the sky.

We're heading for Cherokee, the Indian reservation, miles on down this highway. We've seen the signs – \$\$\$ PRIZES AT OUR CASINO, TRIBAL BINGO – and heard the rumour that tribal elders in full headdress, bows in hand, can be seen walking the streets between the tepees. The Cherokee never lived in tepees but we'll let that pass. On Tasalagi Road, the main street, there are tribal drum sets, beads, feathered headgear, and sales opportunities for any amount of further native American tat strung out as far as the reservation goes. You expected a quiet village in a clearing somewhere, like they had in the films, smoke curling slowly from a fire, horses tethered, children playing? But this is new millennium, a time of economic suicide and endless liquor. Things have moved on.

On the roadside, on a pole near a hedge, is a small sign announcing Bluegrass Ahead. Bluegrass Festival. Bluegrass Parking. Bluegrass Turn Right. The 29th Annual North Carolina Bluegrass Festival, Happy Holiday Campground. Wolfetown Road, Cherokee. Taking a chance we turn in, park the car and pay the thirty dollars for a cyclostyled sheet of adverts for milk, tractors, dried apple stack cakes and account-ants. It has a running order printed in the centre of page one.

The festival phenomenon began at the height of the folk revival when Carlton Haney ran the first weekend all-bluegrass affair at Fincastle, Virginia in 1965. Bluegrass festivals have been steaming steadily ever since. At Cherokee it is in its heartland. The campsite has a lake and some small outbuildings housing site offices and a canteen. Most of the space is given over to SUVs with canvas awnings and the largest collection of motor homes I've ever seen. Foretravel, Beavers, Holiday Ramblers, Safaris, Entegras, Gulfstreams, Monacos, Winnebagos. By the dozen, by the absolute score. A convention of the middle-aged and, as signs everywhere ban it, the alcohol free.

Centrepiece, however, is the Festival stage and in front of it is a canvas awning covering space for around 400 Appalachian guests. All seated. All using folding chairs they've brought themselves. This is how you enjoy bluegrass. You come with your own canvas seat complete with arm rests and integral cup holder. You lounge. You do not stand, you never leap.

The acts roll on, one after another. They nod and beam at the crowd. Talk to them as if they are all acquainted personally. It's so relaxed it's hard to believe these singers are actually on a stage. Everyone knows everyone else and there are smiles and soft applause and quiet cheers. The Isaacs, the suited and mightily God-fearing Doyle Lawson and Quicksilver, the best-dressed band I've ever seen, Charlie Waller and The Country Gentlemen, stand-up bass and acoustic guitar, Larry Sigman and Barbara Poole, Longview and The Osborne Brothers. They, too, sing *Kentucky*, Karl Davis's song still doing the rounds. They do it so slowly, so achingly, and with absolute perfection.

Every now and again a band strikes off into a gospel number or a song that praises Jesus and the singer precedes it by explaining to the crowd how it was when he was saved and how glorious such a state can be. This is about the only time the seated crowd are stirred to action. They rise to their feet, they lift their hands, they praise the Lord right back and shout halleluiah like this was a great country church. Maybe it is. We're deep in the Bible Belt. If I'd forgotten that then now I've been told.

The Primitive Quartet come on, all blue denim overalls with bibs. They sing in close harmony, leaning clustered around a central mic – *Jesus Came Searching, Just look How He Found Me, Ye Must Be Born Again, It's Hard To Stumble On Your Knees* – it's a decent sound. The crowd just can't keep still with all their joining in and counter praising. It's now half a bluegrass fest and half a revival. The spirit is here and it's soaring. The Primitives are followed by an incredibly ancient and thoroughly authentic blind Doc Watson. He is led on stage by banjo player David Holt. He has his guitar in his lap. The crowd is vibrant with expectation.

If bluegrass is a post-War construct then what Watson does is a total throwback. White man mountain music riddled with the blues and with enough high velocity flat picking and occasional forays with the banjo to justify his honoured position at the head of the bluegrass revival. Revival, hell, I never knew this music had been away.

In contrast to his guitar playing, which is truly sensational, Watson's voice is flat and shallow. You might want to get out there in the front row just to be able to stare at his fingers flickering over the fretboard but his voice is not the draw. Not that Watson can't do it. His blues are as authentic sounding as anything knocked out by Alexis Korner, Lonnie Donegan, and even Lightnin' Hopkins come to that. He just lacks the tone, the roundness, the sort of thing that Josh White and John Hammond had but he does not.

He was born in Deep Gap, North Carolina so this place is absolutely home. Doc because the crowds couldn't get their mouths around his given name of Arthel and found the Sherlock Holmes association easier to manage. For years he sang as a duo with his son Merle until Merle's death in a tractor accident in 1985. The two of them adapted fiddle tunes to their acoustic guitars and banjos. They picked and cross picked and zipped and dived, delivering rattling, electrifying acoustic music with enough authenticity about it to delight their audiences. On stage now he's doing *Foggy Mountain Top* and then follows it with *Sitting On Top Of the World*. The black world meets the white one head on.

Sitting here watching Doc Watson, it's hard to believe I was in a car hunting Indians just a short while back. Almost everyone at the Cherokee Festival sells CDs immediately after their performances. The bands stand there behind their folding tables smiling and signing. The gap between audience and performer is tiny. I buy a handful plus a hot corn on the cob to bite into. "Where's that accent from?" asks the woman serving this buttery delicacy, "you sound like you're from Alaska." "Not quite" I say.

Back on stage we've reached the highlight, my highlight, everyone's highlight. Coming on like a diminutive and mightily weathered southern cowboy is the one remaining Stanley – Ralph. He's got the latest iteration of The Clinch Mountain Boys on stage behind him although you could argue that by dint of sheer stage presence he doesn't need anyone else at all. Stanley is a claw hammer banjo player and one of the two or three mainsprings of the whole bluegrass thing. He was there rivalling Bill Monroe, making high keening acoustic music of his own. Back at the beginning of bluegrass there was bad blood between them. Monroe accused Ralph and his brother Carter of stealing his style and left Columbia Records, the label who first recorded him. He signed with Decca in protest. But over the years it's been patched and by the time Bill died in 1996 the world was again a smooth place.

Ralph sings the famous *Man of Constant Sorrow* and then moves to the show highlight, *O Death*, the Coen Brothers' dirge. The crowd are clapping and roaring. It's a great bluegrass moment, an old man still making great music, a Stanley Brother on incredible form.

In the car it's dark, the headlamps light the highway. Our motel room is a way off. But the Lord's up there, he'll see us home.

9 • Bluegrass Number Two

The speed limits flicker. They seem to change every few yards. 30. 40. 25. And then back to 40 again. These are still Indian lands. There's a notice I've seen a few times pinned to posts and tree trunks. RE-ELECT LEON JONES CHIEF. Democracy at work. The Cherokee Nation with an ancestral line that leads straight back to Wales.

Our destination is Maggie Valley and we've a way to go. Earlier we'd pulled onto a side road and among the parked artics and seemingly abandoned trailers found what was advertised as a farmer's market in full swing. Farmer's markets, at least the ones I am familiar with, consist of tables under awnings offering strange cheeses, collector's pasties, vegetarian meat pies, very powerful ciders and chunks of hand-reared salt beef with family tree printed on the wrapper. These markets are common strung along UK suburban streets or spread out across community centre car parks mixed in with cars delivering kids for football practise and aged smokers turning out for bingo.

But in Appalachia things are different. The Western North Carolina Farmer's Market sits on a vast and rambling 36 acre site of truck sheds and warehouses linked by parking lots. This spread of land is festooned with diners, delis, kids play areas, concessions selling tractors, sit-on motor strimmers, domestic harvesters, and long rows of greenhouses full of tropical plants, banana trees, and blossoming pineapples all topped by an artificial forty-foot waterfall embellished with sunflowers and windmills. Inside the truck sheds are apples and peaches in great hills, sliding stacks of pumpkin, carrot, squash and hot banana peppers as far as the eye can see.

At the north end the formality of the serried stalls with their smiling, permanently happy traders gives way to men wearing denim dungarees selling from the back of trucks, tailgates down, flask of coffee on the side. I buy a punnet of apples from a slow, check-shirted local shrunk into his plastic chair. He looks like William Carlos Williams in later life, withered, round glasses, white flaky hair. The punnet weighs[29] a peck. There are four pecks to the bushel. It's an imperial measure that went out with furlongs, poles and perches back home but still hangs on here. I hand him a twenty dollar bill and he gives me something back.

I ask him if he knows the best way on from here to Maggie Valley. A farmer would know the roads and the best routes, wouldn't he? This one does. He brightens and tells me, pointing a bony arm and giving off a sort of hay and tobacco smell that hangs in the smooth warm air. Trouble is I just can't understand, the accent is so wayward. I catch a word, that's all, here and there. That. Hill. Turn. I smile and thank him and go. Back to the car to dig out that huge six foot wide map of the state that seems to alter every time I gaze at its breadth. Maggie Valley. It's there. Somewhere to the north and the west of Asheville. Higher. Thick with trees.

The road turns and rises. Our automatic limousine purrs. These American autos do not do performance. They don't roar and zip. They float and glide. When the gears shift down it's like a Superfortress lumbering. Take off will come. But not soon.

Along the roadside are stalls. This is the land of the free where anyone can be king and everyone needs to start their empires somewhere. Mountain Grown Produce. Corn Grits. Molasses. Honey. Country Hams Sugar Cured. Everything looks as if it were constructed before the war and hasn't been repainted since. We stop at Dude's Jonathan Creek Boiled Peanuts Incorporated. Curb Service. The place is manned by a tall, thin replica of Jed Clampett who sells us a cone made of newspaper and filled with warm wet salted nuts still in their pods. Does he know where Maggie Valley is? Straight ahead.

On the radio a preacher with an accent that could slice the top off a white pine is explaining how once you've let God into your life then the world will never again be the same. It will be full of glory and light. All that weight of sin will be forever gone from your shoulders. Out of the window I can see the sun, falling down through the tree tops and beyond that clear blue. The man is right. Up here, anyway.

Maggie Valley is a community officially about the size of Roath Park Rec on a sunny day (pop 607 in 2000) but actually containing almost as many attractions strung out along the roadside as Pigeon Forge (which we'll get to later) in sunny Tennessee. They sell everything from buckets of fried chicken to Elvis Presley pin-ons.

Here you can experience, jammed in next to each other in a line worthy of Coney Island, the following: The Ghost Town In The Sky Amusements, Miss Caroline's Wedding Chapel, Santasland (open all year), The Cherokee Fun Park, Hurley's Creekside Dining and Rhum Bar, The Brew, Que and BBQ and Bowed Up Archery, which specialises in pistols, firearms and knives. Beyond are opportunities to gamble, to breakfast all day, lodge, spend dollars on fake antiques, mountain foodstuffs, burgers, jellies, fries, cokes, hot dogs, double over easy fried eggs on French toast on plates the size of toilet seats, triple portions of things that could once have been mashed and thrashed chicken but are now shapeless blobs of batter that resemble for all the world the balls of fiberglass putty B&Q sell to repair holes in the side of your caravan.

There was a real Maggie, too. Once. In 1890 Jack Seltzer, a mountain settler, responding to demand from the local Blue Ridge community to send letters back down to the plains, established a sort of post office in his back room. The US Postal Service, keen to expand their reach, offered to make the office official so long as it had a name. Setlzer tried a few and had them rejected as being already in use. In desperation he then submitted the names of his three daughters, Cora, Mettie and Maggie Mae. After some deliberation the postal authorities picked the third. The settlement would be known as Maggie Mae, NC. Maggie Valley it became.

Why are we heading there? It has an Opry, so says the brochure. There might be bluegrass. Heavens, in this place what else would there be? We check into a motel right next to the creek on Soco Road. Just up from the tubing franchise. Rocky Waters. Pool. Cable TV. Air. I never stop where they don't have air. US motels, or at least these mountain versions, have a basic clapped-out primitiveness about them. Back in the 1950s they might well have been at the top end of world progress – drive in, pay your money and the place is yours, none of this checking in, signing forms, bell boy to carry your bags, stuff – but by today they are mostly in creaking disrepair. Rocky Waters just about slides into the acceptable category. Bed, no coffee. I'll put some on tomorrow morning, says the owner. You want something now then try down the road. We do. We find somewhere just beyond the Welcome To Maggie Valley NC Home of Raymond Fairchild sign. Fairchild. This place, small as it is, has a famous son.

If you read the bluegrass histories you'll find them full of feuding musicians, bands that don't talk to each other, disagreements about origins and who invented what in the emerging style. Check the story of Monroe and Ralph Stanley in the previous chapter. Neil V Rosenberg, Professor Emeritus of folklore at Memorial University of Newfoundland and himself a picker of some accomplishment has compiled the definitive account. *Bluegrass – A History*. In it he expounds the style's complex origins. Old time music would have instruments playing as an accompaniment to the verse. With bluegrass the music counterpointed, it improvised, leapt off at tangents, rearranged the theme, then varied it as Bach would, bounced it around it as Miles did, then returned it to where it had started. Charlie Parker might have felt at home if he'd played the banjar. It was folk jazz, although Rosenberg never actually calls it this. It uses new and previously unfamiliar instruments such as the dobro, the lap-held guitar played with a sliding steel, and the high musical flickering of the mandolin. Bill Monroe's instrument. It fitted the emerging sound to perfection.

Bluegrass began with this man. It was he who came up with the name, bluegrass. Why that, he was asked. "I'm from Kentucky, you know, where the bluegrass grows, and it's got a good ring to it[30]." Bill Monroe formed his Blue Grass Boys in 1939 and by the end of World War Two was fronting a band that contained, among others, Earl Scruggs on banjo and Lester Flatt on guitar. Monroe's was the classic bluegrass line-up. He took old time mountain hillbilly music and altered its sound, adding new instruments (mandolin, dobro), and changing the way it was played. He was much imitated. In the record stores they added a new section. Bluegrass as a distinct entity was born.

Bluegrass, Rosenberg proposes, contains as much Christianity as it does because it has become a substitute for actual church attendance. Fundamentalist Protestantism has also suggested that church attendance is not necessary for salvation. Salvation is a matter for the individual, for that person's faith and their belief in the Good Book and their expression of their belief through their music. Gospel bluegrass becomes the ideal vehicle. Almost without exception bluegrass singers have an element of religious music in their acts. A God spot. Their audiences can praise the Lord without having to turn up somewhere neat each Sunday and can do it from the lounging depths of their festival chairs.

Observers have noticed that right across the Bible Belt South there might be more churches than anywhere else in America but attendances in the mountain regions are uniformly low. Maybe. But this doesn't explain America's latest piece of expansionism – the rise of the giant megachurch which occupies acres and has pews inside for congregations of several thousand. There are a few not far from here – in Greensboro, in Durham and in Hendersonville. They have charismatic pastors. They deliver optimistic messages. They welcome all. Here you can experience religious fervour in the company of thousand-strong crowds. America, land of contradictions.

But there's evidence, too, that among the strange and non-conformist Pentecostal sects in the mountains, where men of God prove their faith by drinking poison and handling venomous snakes[31] this music of dobro and banjo has entered the service itself. The faithful love nothing better than a Sunday morning listening to four-part or even five-part bluegrass harmony and banjo-accompanied recitations of *Come On Dear Lord And Get Me* and *I Live For Him, Cause He Died For Me*.

On the road into Maggie Valley, what did the sign say, pop 607, I count the churches – The First Baptist, The United Methodist, Mount Calvary Christian Fellowship, St Margaret's Catholic, Victory Baptist, Peachtree Methodist – they can't all be full of Sunday bluegrass. They can't all, each Sunday, be full at all.

At the Maggie Valley Opry Raymond Fairchild is on stage. The

Opry House is a wooden shed set back from the highway and with an extremely large and hopeful car park out front. Opposite and down a bit is its main rival, the much more attractive looking Stompin' Ground. Here the traditions of country line dancing and bluegrass clogging are irreverently mixed. But we've gone for authenticity, as much as that might be possible in this sub-Disneyland of a town. Given a chance, the space and the investment, this little habitation would make itself twice as vibrant and four times as dreadful as it currently is. Already there are plans for more rides and roller coasters, more hot dog concessions, more stores selling plastic doo-dahs, inflatable Christmas trees, portable wine coolers, devices to flatten your dollar bills, battery-operated shoe-stretchers, grape polishers and gloves that light up in the dark. This is all backed up, of course, by stacks of authentic mountain merchandise assembled in China and shipped here by the container-load.

Fairchild, it turns out, actually owns the Opry House. It's his franchise, authentic hillbilly entertainment as a tourist offering. He's in competition with tube rafting, burger consumption and visits to see the denizens of Santaland. The fact that Fairchild is a primitive banjo genius is a bonus.

As a picker he began by listening to Bill Monroe and Earl Scruggs on the radio. Not the family radio, mind you. Electricity did not at that time run to Cherokee where Raymond had been born to a white and largely absent father and a caring Indian mother. He sneaked a listen in the bar and at the country store. He loved what he heard. He bought a Silvertone mail-order from a Sears and Roebuck catalogue and largely taught himself. Booklearning, as it's called up here in the mountains, was not a strong point. Written instructions meant little. Watching others was how our man progressed.

He played with The Crowe Brothers, visited Nashville, sat in with the greats, showed them how fast he could play and how his nascent, self-taught style could match theirs. He got a contract and made a few records. He was good enough to be inducted into the Society for the Preservation of Bluegrass Music in America Hall of Greats although, given the size of bluegrass's totality, that wasn't the mighty honour it might seem.

There are rumours, deep inside his lengthy biography, of him hunting ginseng roots in the Pisgah forests and concocting his own highly-secret stay-alive tonic. If true, it worked. In his sixties, Stetson, range-rider fringed Indian suede jacket, de rigueur cowboy boots, he still looks as if he could kill a rattlesnake with his bare hands.

Fairchild is backed by The Maggie Valley Boys. This duo comprises Wallace Josh Crowe on guitar and Cody Shuler on mandolin. Shuler will go on to greater things. Fairchild who hates travel will stay in Maggie. The show is as much talking as it is playing. There's something about age that brings this on. Once they pass six decades singers seem to acquire the desire to tell their audiences tall tales, to explain their lives, to joke and anecdote endlessly filling their stage slot with material that is not the music the audience came to hear. The late BB King, having achieved treasure of the nation status, spent almost all his stage time doing just this. He squatted, they all squat when they're old, legs spread, full sized wall clock at his feet because his eyes had gone, squeezing starts out of his guitar but never finishing them. The riffs fluttered. The tall tales drowned them out.

Fairchild tells us how it used to be in Appalachia, throws in jokes he's picked up on the road, runs his left hand along his banjo's neck thumbing out a single note. This man is renowned for his speed, a sort of North Carolinan Django Reinhardt who can outplay a rushing train. He rocks into it. *Duelling Banjos, Orange Blossom Special, Whoa Mule*, banjo versions of Boots Randolph's *Yakaty Sax*, stuff you know such as *Foggy Mountain Top*, and *Little Maggie,* stuff you don't, *Pat's Train Special, Rabbit In the Log*. His act highspot is a pretty awful exercise in talking banjo where he gets the instrument to approximate the voice of a six year old asking for a drink of water and has the small audience, all except me, smiling with delight. This, naturally, only encourages him, and we get a whole extension of the six-year old idea with the voices of animals, dogs, cats, horses and shrieking women added for good measure. Raymond Fairchild novelty banjo picker rather than Fairchild the authentic voice from bluegrass history I would much have preferred.

During the break Fairchild and his boys follow the now expected bluegrass tradition of selling merch from a collapsible table. Raymond has arrayed three CDs and a postcard. We buy one of each. They all date from the long past and feature accompanying musicians largely not present tonight. Not that this slows anyone down. CDs are duly autographed by the master and then by the accompanying musicians, men who do not actually appear on the recordings they sign. *Mama Likes Bluegrass Music. Picking & Singing In Maggie Valley. King of the Smoky Mountains.* All overstocks for the sixties, at last leaving the USA.

"So what's the bluegrass scene like back where you come from?" asks one of the boys, making conversation. Our fellow audience members have gone out back for a fag or to use the distant facilities. "Pretty sparse," I say. Everyone smiles. Then it's back to more high speed picking and nasal singing packed about with stories and jokes I don't fully understand. Is the music the genuine article? I'd like to say that I'd discovered another Roscoe Holcomb, the banjo player and singer from Kentucky who'd been described by the man who discovered him as "the end of the line". Holcomb, the highest of high lonesome singers, a man about whom it was said that once you heard his ancient music then there was nowhere else left to go. But no, not quite. Holcomb died in 1981 and bluegrass went on beyond him. Fairchild isn't in that class. He's much keener on keeping the wolf from the door.

If you want to hear Holcomb then try to track down his Smithsonian recordings issued as *An Untamed Sense of Control.* These were recorded in the sixties and the early seventies and produced by folklorist John Cohen. They capture perfectly that rough-round the edges authenticity that was once so sought after by early folk fans, those around at the time of the emergence of the singer songwriters in 1962. If we have to label them Holcomb's songs are pre-bluegrass. They owe a lot to black music but also contain the same nasal twang to the vocals that Bill Monroe perfected. The banjo plays blues parts allowing Holcomb to sound something like a cross between Mississippi John Hurt and Burl Ives. Hearing him at length requires a little determination. Even the liner notes suggest that Holcomb's music makes great demands on the listener. "His ideas about music were shaped before the advent of radio and phonograph told home musicians what their music was supposed to sound like," writes John

Cohen. Holcomb's version of *Man of Constant Sorrow* makes The Stanley Brothers sound like Only Men Aloud. This might be genuine mountain music but it's hardly easy listening. I bought a copy on the way here from some roadside stall, lost among the mountain cookbooks and jars of mountain jelly. A gem.

Then we're back to our creek side motel. I stick the CDs in a suitcase which already has more of them in there than it has clothes. I'd been hoping to find a coffee stall open somewhere or even a machine selling canned Coke but there's nothing. Maggie Valley, town of plenty, you've failed me. Up here in the night time mountains are just trees and stars.

10 • Bluegrass in Pontypridd

Rhodri Morgan is on stage. He is explaining how, during the nineteen-sixties early days of post-industrial urban redevelopment when the slums were being cleared and replacements were underway, he managed to convince a highly sceptical contruction industry to build north of Cardiff. There'd be no money in it for them, they'd first imagined, but with a few tax breaks and some pushing they finally agreed. The estates of Caerphilly were the result. A dormitory feeder for the rising Welsh capital. And despite being literally on the far side of a mountain (Caerphilly Mountain, southern extent of the coal field, 271 metres high) were actually only a small vroom in your car from the joys of metropolitan sophistication.

I'm at public meeting to discuss Cardiff's LDP, the Local Development Plan. This is the formal local authority proposal for how we are going to get from 2013 to 2026, albeit with a fractured economy, a blossoming population, and the desire among every single one of us to have our own house, car parking space and giant widescreen TV. The new snow line, as it's called, turns out to be just that further on up from Caerphilly in recidivist Pontypridd. That's how it's labelled here. South of Ponty new houses will sell. To the north you are in payday loan country. Thin roads, rising hills, conifers in increasing density. Work is scarce. Infrastructure poor. Deprivation is rife. The Welsh Appalachians.

Except that despite the converted Wesleyan chapel that is the Muni, the museum, and the soggy-carpeted heart of patriotic Wales, Clwb y Bont[32], Ponty is no local version of Appalachia's Asheville. Rather than boutiques, delis, music stores, and hippie emporia the town majors on fireplaces, fast food and charity stores. Despite this Geoff Cripps and the enlightened management the Muni have managed to book The Cherryholmes. Nashville reaches the valleys. The wilderness tamed. For their performance there's a full audience of South Wales locals, handle-bar moustaches and plump thighs, t-shirts celebrating the Abertillery Blues Festival, beer in their hands. We're not going to stand if The Cherryholmes sing about Jesus. We're going to sit and thrill.

The Cherryholmes are a family band as are so many acts in bluegrass. Ma and Pa plus four siblings. They look alike, the siblings, and they sound the same. The six piece would have been seven if daughter Shelly hadn't died at 20 back in 1999. It was her death that started them. A family bonding exercise led to father Jere allocating an instrument to everyone and the band was the result. They sound as slick and professional as anything that's rooted in history and been on the road since the start of time.

Jere has a ZZ Top beard and plays a compact, upright electric bass. He comes on in Stetson and western jacket, rhinestones spangling. Between them the rest play fiddles, guitars, mandolins and banjos. They all sing. Is this Tennessee or top of the trail North Carolina? Both. Their harmonies soar, bend, shiver and fall. The sound is a bluegrass that owes as much to its Irish roots as it does to the country sophistication of Nashville where the band are now based.

The Cherryholmes act mixes everything from banjo breakdown to clog dancing, yodelling cowboy to bubble-gum country, four-part acapella harmony to everyone soloing like this were *Thank Your Lucky Stars*. They are immensely hard-working and they win prizes. They did the Opry in 2003 and have been nominated for some award or other every year since. They played Ponty in 2008 and again now in 2010. They've put out seven albums and there they are, in true bluegrass style, standing behind an unfolded table flogging copies straight after the show.

In 2011 The Cherryholmes will hit the wall. Like so many others in the music business they will allow the endless road to get to them. As a big family unit they will pack it in. Solo careers will follow and there will still be occasional revivals but for the most part one of the most listenable bands in bluegrass will hang up their boots. Hard to believe when you hear them now in 2010 on the Muni stage. Their Welsh audience are on fire.

The place of bluegrass in the souls of the Welsh is a bit stronger than many think. There are at least three annual festivals: Gower, just up from Three Cliffs Bay, North Wales at Conwy and the surreal sounding Coastline Bluegrass Festival at inland Llangollen. Some of these have been going for more than a quarter of a century. There are also a number of home-grown Welsh bluegrass bands including The Beef Seeds, Conwy Mountain Bluegrass, The Garth Mountain Boys, and The Grass Snakes. Middle-aged men in cowboy costume, *Oh Susanna* rehashed, easy listening folk music? All of those things and none. Whatever it is, bluegrass in Wales has few native antecedents. Unlike the traditional musics of England, Scotland and Ireland ours has distinctly failed to take over the world. We have no preachers who dance with serpents. Our banjos are throwbacks from the Black and White Minstrels. The fiddle reached here only after it had got to everywhere else in the entire Western world.

Welsh music is rooted in the bardic tradition, with the harp at its centre, music created to accompany the recitations of poets at the princely courts. *Cerdd dant*, string music, and *cerdd dafod*, tongue craft were (and still are) the two parallel arts of string playing and verse creation. Both deliver the goods in a highly regulation fashion. The tradition is old, amazingly so. Quite often the poet and the harpist were the same person. There are records of such activity taking place in the sixth and seventh centuries. There are extant words but only guesses when it comes to how they were sung. Harps then were small enough to sit in your lap, similar to but perhaps more delicate than those in use in Ireland. The strings were made from twisted horse hair or gut, rather than brass. They were plucked with fingernails instead of fingertips. The sound was bright and loud.

Back at the dawn of Welsh time the harp sat at the centre of Welsh life. Although, being Wales, there is argument about that. Some historians suggest that the Welsh actually played the *crwth*, a predecessor of the violin where all four strings were sounded simultaneously. However Venantius Fortunatus, a sixth century bishop of the early Catholic church, claimed that both the *crwth* and the harp, instruments not seen in Rome, were played by the Barbarians, in other words the Celtic Brits, the Welsh[33]. Whichever way it went it's the harp that has persistently triumphed in Wales.

By the reign of Charles I (1600-1649) the 95-string triple harp had arrived and pretty much ousted its earlier and much smaller predecessor. The instrument was impressive looking and still light enough to be carted on your back. In addition to appearances at royal courts and in the drawing rooms of the gentry harpists did the rounds of fairs, festivals, markets days and taverns. They competed at local *eisteddfodau* and were regarded simultaneously as entertainers and bastions of cultural tradition.

Traditional music in Wales was severely threatened during in the mid-nineteenth century by the rise of non-conformism and that religion's damning of anything that smacked of what it regarded as loose morals: dancing, singing, smiling and especially drink. The arrival of the more formal-looking new pedal harp didn't help either. Harp music, indeed Welsh music as a whole, moved in the direction of the concert hall.

There were some who kept tradition alive, against all odds. Nansi Richards (1888-1979) saw in a recovery of interest in the triple harp and passed her enthusiasm on to more recent masters such as Osian Elis, Elinor Bennett, Catrin Finch, Robin Huw Bowen and others. Yet the harp did not return to the parlour and the pub. It remained, as it largely does today (with the exception of Catrin Finch's innovative popular work), a feature of the concert hall, the church service, the formal reception, the wedding, the dinners given for visiting dignitaries, and the occasional appearance on *Songs of Praise*.

In the 1974 Oriel Bookshop down on Charles Street, that centre of Welsh culture and poetic endeavour that I managed on behalf of an enlightened Welsh Arts Council, I'm putting books out on the shelves. My brief is to cover the Welsh universe in both languages and to add value with material from other Celtic places. I'm also stocking art, photography, architecture, local history, plus poetry: everything published in the twentieth century, small press, big press, obscure, obvious. Faber's complete enchilada as well as a whole shelf devoted to the concrete outpourings of Bob Cobbing, Tom Phillips, Ian

Hamilton Finlay and Edwin Morgan. Sales are good among the material for Welsh learners, Welsh children and lovers of Welsh poetry and fiction. The books in Irish I've imported are going like Guinness among the attendees of the Catholic cathedral up the road.

In the record racks I have every spoken word album issued – all the labels: Argo, Caedmon, Folkways, the Dial-a-Poets from New York, world sound poetry from Fylkingen in Sweden. From Ireland's Claddagh I've imported albums featuring James Joyce, John Montague and Austin Clarke. Chancing my arm I'm also trying out the first lps from Seán Ó Riada's Ceoltóirí Chualann successors, The Chieftains. Instrumental tradition. I play them as background. They sell like rockets.

The stock arrives in great crates. Sometimes customs open it and impose taxable additions but mostly they don't. No other specialist stores seem to be finding this material. I have the stage to myself. Oriel, market place of the Celtic world.

But we need, also, to look after our own. I pile them in: Sidan, Bois y Blacbord, Tecwyn Ifan, Hergest, Bran, Edward H Dafis, Tony ac Aloma, Meic Stevens, Hogiau'r Wyddfa, Teibot Pws, Y Diliau, Tryfan, Heather Jones singing her Joan Baez popular best, Geraint Jarman doing Welsh reggae, The Hennesseys trying to recreate Ireland in Wales. What's missing is much that connects with deep tradition, ours.

I hunt and then I find it. Recorded in 1954 for the Smithsonian Institute in America, almost by chance, while the singer was there studying philosophy at Princeton. Meredydd Evans, *Welsh Folk Songs*. Issued as a ten inch album by Folkways. Replete with lengthy notes, lyrics and cultural history. The unaccompanied voice relays traditional songs that were all but lost in the Methodist Revival and puritanical reforms of eighteenth century Wales. A rare gem. I buy in twenty and sell two. Welsh traditional music here does not have legs.

Or didn't then, forty years back.

As in Ireland Wales had seen an early twentieth century establish-ment of a number of national institutions. The National Library of Wales, the National Museum and the University of Wales were all founded before 1910. The Welsh Folk-Song Society (Cymdeithas Alawon Gwerin Cymru) had also been created in 1906. Like the other institutions it formed part of Wales's search for national identity. By the time of Meredydd's recordings the Welsh Folk-Song Society had done sterling work. It had collected more than 600 songs. Ancient airs, ballads, the essence of Wales' cultural past all now rescued and preserved. Naturally the material was entirely in the Welsh language. As three-quarters of the Welsh population did not speak the tongue this historical collection remained secure but corralled.

From the seventies on, however, on the back of a huge increase in interest in all other things Welsh (including a large boost of concern for and learning of the language) Wales has witnessed a do-it-yourself, traditional music rise of significant proportions. Societies, players, collectors and instrument makers have all contributed to the establishment of an apparently unbroken folk music tradition, old as the hills and the envy of the Western world. Today we have them – the *crwth* players, the pibgorners, the pipers, and for that matter the fiddlers, the guitarists and the bodhran beaters. The music they play simultaneously aches with oldness and ripples with modernity. It references the traditions of the eisteddfod, the tavern and the ancient princely courts.

Recordings of the work of Nansi Richards and other traditional harpers have been collected and reissued. Dancers, guitarists and fiddlers across the country have begun retreading the older songs. Yr Hwntws, Swansea Jack, Mabsant, Cilmeri, Plethyn, Aberjaber, Calennig, Ar Log. Dafydd Iwan with a Welsh Bob Dylan guitar. Twm Morys, masquerading as Bob Delyn, playing ancient harp and surrounding it with rock music and recited poetry. Bragod, which consists of Robert Evans doubling on lyre and the prehistoric-looking *crwth* to accompany Mary-Anne Roberts' vocals, reinventing the earliest songs where not a trace of how they originally sounded remains[34]. By the turn of the millennium the revival had hit second gear with the arrival of Allan yn y Fan, Calan, Crasdant, Plu, 9Bach, Gwenan Gibbard, The Gentle Good, Gwyneth Glyn and a host of others. Today it's a vibrant scene.

Yet somehow it does not travel. Nothing like as well as we could wish. Unlike the world famous singers who front the traditions of Ireland and Scotland, Wales keeps its head down. On Celtic music CD compilations issued in America it's pretty much always Ireland 9, Scotland 7, Wales 1, if at all. Even Brittany, a land denied by French centralism, punches well above our native folk music weight. Does Welsh traditional music somehow lack the slippery spark, the warmth and the distinctive soul-filled drug that is there at the core of, say, Irish music? Have a listen. You decide.

On the radio I'm listening to Gorky's Zygotic Mynci, a sort of 1990's Welsh mixture of Captain Beefheart with The Incredible String Band. They've broken up but their weird, off-the wall psychedelic folksiness endures. If anyone we've got (or had) could take the cultural place of bluegrass's Cherryholmes then it's them. "So I ran off on Thursday with a dance troupe from Spain where wine, dance and music is the name of the game".

11 • The Irish Connection

In front of me sits Gerry Adams. I know it's him, he's been hugged and cheered and hand shook by many of those around him. I've even shaken his hand myself. It's 2008 and this is the Royal Hospital, Kilmainham, Dublin. We're in the grounds converted on this occasion for outdoor concerts. Tiered seating for 10,000, wooden ramps, safety rails, stewards wearing steward armbands, the half shell stage lit in anticipation. The audience swells. There are more faces I recognise than you can shake a stick at. Bertie Ahern, U2 manager Paul McGuiness, Bono himself. Someone who looks just like Seamus Heaney but, hell, could it really be him? If Yeats were alive he'd be here, so perhaps it is.

We've come for the first Leonard Cohen concert tour in decades, the first break in silence this side of the Atlantic in an age. Cohen, the most miserable man on the planet, at 73 is back on the road. He's here because he needs the money. Ripped off by Kelley Lynch, his former lover and manager, fortune spirited away while our man was lost to meditation. Tonight he has a full house, the rain stays away, the coffers spin. Boosted by this later-life roar back to popularity Cohen will begin to tour with revived vigour and apparently no end. He'll return to Europe and spin on around the world again and again. As I write – he's in New Zealand. Where next? Chinese moon base. Then with the Yankees to Mars.

The show is as slick as anything Tony Bennett can do. Cohen in fedora fronting a hand-picked band of class musicians breathing through a repertoire of twenty-three songs. Cohen, poet of the mind. Behind him The Webb Sisters chant and purr. On stage with him collaborator Sharon Robinson's voice holds his to the melody when Cohen's age or simple inability cause it to wander. The effect is as satisfying as just about any musical thing I've experienced. The crowd love it. There are thousands of them here because they began following this man when he emerged from Canadian obscurity in the sixties and still do. There are thousands, too, who are completely new to this highly turned form of musical depression. They've been carried forward by its ultimate professionalism and the feeling that this is something the twentieth century was famous for. Now he's here in the new millennium, and before the old world completely fades, they'd like to experience what he does. See him before he dies.

Cohen began as a poetry writing guitar playing singer-songwriter with no voice to speak of but a great line in lyrics. Where Dylan took surreal leaps into the wider world Cohen turned back and looked inside

The early singer-songwriters – Tim Buckley, Bert Jansch, Tom Paxton, Eric Andersen, Mark Spoelstra, Gordon Lightfoot, – along with scores of others – had their roots in the folk tradition. You could hear it in some of the tunes they lifted and repositioned, the melodies and the ideas for melodies that they reworked. They played guitar and they sang alone. They toted their instrument cases down the roads that led from gig to gig. A bar, a club, a university hall. There was a bohemian romantic glamour in the way they engaged with the world. Whole generations wanted to be just like them.

Cohen fitted perfectly. He could barely sing and played guitar like a beginner. But he had the look and the lyrical message that reached beyond tradition and motivated thousands. They travelled the road together – Baudelaire, Rimbaud and Cohen, all brothers.

What Cohen was not, however, was any kind of folk musician reworking his heritage and nodding back to those who had gone before. Cohen made everything brand new. There were no lifted guitar riffs, fragments of ancient tin whistle melody, nor heroic tales retold in new language. Here in Ireland he was the opposite of most of the traditional singers around him. Ireland's music took hundreds of years of maturing to reach the twentieth century. Cohen began in 1967 with an album produced by Paul Simon and in the forty years since then has barely changed a stylistic thing.

I'm here as a diversion on a trip west. All musics move west, towards the setting sun, Buddha and enlightenment, the place where the world begins and ends. It happened in America, landing at Charlotte in the Carolinas and then moving on in, to the mountains and beyond. Here I am set to cross Ireland's bog-ridden heart in the same direction, in search of the music that started it all.

Ireland is green and vacant and full of rain. It comes in, not like the deluge in New York that drowns whole neighbourhoods in an instant, but as a soft and insidious mist that drifts into every part of your being. You want to get wet? Come here. Ireland's people have made music for as long as any of them can remember. They follow a rich tradition and their music can be heard nightly in sessions the length and breadth of the land. The same jigs and reels and hornpipes emerge diddle-diddley in the music of Ulster and Leinster and Co Clare and then again among Irish ex-pats in America and across the rest of the world.

Irish music began with the harp. At least that's what the nation thinks. It has the instrument as its national symbol. It's on its official communications, its coins and its beer. There's a fourteenth century example housed at Trinity in Dublin[35]. Named after an early Irish King, Brian Boru, it is 70 cms. high, thirty bronze strings, to be played with your fingernails. It's the source for the instruments today wielded by Breton Alan Stivell and Welshman Bob Delyn. Welsh singer Georgia Ruth plays one on her prize-winning album *Week of Pines*. It held sway as Ireland's main source of music making for centuries until it was superseded by uilleann pipes, accordions, concertinas and fiddles in more recent times.

The music itself can track a history back to at least the eighth century. For more than a thousand years it has been at the mercy of wars and famines, invasions and rebellions, religions, agricultural revolutions and the ways and politics of man. Folk music it has always been and, until the twentieth century, was exclusively the province of the working poor. A people's music, used for telling tales, for lamenting love, for fomenting revolution, for elegising the dead and celebrating great battles, for getting through the day. God was praised and so were his crops. You danced to it. It was in your blood.

The Irish – the Irish speaking Gaels – developed a music that ran from south west Munster to the Hebrides and that shared a commonality with Gaelic speaking Scots. Even today you can often be hard put to tell the folk musics of the two countries apart. It was a music constantly under threat. Puritan Cromwell banished it, sending musicians to the West Indies. William of Orange tortured Catholics in an attempt to convert them to Protestantism. The art of the harper faced extinction. The ascendancy of the English tongue as the working language of the country which had a dramatic effect on the content of the oral tradition did not help either.

Historically Ireland has not been a kind place to its people. It lacks industrial resource, there's nothing here to mine or to make. Its crops grow badly and barely support subsistence. When times are hard the Irish leave. They did so at the start of the eighteenth century. Thousands of Presbyterians fled bad harvests and religious confrontation to settle in the Appalachians. Their Catholic contemporaries went from the south, chasing the fish, to Newfoundland. The great famine of the mid-eighteenth century saw the Irish population drop further, this time by a quarter, with at least a million fleeing the country to any land that would have them. Hundreds of thousands chose Amerikay. Music in Ireland became a pale shadow of its former self.

Home Rule, however, was to be its salvation. The rise of Irish identity and the desire to remove British colonial rule became increasingly apparent towards the end of the nineteenth century. The Gaelic language, up until that point in retreat, was now seen as an instrument of redemption. The newly formed Gaelic League looked to the glories of the Gaelic past as a way of promoting the nationalist agenda. Traditional music, folk music sung through the medium of Irish, was something to be revived and celebrated. The League introduced the *céilí*, an organised evening of singing, playing and dancing. It became a fixture among Ireland's increasing urban communities. The language was the driver but the music was the main beneficiary. The League set standards and formalised both the music and the dance steps that were to go with it. Spontaneity was for the kitchens west of the Shannon.

Urbanisation itself set the scene for a change in the relationship between the musician and the audience. As we will see also happening in the American Appalachians the arrival of radio and recordings began to erode the need for the musician to be the sole keeper of the oral tradition. In Ireland, as they did elsewhere, recordings took the place of memory. Music increasingly became an act of performance without the need for dance to accompany it. In urban places, in pubs and taverns, musicians sat in circles playing. Around them their audience drank and politely listened.

The early twentieth century was, in its own way, just as difficult for Irish music as had been the times under Cromwell. At first the British Black and Tans broke up local dances as places where independence might ferment. They were succeeded by the newly arrived Irish Free State which gave in to the demands of the Catholic Truth Society of Ireland and, with its Dance Halls Act, moved against what was seen as the immorality of unsupervised dancing. Traditional Irish music once again suffered.

Its salvation was the setting up of an indigenous radio station. In 1926 the forerunner to RTÉ, 2RN, began to broadcast folk music and to offer it some sort of status. Nevertheless the music remained a sub-class, no match for the sounds of serious music. It was derided by educationalists, uncelebrated, and certainly not a thing you'd give your artistic life to.

Until, that was, Seán Ó Riada came along and blended Irish traditional playing with the concert hall. He scored films and presented fiddle tunes on the stage with the players dressed in white shirt and tails. He helped usher in the great traditional music revival of the 1960s. In that decade the old and unamplified folk music of Ireland found a new place for itself. Its players realised that their music could serve both economic and cultural ends. It was as Irish as the peat bogs and it was also saleable. Tourist Ireland of the welcomes was born.

Today Irish music can be heard in pubs the length and breadth of the land. It's played as much for locals as it is for visitors. It has had a stream of internationally successful popularisers: The Clancy Brothers, The Dubliners, The Chieftains, Planxty, The Bothy Band, Clannad, Mary Black, Sharon Shannon. And it's had a host of those who have gone one step further, adding electric instruments and taking the music to places where the djs play and the lights rock along in time. Ó Riada might have welcomed it but the musician who played the Brian Boru Harp, back there at the start of it all would surely have begun to spin. Horslips, The Pogues, Moving Hearts, The Afro-Celt Sound System, Hothouse Flowers. Sinead O'Connor on a good day. Van Morrison when he remembers.

The drivers of Irish traditional music remain the pipes, the concertina and the fiddle but they've been joined by guitars and banjos, bodhrans, bouzoukis, mandolins, tin whistles and flutes. These things are rarely electric. They work in places where the power can't reach.

Back on the trail we've borrowed a car and are heading west. There are motorways but in Ireland they don't run straight. Irish roads are like the lanes of Wales. They turn as the fields do. They overgrow with greenery. They are full of slowness and gleam. We're heading for County Clare. For the music, the sessions. You read about these things. We drive towards Lisdoonvara. Fort of the Fairy Hill. A spa town and a place where the music spills out and flows on into the Atlantic and heads west to America. Lisdoonvara, near the Cliffs of Moher where Europe ends.

On the player is Doc Watson merging his music with that of The Chieftains[36]. Last heard at Cherokee with David Holt playing blues, ragtime and old country. From the speakers of our Irish Prius he now sounds as native as Paddy Maloney. *The Fisherman's Hornpipe. The Devil's Dream*. Watson could have come from Lisdoonvara. Fled to the Carolinas to avoid the matchmaking festival. Rocking the Irish blues now in the distant Smoky Mountains.

In the west of Ireland, like the west of Wales, there are tourist signboards everywhere. Horse Riding. Restaurant. B&B. Bike Hire. Holiday Information. Hotel. Café. Crafts Gallery. But where in Wales they spread out along the roadways here the Irish collect them. They mushroom in great arrays at junctions.

There are signs celebrating the filming of episodes from *Father Ted*. There are directions to taverns. There are markers for the deaths of Irish patriots. There are handbills for Munster Rugby, for Saturday nite traditional sessions, for Madam Lee the fortune teller. Lisdoonvara is in the heart of the Burren, an area of limestone pavements of great natural beauty. The town itself is deserted. The music festival that Christy Moore sang about here, the Irish Woodstock, came to an end in 1983 when eight people died swimming in the sea and Irish hells angels caused havoc. Instead Lisdoonvara now majors on love. Come here if you are on your own and lonely. But not this week. The annual matchmaking festival has just ended.

Down the road at Doolin, where the land runs out, are a scattering of pubs and restaurants, all pumping the Irish tradition. It ought to be like Beale Street in Memphis or the Lower Broadway honky tonks in Nashville. A short-sleeved roll from bar to bar, sampling the beer-driven music, fed up with this one, move on to the next. Dozens line the streets. But here in Doolin the air is, as ever, full of drizzle. There are only four pubs. The same two or three sets of musicians move between them. Do that yourself and you'll likely follow the same band from place to place. Same music. Different beer. But when the bands play the magic is palpable.

In the rain damp Doolin record store at the cliff edge – opened to underline the fact that despite the thinness of variety this is an Irish musical capital – the Magnetic Café is selling coffee and CDs. Own label plus rarities. You can buy an instrument here if you want to join in. Dulcimer. Banjo. Mandolin. I stick to tea and cake and watch the sea out there, thrashing and churning, in great sloops and draws. It looks as if it goes on forever.

But out there, among the swells and storms, is Inishbofin, legendary island, home of fiddle player Dessie O'Halloran, the roughest of singers on Sharon Shannon's famous *Diamond Mountain Sessions*. Here Shannon, a County Clare non-singer playing that most uncommercial of instruments, the accordion, assembled a stellar cast of international accompanists to take Irish music to places it had never before reached. Mark Knopfler, John Prine, Jackson Browne and others had septuagenarian O'Halloran with them on this unlikely million-seller. O'Halloran sings *The Way You Love Me*, unfettered by sophistication or artifice. Its melody gets under your skin. Despite O'Halloran's wayward voice and almost inarticulate diction the song was released as a single and reached no 4 in the Irish charts.

On Bofin itself, reached by a boat out of the harbour at Cleggan, the rain continues its glorying of the Irish green. O'Halloran, who was born here and regularly returns, is not in residence when I visit. The Inishbofin Céilí Band who have been playing all summer in one or other of the island's three bars have gone off to tour Europe. Dessie is with them. I buy his solo record at the community centre. *The Pound Road*. The road itself runs right across the island. I walk it. Dessie's tuneful, endearing, creak of a voice running in my head.

If I was looking for a place where all these musics I am following come together then it ought to be here. But somehow it's not. Ireland is not full of bluesmen nor new generation rock and roll. It's replete with its own sounds. The world glories them as Celtic Music. A new genre of harp and pipe and Celtic heartbeat. Ethereal voices. Enya. The swirl of the past. As false a categorisation as calling The Johnny Burnette Trio 'easy listening' which is what I saw recently in HMV's struggling store in Cardiff.

Back in 1971 the Breton singer Alan Stivell released what turned out to be a ground-breaking instrumental album – *Renaissance of the Celtic Harp*. It was as haunting and engaging as anything ever recorded on the ancient instrument. With it he popularised not only the music of Brittany itself but the idea that the six or so Celtic nations all had music drawn from a common root. What you heard in Ireland could be experienced in mirrored form in Scotland, and again in Wales, Cornwall, and beyond. The opening track, *Ys*, celebrated the fifth century capital of Cornwall or maybe that was Brittany. No trace can now be found. It was a lovely idea and it suited the great Celtic renaissance moving in the world at that time. We six Celtic brother countries with our non-English tongues can all understand each other. We have the same beards, the same locks, the same furrowed brows. We live for a world where our identities will become, as Margaret Thatcher was eventually to say about a different cause, paramount.

The Q Celts[37] of Ireland, Scotland and the Isle of Man would hold common cause with the P Celts of Wales, Cornwall and Britany. At a conference held in the early seventies at the Reardon Smith Lecture Theatre in Cardiff bards from all six nations gathered to bend their verses into a homogenous whole. The Irish were the boldest. The

Cornish uncertain. The Scots knowing. The Manx reticent. The Welsh serious. The Bretons full of joy. Celtic would be what we spoke. But in the event it turned out that no one could quite understand anyone else. Instead this Celtic world settled on an alternative lingua franca, English.

The melodies of these nations' respective musics also turned out to be less compatible than many might have wished. According to June Skinner Sawyers in *Celtic Music: A Complete Guide*[38], the P Celts, the Gaelic, present an extended range of more than two octaves in their melodies. The Q Celts, the Brythonic, close this down often to little more than a half octave. The musics are, Skinner concludes, not the same. Not that any of this stops musicologists from looking for trails and similarities and declaring the missing link to have been found. Stivell one year, Meic Stevens the next, The Chieftains when all else fails.

In the pub, back on dry land at Cleggan, they've got Johnny Cash coming out of the jukebox. Country music's John Wayne, made more albums than Mantovani. He's singing *Danny Boy* with a sort of cod lilt added to the top of his fractured Tennessee twang. American Celtic. A new world music.

12 • Flying To Nashville –
Country Music's Heart

I've seen my first cowboy. In the transit lounge at Toronto where we switched planes before heading south. He was sitting in the far corner up beyond the stall selling souvenirs embellished with the word *Canada* as if saying that alone would make America go away. He's there in tooled boots, western shirt embroidered with roses, a bolo bootlace tie, and a black Stetson hat. His guitar is in a hard scuffed case on the floor beside him. He could be posing for the cover of his latest long player, if such things were still made. The past's romance is still present. He sucks on a toothpick as if it were a cigarette and then brushes lint from his knee as if it were ash.

In Nashville itself there are more. Big hats are de rigueur. There are rhinestones on the walkways. A man in full Indian headdress is collecting his case from the carousel. Men lounge in white linen suits. Everyone wears boots, not trainers. The humidity is air-con cushioned. There's high blue outside. As you drive into the city and it's like approaching Oz, a kingdom of rising glass and steel glowing up out of the plain. Like the cover of *Nashville Skyline* ought to have been. AT&T's Batman building. The Fifth Third Centre. The Snodgrass Tennessee Tower. The Life & Casualty. The Pinnacle. In the foreground are the trusses of the Shelby Street Bridge, once the world's longest pedestrian river crossing. The *General Jackson* river boat sails under, plying the Cumberland River. This is a Martian City – a glowing place. Captain Video is in his hover plane coming to greet you. Flash Gordon flies his rocket to protect this Confederate slice of the southern world.

For decades I'd understood this city, if I'd understood it at all, from Chet Atkins' guitar, George Jones' voice and *Nashville*, Robert Altman's 1975 multi-layered film[39]. The film was famous not for its music but for its plot's labyrinthine mix of city politics, Christianity, and just how it is in the music business down south. But now that's all been blown out of the water by the high definition arrival of *Nashville*, the TV series and I've been glued to the screen. Nashville, city of musical cliché, is depicted as home of overproduced, layered, radio-friendly country cross-over pop and broken romance. Nothing rough, high voiced or redolent of the rootsy material I've been chasing. That doesn't sell to satellite TV's demographic. In Nashville, as they always have been, the edges have to be smoothed. The easy sentiment might still be there but it's dance friendly now, full of woops and smiling faces.

On the small screen *Nashville* takes over from *Dallas*. It's a trashy, easy watch featuring cheerleaders, milfs, divas, quiffs and suntanned hunks in western jeans. The music might be composed by Elvis Costello and John Paul White of The Civil Wars but it sounds much like the series looks. Slick and shiny. Nothing to shock, everything to love. Nevertheless *Nashville* does foreground a few of the city's great musical institutions: the Bluebird Café, the Opry at the Ryman and Music Row. And I counted the hats too. Everyone wears one.

The big hitter of the moment in the real world is Taylor Swift. She's on the billboards down Music Row and all over the music press. Since she was discovered back in 2006 she's sold more than twenty-six million albums and seventy-five million digital downloads. She's taken country beyond itself to that place where bubblegum meets rock. She's provoked the Southern Baptists to call her "the whorish face of doomed America". There are posters advertising what she does and how she looks right along the airport malls. She's TV *Nashville*'s young star, Juliette Barnes, to a tee.

Why is this city so famous for its music and why is it here, on the plains of Tennessee? Like so many American cities this one began as a fort, built in a clearing on the Cumberland River. Fort Nashborough was named in honour of the Revolutionary War General Francis Nash. By 1794 that name had shifted in favour the present Nashville. The fort is still there, or at least, a pretty decent replica is. It isn't exactly where the original was but almost. It's free to walk through. An American castle in extant wood sitting by the water. It is overlooked by passing pleasure boats, and crawled through by visiting children. Nashville itself developed on the back of cotton. It became a railroad hub and a centre for trade. Enamoured of status the local administration built a life size replica of the Parthenon as the centrepiece for an exhibition celebrating Tennessee's hundredth year as part of the Union. It sits in Centennial Park at the top of the slow rise of 26th Avenue. Glowering power by association.

The music of Nashville has a long history. In the nineteenth century the Fisk University was established here. This was the first higher educational institution open to blacks in post-slavery Jim Crow South. It produced The Fisk Jubilee Singers. The Jubilee Singers were an acapella choir of eleven voices who rose to fame for their singing of spirituals. In this era the songs of slaves and former slaves were largely unknown outside those communities. The Fisk Jubilee Singers were exotics. They opened their black music up to whites who had never heard such singing. They became enormously popular. They toured America and then travelled to Europe. They famously performed before British Prime Minister William Gladstone who was accompanied by a black-clad and unsmiling Queen Victoria. Their act went down well. "They are real Negroes," the monarch wrote in her journal. She commissioned a painting of the Fisks in their honour[40]. Nashville had made its first move on the road to musical fame. Country hadn't arrived yet. But it would.

In the early twenties the National Life and Accident Insurance Company whose slogan was 'We Shield Millions' (WSM, remember that) was looking for promotional opportunities. How could you sell insurance to country folk? Someone came up with the idea of starting a radio station. In the twenties radio – rather than recordings – was cutting edge. Radio had fidelity. It crossed open spaces. It was free. Recordings were created using acoustic equipment and, despite claims to the contrary made by their manufacturers, lacked a certain veracity. They simply didn't sound as good the music on the wireless. Furthermore they were costly to create, difficult to market, fragile and cost the user in equipment. They did, however, operate where there was no electricity. Turn the handle and sounds came out. But National Life opted for radio. They opened a studio on the fifth floor of their office on the corner of 7th and Union and began broadcasting from there. AM 650 WSM was born.

In 1925 George D 'Judge' Hay, a professional broadcaster hired by the company, began to programme hillbilly music and created a programme he called *WSM Barn Dance*. It was a successful formula. In 1927 after listening to an hour of the music that preceded his own broadcast, opera as it turned out, Hay was heard to say "For the past hour we've been listening to music taken largely from Grand Opera. From now on we are going to present Grand Ole Opry." The name stuck.

Today the Opry is an institution. It is country music's major edifice. Its story is well and regularly told, often by the Opry itself, an organisation that is a master of self-promotion. By the nineteen-thirties Opry shows had been expanded to four hours and moved to Saturday night and was broadcasting to thirty states. It shifted to national radio in 1939. It featured fiddle players, banjoists, singers of old time music and a high preponderance of square dance players. The idea of a knees-up in a country barn persists in the show's fabric right through to today. You can get a flavour from the names of some of the early Opry stars: The Binkley Brothers' Dixie Clodhoppers, The Possum Hunters, The Gully Jumpers, The Crook Brothers, Uncle Dave Macon and The Fruit Jar Drinkers. These guys do not sound as if they are familiars on the sophisticated stage of Carnegie Hall.

The Opry grew and developed its own management and institutional status. Being a member, i.e. someone who had played from the Opry stage, brought fame and status. Despite pressures from television the show remained a radio medium, as it does today, funding itself through the advertising it pushes between acts. Its format was slick. Its performers never less than the best.

When it outgrew its studios in 1934 the Opry moved. This was first to Hillsboro Theatre and then to a variety of venues, none ever suitable for long, before settling in 1943 in the place it made famous. The Ryman. The mother church. Country music's beating heart, if you believe, that is, that a music that majors on saccharine heartache backed with betrayal and sung by straight-laced good ol' boys with half an eye on the whiskey bottle and the other on God can have a heart. But I paint a cliché-ridden picture.

The Ryman was not the end. The Opry carried on growing and by 1974 had become too big even for the Ryman building's 51 year old, 3000-seat capacity. The Opry moved to a new, much larger and purpose built concrete-slab of a building out of town at Opry Mills. An hotel and theme park grew up around it. The theme park was replaced by the Opry Mills Mall in 2000.

The Ryman, the district around it no longer rough, run-down and threatening as it was in the seventies, markets itself in bright, tourist destination Music City as 'Historically Cool since 1892'. Quite how this figures for a building that started out as Captain Thomas Green Ryman's Union Gospel Chapel I'm not sure. The Chapel majored on hellfire and damnation preachers before changing its name to the Ryman Auditorium and becoming an actual opera house in 1904.

Despite the Opry having moved, this epicentre of the city's main business retains considerable glamour. A six foot square of the original stage was removed and installed in the new operation at Opry Mills. You could stand on the stage of the new concrete Opry and be on the same boards as Richard Nixon when he played his piano at the building's 1974 opening. Or better, imagine yourself channelling The Louvins, George Jones, Eddy Arnold, Cowboy Copas, The Everlys or Patsy Cline. Back at the Ryman, with its stage repaired and the new wood shining, you could do the same thing. How many places does the past infect?

On the Ryman tour we get shown dressing rooms, and doors, and places where the famous walked, hung their coats and tuned their guitars. You can pay extra and get a recording done of yourself karaok-ing to backing tracks of everything from *D.I.V.O.R.C.E.* and *Amazing Grace* to Carrie Underwood's *Jesus Take The Wheel*. My wife Sue and I settle for a photo of the two of us holding guitars and in front of the Ryman's main stage mic. There we are, Keith and Candice-Marie, a long way from home and doing a country version of *The Zoo Song*.

The Ryman was refurbished in 1994 and now features regular

concerts by headline acts, not all of them country by any means. There's nothing on when we visit which is often how it goes. Concert halls on dark nights are pretty synonymous with one of the themes of this book, car parks that once had famous buildings on them. Check ahead two paragraphs and you'll see it happening again.

Nashville heats up. Downtown fills with visitors. I guess I should have worked it out at the hotel when in the foyer I encountered around a dozen girls all attired in the same white dresses plus boots and then ran into a gang of young men all wearing the same t-shirt. Nashville as party land, just like we have back home. You can come here for a stag or a hen and spend your time out on the streets whooping. The difference is that in American you don't drink until you are twenty-one and you never carry alcohol with you on the streets. The passion for getting yourself blasted into a place where the mind no longer functions might be popular but it isn't, like it is the UK, quite as culturally central.

That's not to say that the city does not offer opportunities to party. There is a preponderance of Nashville stretched limos and open-topped party cars along with a number of twelve-person party bikes, bars on wheels where drinkers sit and peddle while the barman steers. They roll by, their occupants shrieking furiously as they go. When the sun shines Nashville shakes.

I go looking for the National Life and Accident Insurance Building. It's gone. In its place is a parking lot. It's around the corner from the Doubletree where we are staying. When I arrive there's nothing to mark it. History hangs in the empty air.

Out at the Opry itself, the new one, the atmosphere is markedly different. The building sits at the end of a parking lot that is longer than anything I've previously encountered. The gps shows the nearby Interstate but depicts the open acres of car park and white space. There are other cars, certainly, but enough spare slots for attendees at a six nations rugby international, should one ever be played here, all to have a space of their own. We are outside Opry Mills, a granddaddy of a shopping mall where security staff have electric carts and the multitude of stores all blend into a homogenous flow of stacked goods, glass, lights, encouragements to buy and opportunities to buy some more.

You can purchase virtually anything here except books, or music or electronic goods, things that might tempt me. Instead it's Starbucks and other old familiars. The western world turns into a uniform gloop as its molecules coalesce and its edges all soften.

As an institution the Opry has always suffered squabbles and difficulties. Who to invite, who to ban. How many times you had to play there in order to maintain membership. How many exceptions could be made. During the long-haired sixties when country music rolled off into rock the new electric popularisers were resisted. Music with drums was disliked. The Byrds, who played at the Opry when their country album *Sweetheart of the Radio* came out in 1968 had a tough reception. Earlier, in 1965, Johnny Cash had managed to smash a floor light with the microphone stand and got himself banned. The Opry was for the upright and the God-fearing. Most of the time.

Looking like a brutalist housing project with banners stuck around it in an attempt at user friendliness, the new auditorium attracts the middle-aged and the elderly. They are here in droves. Coming in on sticks and using battery-powered personal mobility devices. Ryman Hospitality, which owns the Opry along with the Ryman itself, WSM, the *General Jackson* showboat, plus any number of Gaylord hotels and golf courses, has business set as smooth as it gets.

The Opry today is sponsored by Humana, Dollar General and Cracker Barrel. In UK terms that would be Spire, Poundstretcher and Harvester. It runs two shows nightly, four days a week. You enter via the merch store and seamlessly roll on into the main auditorium. Opportunities to upsell, onsell or just plain sell abound. Do you want the Opry Book at reduced price? How about a Hatch print poster of tonight's programme? Buy the two for $20, that's 25% off, folks. The trick is to do this with style and not come over like Ryanair. Somehow it manages it.

The Opry started as a radio show and it still is. Between acts that run on rails are the adverts, mostly voiced over by the session's mc. *Sign Up To Humana For Your Health Plan. Being Healthy Has Its Rewards. Durango For Your Footwear. It's Not A Boot It's An Attitude.* The show is presented with a full band in an auditorium that reminds me of the old Cardiff Capitol.

We get slick Charlie Worsham doing post–Garth Brooks mainstream country; Sara Haze treading Taylor Swift's dance pop footsteps; The Del McCoury Band on top form presenting faultless bluegrass; Connie Smith, the most famous and simultaneously the most ancient, what Dolly might have turned out like if she'd stuck to pure country; John Conlee who gives Connie a run for her aged money in a suit that doesn't fit; Moe Brady the sentimental cowboy; the large Willis Clan with dancing children and upbeat smiles; and then the star, "I'm just 22", Scotty McCreery, winner on *America's Got Talent* and with a voice to match. The route up to stardom is no longer the old one. Today you have to do it via TV talent shows. You need to be young. And in the Bible Belt, this Nashville place, you also need to be outwardly Christian and not look too much like a redneck drunk.

Have I just heard the sound of this year's country music? One side maybe. The other you experience at a cramped 90-seat diner a few miles south west of here. The Bluebird Café. Its rise to stardom has been inexorable. It originally opened in 1982 as a gourmet restaurant but along the way acquired a reputation for presenting acoustic music and, in particular, new material sung by the composer. On the route from 1982 to today the Bluebird has done nothing but bounce bigger. Early on it hosted Kathy Mattea and Garth Brooks. These days LeAnn Rimes, John Prine, and JoJo Herman regularly sing here. If you want to hear newly written original, country-tinged music then this is the place. It has strict attendance and silence policies, a crisp management and succeeds in presenting two shows each evening, with food, every night of the week. Peter Bogdanovitch set his film *The Thing Called Love* here. The TV series *Nashville* features the Bluebird in most episodes. Viewers know the place like they do their own living rooms

The Bluebird stands in a row of shops on a busy main road. We're attending an early evening open mic night with the expectation of seeing the new when it is still sparkling. The huge snaking queue outside stands in blinding sun with a gun-toting security guard snarling instructions to stay in place and tighten your lines up and then meekly offering fainting customers free water to help them survive. After about an hour of this and the stress of thinking that you won't get a seat we all get in.

The Bluebird inside is pretty much as it is on TV except more crowded. Singers night organiser Barbara Cloyd takes the stage to tell us that she has a list of 45 acts each of whom will present a single song. In the two hours available we should get to hear 35. That's cracking along.

We begin with a couple of ancients who clearly haven't listened to any music for at least fifty years. They bang out a full of smiles rousing folksong much as The Weavers might have done. There's a preponderance of serious looking handsome young boy start-ups and long-haired earnest women who extend the path already trodden by Joni Mitchell, Kate Bush and Alanis Morissette. Many are students of the Nashville music and songwriting colleges — such as Mike Curb's College of Entertainment and Music Business — that have sprung up around Music Row. Nothing sounds country, no Faith Hill, no Taylor Swift either, although she, too, was discovered here. A pattern of alt country is emerging. There are warblings and weak chords. Occasionally something stands out but as soon as it has arrived it's gone. It's a production line. Everyone is so excited to be at the new centre of Nashville's songwriting world, the Bluebird. That's what they all keep on saying.

The real commercial musical heart of Music City is actually along what's called Music Row. It's here that the music companies have their offices and where the artists come to record. Doing something you don't do in Nashville (or indeed do much in any American city) we decide to walk. This is an urban ramble through rising humidity. We go out along the city's flaky sidewalks to pass under the Interstate that flies above on legs. Apart from the cars we're mostly alone.

At the end of Lower Broadway we stop at Legends Corner for a drink. It's 10.30 am. Fiddle player Katie Marie and her accompanists are already in action. It's standard country but she knows how to play. The audience is about six strong. Sue and I from Wales at three thousand miles distant and then some guy in boots from Hawaii which turns out to be further.

The walk takes in further slices of the vanished. On McGavock Street at no 1525 is the Beaman Toyota parking lot right in the place where once stood RCA Victor's original Nashville studio. It was here in 1956 that the just captured from Sun Elvis Presley recorded *Heartbreak Hotel*, one of the foundation stones of rock and roll. You'd think there'd be a marker but there's not. The car salesman, a fat friendly guy, hunts the history on his phone but comes up with nothing. "I've been here a while and I've never heard of any studio," he says. "The Beaman family have had their business here for thirty years. Didn't know Elvis had a connection." History again lost in the redevelopment dust.

Music Row was originally settled along 16th and 17th Avenues. They were suburban, residential, and leafy. Despite all their fame they still look like that today. As an aid to tourism the Avenues have now been renamed Music Square East and Music Square West. The first to settle here were the Bradley brothers, Owen (1915-1998) and his younger sibling Harold (1926-). They bought a house at 804 16th Avenue South and moved into the business of creating scores for film and television. They built a studio in the basement. Their interests soon morphed into country music. Owen played piano and Harold played guitar. They established themselves as the core of the first country music rhythm section. The entire Nashville edifice was born.

In 1954, outgrowing the basement Bradley added a Quonset hut out back and built a larger studio in that. A Quonset was a US Army pre-fab building made of corrugated metal and with a curved roof much like the British Nissan hut on which its design was based. It gave you space for small financial outlay. The Bradleys' hut became the most legendary place in Nashville recording more stars than any other studio in the world. Patsy Cline's *Crazy, I Fall to Pieces,* and *Walkin After Midnight* were made here. So, too, were Lynn Anderson's *Rose Garden*, Johnny Cash's *Ring of Fire*, *A Boy Named Sue*, and *Folsom Prison*, Tammy Wynette's *Stand By Your Man* and *D-I-V-O-R-C-E*, George Jones's *White Lightning*, *A Good Year For The Roses*, *Golden Ring* and *He Stopped Loving Her Today.* The studios were used by Bill Monroe, Marty Robbins, Bob Dylan, The Byrds, Buddy Holly, Brenda Lee, The Beach Boys, Conway Twitty, Simon and Garfunkel, Ernest Tubb, and, it seems, everyone else you'd ever heard of.

Bradley's success attracted others. The best place to open a new shoe shop is right next to an existing one runs the economic trope.

Studios along the strip flourished. They turned residential suburbia into a mecca for country's stars. RCA opened what was to become its Studio B, a place where Elvis could record when he was away from Memphis. Columbia came. Countless independents set up shop here. Country's Nashville sound took hold.

The step across from the Heartbreak SUV retail car park to the top of the strip isn't far. Here, in 2003, in one of those municipal fits that no one in retrospect can understand, the city of Nashville commissioned Alan LeQuire to create a Music City celebratory piece to mark the importance of Music Row. LeQuire is a public artist with a reputation for using human forms at large scale. He should have been perfect. Musica, the resultant country music epic, sits in the centre of a roundabout outside Owen Bradley Park at the top of the row. It is a hideous forty-foot tall set of hand-holding bronze dancers. Men and women, nine of them, nude and clueless. Locals regularly dress them in appropriate clothing. As we pass they've been done out in red tee shirts supporting Stand Up To Cancer. If there's a connection to Country then I can't see it. They look more like vigorous Olympians preparing for their big day.

Nearby is a diminutive park named after Bradley. It is headed with a Gary Ernest Smith's 1999 statue of the man himself at his piano. The names of some of his many many hits are engraved into the paving around him. It's a musical memorial but utterly silent. On the still leafy and well-kept row itself there's plenty of evidence of contemporary activity with studios and music publishing houses open for business all around. But we're seeking the past.

While I'm photographing a sign marking the establishment of BMI (Broadcast Music Inc.) in Nashville in 1958 we are approached by a baseball-hat wearing, side burned local in jeans who'd previously been valeting a car. "You want to see a real historical studio? You heard of the Quonset hut?" We nod. "I can show you where it is, son," he says to me. "Back of that parking lot. You can still see a piece of its curved roof. I worked there. I was a session drummer on all those hits. Jim Isbell. I'm in all the books. You look me up." I do and he was. Drummer on everything from Gordon Lightfoot to Tony Joe White.

Owen Bradley's genius was to recognise that the rough, hillbilly, scratchy sounds, all fiddles, errant voices and steel guitars, which had marked the music so far, had to go. To broaden the appeal and to sell more records you needed sophistication, musical arrangements, piano parts, strings. You needed to put the singers out front and drop all those hick-sounding names. Up at RCA B his cue was picked up by guitarist and producer Chet Atkins who, along with slip-note session pianist Floyd Cramer, played on and created most of country hits that Bradley didn't. This was the Nashville Sound, countrypolitan, maker of more hits and more bucks than old time music had ever done.

The hits were controlled by the label's New York headquarters. They were in the business of making money not art. Countrypolitan singers had little control over the material they were required to use. We got Patsy Cline, yes, and Tammy Wynette but we also got Jim Reeves and Waylon Jennings' pre-outlaw mainstream pap.

The remains of the Quonset hut are hidden round the back of Mike Curb's College of Entertainment and Music Business which bought the studio space from Columbia a decade or more back. Hard to discern but there, a many-times painted arc of history.

The Row like many other parts of Nashville is littered with garishly painted ten foot tall Gibson guitars. These Barry Island funfair additions to country music's backdrop arrived in 2004 as part of a project called GuitarTown. They are supposed to mark significant spots and are individually designed. They have that feel of community art about them, of colour splash that works well amid urban decay but maybe not here in Nashville's well-to-do Row. There's one right outside RCA's Studio B decorated with a picture of Elvis and a street sign saying 'Lonely Street'. Up the neck run the words 'Heartbreak Hotel'. Not actually recorded here, as I've discovered, but let's bend the past a little once again.

Studio B is now on the tourist trail with daily bus trips up from the Downtown, the only way of access. Inside are giant photos of the stars who recorded here and a chance to look into the cramped spaces that produced so many hits. Add Eddy Arnold, Elvis Presley, Waylon Jennings, Willie Nelson, Roy Orbison, Dolly Parton, Jim Reeves, Charlie Pride and a host more to those who worked round the corner at Bradley's barn and you've got country pretty much sorted.

When the unending sameness of countrypolitan fell apart in the 70s and pop music began to swamp the Nashville world the answer was the creation of The Outlaws. These were Nashville outsiders (or insiders at last let off their a&r leashes) playing a rougher sounding, more exciting country music. Waylon and Willie, Jessi Colter, Merle Haggard, Kris Kristofferson, and others. They were followed into the 80s by the advent of country music that attempted to crossover into the mainstream – country pop. Dolly Parton's dreadful disco. Kenny Rogers bland slush. Alabama and Ronnie Milsap's almost rock music.

In the 1990s Garth Brooks, Shania Twain and Faith Hill took a new form of highly produced, stadium show-biz orientated country out into the million seller lists. Nashville could still turn in a country dollar. In the new millennium it still does with its roster of country dance pop crossover singers including Lee Ann Womak, Carrie Underwood, and the inevitable Taylor Swift.

If this high-powered enormously high energy whap isn't for you then there is an alternative. Alt country, of the kind experienced at the Bluebird and with a beating heart in the bars and hideaways of east Nashville. This is a music that looks to its American acoustic roots but often does so with a drummer and a distortion laden amplified guitar. It's a parallel world to the money spinning still created by Music City. At its origins are clear and total outsiders, men with guitars, like Townes van Zandt, Gene Clark, Joe Ely and Steve Earle. At its core are cowpunk bands like The Long Ryders, Uncle Tupelo, Son Volt, Wilco, The Jayhawks, and The Drive By Truckers. Practitioners include Mark Olson, Bonnie Prince Billie, and the most famous exponent, some of the time, Ryan Adams. The music travels. It says something. Its sentiment is not that of Nashville. It'll never be famous.

Just down Deaderick Street from the hotel is an old boy sitting on the wall. He's weather-beaten, unkempt and clearly down on his luck. He's strumming a well-used guitar and has got a hat for coins on the sidewalk in front. There was a notice in a nearby store advising against giving money to vagrants: 'most of them are professional con artists', but not this guy. The spot he's chosen is not audacious. Passing trade is low. I listen and he's okay. *A Good Year For The Roses*. He does it sweet, more like George than Elvis. He finishes and raises a left hand to touch the brim of his Stetson. I give him $5. So he'll spend it on beer, who cares?

13 • Memphis – Only Just Tennessee

For years I could never figure David Ackles. To start with he'd given up recording by the time I'd discovered him. Four albums was all he ever made and only two of these did anything. In fact there was only one that actually echoed down the years. *The Road To Cairo*. Picture of him on the cover, standing in a bed-sitter somewhere, behind a sheet of smashed glass. What was this smoky voiced Leonard Cohen sound-alike doing rolling along an organ-filled road to the Egyptian capital? How could this be hip? "I know this road, it leads straight to Cairo, twenty-two miles up ahead". Julie Driscoll[41] made a minor hit out of it in 1968 but it was Ackles who'll be remembered. If for nothing else then for this.

Truth was that Ackles was a better songwriter than his label (Elektra) had allowed for. He got hung up creating overly-Gothic, Brecht Weill, theatrical songs with hugely complex orchestral arrangements. Out here in listening land all we wanted was to hear was more of his Al Kooper-driven stripped-back country rock. Didn't get it. Ackles gave up in 1973. And here I am now on the road to another city named after one in Egypt. Memphis.

Ackles' Cairo was in Illinois. The place I'm heading for is in Tennessee. For all the world, though, it feels like it's Mississippi. There's a great meandering river, a flood plain, high humidity, cotton fields as far as the eye can see, and a palpable lack of money. That's what it's like in Mississippi, the state of the Union they prefer not to celebrate. But Tennessee, that place has a saleable buzz. *Tennessee Waltz, Tennessee Blues, Tennessee Flat Top Box, My Tennessee Mountain Home*, and the song that celebrates just where I'm going, *Memphis, Tennessee*.

The road we've been on is the 40. It scoots west from Nashville passing the farms and the fields that made the state famous. In the distance the sun flashes from the chrome of rigs lined up by the hundred at a giant distribution centre. There are bushes, just a few. Direction boards for Jackson, for Humboldt, for Milan. Actual habitation is scarce. At succeeding junctions there are clusters of signs for Cracker Barrel, Wendy's, Taco Bell, Ruby Tuesday's, Motel 6, and Quality Inn. Then suddenly it's in front of me. Exit 56 from the 40. Brownsville. A name I recognise from my past of browsing ancient blues. I dredge the memory and come up with a bunch of names. Charlie Musslewhite. Bukka White. Furry Lewis. Sleepy John Estes. America littering her landscape with singers once again.

I find Brownsville's West Tennessee Delta Heritage Centre (WTDHC) just behind MacDonald's. It has an empty parking lot large enough to accommodate bus fleets. Would I expect anything else? Inside, beyond the welcoming life-size wire sculpture of a banjo-toting figure constructed entirely from disused heating elements[42], are more free information leaflets than any visiting human could ever require. A trained Hospitality Ambassador of uncertain age tells me to take as many as I like.

The displays are copious. Cotton farm machinery, mannequins wearing ancient bibs and overalls, Newman Walpole's White Oak basket collection, bags that once held fertilizer, log books done in long hand and then the music. This is a stop, after all, on the music highway that connects Nashville with Memphis, kingpins at the heart of American song. The WTDHC has displays that reference Tina Turner (born in Nutbush, TN), and Carl Perkins (Tiptonville, TN) and then a life-size cut-out of Elvis (born Tupelo, MS but spent most of his life up the road in Memphis, TN). The cut out is wired and spookily mutters uh huh huh from time to time.

"You enjoy yourself," commands the Hospitality Ambassador, as if she were working at Disney. Out back in the parking lot stands the museum's centrepiece, the home of Sleepy John Estes. It's a white-painted and pretty bust-up shack. Inside against the walls there are worn out wooden chairs along with a bed that you really wouldn't want to be spending the night in. Photos show Sleepy John as a thin-faced, bent black man wearing braces, dark glasses and a straw hat. I'm overawed. Here he is. His home, his birthplace, the original. But then it can't be quite that. A black-top car park has been constructed right under the building. This shack had to have been moved in from somewhere. I ask the Hospitality Ambassador. She swears "that shack, honey, is real and right where it always was. Sleepy John, he lived right in that place." I start to tell her that I heard him in Bristol, UK, in the mid-1960s but she glazes over. There ought to be some facility to hear him playing but there's not.

Estes was an old man all his life. It was how he looked. Born 1899, son of a sharecropper, he was blinded in one eye in a childhood rock throwing accident. He was sleepy either because he suffered from a blood pressure disorder, as some commentators have it, or more likely, as blues historian Bob Koester claims, he simply enjoyed withdrawing from the world. He made his first record as early as 1929 and sounded then almost as old as he did on his post-war revival tracks. His best work was made with accompanists. These included harmonica player Hammie Nixon, mandolin and guitarist Yank Rachell, and pianist Jab Jones. This was for the Decca and Bluebird labels in the 1930s but such esoteric recordings never reached the South Wales of my blues-ridden youth.

What were generally available were the recordings he'd made for Sun and Delmark, the products of his rediscovery by Sam Charters in 1962. Estes, long thought dead, a rumour given credibility by Big Bill Broonzy's insistence that he'd attended his funeral, was discovered completely blind and living in rural poverty. Like many ancient pensioner bluesmen Estes was lifted from decrepitude, given a new suit of clothes and put out there to shine in the glory of the 60s revival. He appeared at the Newport Folk Festival in 1964 and then went on tour of Europe. Delmark recorded him extensively and although the essence is there and the crying vocals still delight his best work remained behind him. He died of a stroke in 1977.

I'd heard him live back when those around me, young men thrilling up to the early American blues in Mod-era Britain, thought of him as a hero. He was a magic man from mysterious blues history, discussed with reverence in the pages of *Melody Maker*, and sought out by blues collectors with unashamed zeal. Estes was ace, the genuine article. And here he was, in a parking lot just off the 40, ragged past all on display. Authentic as it's possible to be. I listen to him again now, as I write, in 2015, decades down the track. Real, yes. Brilliant? Maybe not.

Memphis. Here it is. I can see it right ahead. It's built on one of the Chickasaw bluffs overlooking the Mississippi River. The Mississippi, the wide-water snaking rip up the centre of the United States. Known to me and most Brits first for its association with riverboats and cowboys, gambling and Indian wars, black and white minstrels, Stephen Foster songs, banjos, and cotton. 2340 miles flowing from northern Minnesota to New Orleans and the Gulf of Mexico. It's a continent divider, a place of adventure, history, death and legend. Suddenly I want to see it. What's pulled me here is the music not the water but now it's the water that draws me in.

At its edge on Riverside Drive where we park the car are a string of riverboats – some plying for genuine travelling trade, others as beached casinos, bars and restaurants. The brown river stretches out beyond them and it's hard to see the further bank. The tows, flat, wide barges laden with grain and cement, are pushed southwards in great strapped-together conglomerations, nine, twelve, fifteen or more at a time. At Memphis we're three hundred and fifty miles from the sea but the Mississippi is still as wide as an estuary. The great Hernando-Desoto road bridge takes the 40 on over to West Memphis leaving Tennessee for Arkansas. The river is the state line. To the south is the Harahan railroad bridge and crossing it a train of freight trucks about as long as the rail distance between Cardiff and Newport. The cars don't stop rolling, no head nor tail. The humidity makes you sweat just standing.

Why come here? Memphis, home of the blues, where WC Handy lived and BB King has his base. Best known for the grave of Elvis Presley and that singer's mansion at Graceland; for its world-famous legendary recording studios – Sun, Hi, Stax, American; for the rock and roll that grew here; for Jerry Lee Lewis, Otis Redding, Johnny Ace, Memphis Slim, and Aretha Franklin; for Booker T. Jones and his Hammond B-3; for Beale Street and the Memphis Blues that almost any Dixie jazzer will be able to hum; for its place as the spiritual and psychic centre of the music that, for much of the latter part of the twentieth century, drove the world.

I've come to Memphis because I'm tracking what I've been listening to for more than fifty years. From the valve-driven, cardboard speaker of my grandfather's steam radio; from the diddle-diddle of the Irish music pouring out of Cardiff's east city pubs; from the chords and guitar picking in the polo-necked British folk clubs; from the British blues rocking out of South Wales dives and late night valley bars; from the harmonica playing of Andy Fairweather Low at the Moon Club; from the revered and pain-killing harp music enshrined in the Welsh tradition; from the Welsh street cloggers and the guys who heard *Green Onions* in 1962 and have been playing its skin-thrilling melody ever since; from the wailers and the shouters and those who could tap a whole evening's dancing just by banging on a bin lid; from Duke Ellington, Captain Beefheart, The Fall, and Tom Waits. From all these things in my musical blood and my ever-open ears. Where did they lead? Where did they come from? Here.

The reason why Memphis became so much more a multi-faceted music city than Nashville, centre of the recording industry, the real Music City, two hundred miles back along the 40 to the east was a matter of geography. Given its prime position on a flood-free bluff overlooking the all too often errant Mississippi River what else could it do but succeed? This was a place where the river had created large and flat fertile lands. Memphis became the area capital, despite being mostly in Tennessee with just a slice over the water in Arkansas and none in Mississippi at all. The climate was hot and humid. Ideal for growing that great nineteenth century cash crop, cotton. The plantations were many. They were worked at first by slaves and then, later, by freed blacks paid a pittance. Memphis was the marketplace, the trading centre, home of warehouses and great transport links down that wide wide river. The city traded in lumber and for a time was the largest mule market the world had known. You want to buy a mule, you go to Memphis. You can get them on Beale Street like no other.

It was here in this city that the blues came up from the delta and mixed with the backwoods, old time music brought in by whites from the north and the east. A melting pot. One of those places where disparate populations slid into each other with no effort and little abrasion. Except here they didn't, not quite, and, when it came down to it, not at all. Memphis in the hard years of the fifties and the sixties before segregation ended was a place of lynchings, Klan revivals, cross burnings, political denunciations from city hall and civil rights violations by the thousand. It was here, after all, that the black civil rights leader and inspiration to the nation Martin Luther King took an assassin's bullet. He was shot on the balcony of the Lorraine Motel on the fourth of April, 1968. The American world after that was never the same.

It's hard to credit, from the perspective of the multi-racial twenty-first century, just how far blacks were from whites back in the mid-twentieth century US South. If you were white you only ever heard black music in the distance. You never attended a black club, never looked inside a juke joint, never dined with a black man, not on your life. When the founders of the multi-racial Stax record label first met with the head of Atlantic Records to discuss business they did it over a meal. As this was at the start of the sixties they had to meet in a private, at a rented hotel room. Not one Memphis restaurant would indulge them. Dinner came courtesy of room service. According to author Robert Gordon[43] integration in Memphis in 1961 was a thing of the distant future. White Stax founder Jim Stewart in the company of future black stars Carla and Rufus Thomas had to use the service elevator to access Atlantic boss Jerry Wexler's room at the Claridge Hotel. Even then the management reacted by sending the police around to harass them.

But I can see no sign, out on whooping Beale Street, that integration is nothing but how things now are. If I dig deeply, though, I'll find the old divides still present in some quarters, but that's another story. Meantime, in the still sunlit evening, the cops watch from cars with Memphis painted large down their sides. The street is a rioting ruckus of partying visitors all intent on having a real good time. Beale developed as Memphis' black heart. In the nineteenth century Robert Church, the first black millionaire from the south, purchased land around it. Built an opera house. Established a park and auditorium at the corner of Beale and 4th. Encouraged musicians to attend. The clubs and bars and entertainment stores followed. In 1916 Memphis native WC Handy wrote *Beale Street Blues*. Louis Armstrong made it famous. The black blues flocked and the street began to rock.

Despite a chequered redevelopment history the street today looks a little like Broadway, Cardiff might if South Wales had the weather. Nothing matches, there are signs and street life everywhere, punters bouncing, men with guitars, stores selling records, hamburgers, creole cooking and booze and booze and booze till it pours from your skin. The place has been declared home of the blues by Congress and is a National Historic Monument. Having a good time is an essential component. State sanctioned fun, what a concept.

At the Jerry Lee Lewis Café and Honky Tonk we get red hot creole fries and fiery Cajun sauce and put it out with Miller Lite. What I can't subdue, however, is the floor show – a rock and roll costumed Jerry Lee impersonator setting fire to his piano while playing a pretty accurate rendition of *Whole Lot of Shakin*. Down the street, past Buddy Guy and Muddy Waters look-alikes with their roaring leads and street amp distorted blue voices, is BB King's Club. The master died in 2015. In his place one of hundreds of imitators who have followed his electric lead plays instead.

King's BB is short for Blues Boy and he made his name on this very street. His distractive electric guitar sound, the one that launched Albert King, Freddie King, and host of others, championed in the UK by Clapton and then just about every other British blues guitar toter, King acquired from Bukka White. Bukka didn't teach King to play as many claim but he was a guitarist that King certainly watched. Bukka's steel slide was something that BB says he tried to copy but couldn't. So he came up with the nearest approximation he could manage to that sliding sound: a distinctive vibrato made by applying a shaking hand to the solid fret. With their lack of roughness and their totally competent delivery do King's electric blues sound like anything that came before? They certainly don't.

At his Beale Street club I enjoy the fact that everything is calm for once. Sophistication as refuge from the barbarous magnificence outside reigns. Soul food is served while the band plays hits from Motown and Stax. The accommodation comfortable. The beer is served with a glass. The blues are at one remove, but never too distant. In Memphis that just can't be done.

The joys of Beale are many. Schwab's Dry Goods Store is one of them. Established by Jewish immigrant Abraham Schwab in 1876 the multi-floored enterprise has only just left family hands. It began as a men's haberdashery and retailer of overalls and moved sideways into retailing what it terms dry goods sometime in the middle of last century. Inside it resembles a vast pound shop, nothing expensive and almost everything junk. But what junk. Voodoo paraphernalia, washboards, harmonicas, American hats, hot foot powder, black cat bones, Guatemalan kick bags, portraits of Elvis, fish made from bottle tops, attraction oil, old time candy, walking sticks, handcuffs, cheese-burger hats, bull castrators, tins of Memphis air, things for getting stones out of horse's hoofs, books about the blues, Barbie Doll candles, Do As I Say incense, bogus antiques, domination talc, graveyard dirt in packets, success powder and sunglasses for viewing Venusians when they land.

Down the road from Schwab's is Handy Park, grand entrance, battered public land beyond, statue of the great man, outdoor beer sellers, burgers, grass worn flat and brown, musicians on the stage. The music is the blues end of hip hop with street dancers out front break-ing, locking, popping, gliding on tip toes then spinning and turning like funky fish. The whole thing is about as far as you can get from my idea of a park. No trees, no pathway, no formality, not enough space to exercise, the green a poor and failing echo of what it could have been. Ornamental parklands, sports fields and great green swards are what the British do. In the American South you simply have useable public space and it's here that locals hang out.

Memphis is a city of some size. The population at the last count was 670,000. It rises to three times that if you include the greater metropolitan area. This makes Memphis bigger than Manchester. What it feels like, however, is nothing like that. Newport, Mon., with heat and music. Reading, Berks., with a really broad river. Swansea, flat and without the sea. All three with soul added in spades.

Soulsville, USA. This is what the 1960s Stax record company labelled Memphis as a riposte for Motown calling Detroit *Hitsville.* Suddenly in the dance halls of Cardiff Wilson Pickett was king, Booker T. was all over the airwaves (despite being described as without imagination by the British music papers), and Sam & Dave were the new Allisons. That soul music was a direct progression from the music they played out there in the delta was hard to discern among the ultra violet lighting in the club basements of Charles Street. There teeth and dandruff glowed so brightly, for a brief moment, before being drowned in the strobe and electronically controlled multi-light flash that followed.

It's easy now to go back and listen to Cream and hear them effortlessly switch from what were once acoustic delta blues (*Crossroads*) to Stax's vision of the blues side of soul (*Born Under A Bad Sign*). How we travelled from sitting up there on top of the world to the land of a thousand dances[44] was pretty much a straight road, although we might not have seen it as such at the time. But now, here I am in blues city and the spectrum and development of the music is obvious.

The classic funky, horn-embellished, organ-driven, gospel-derived call and response music that had begun to appear from Fame, Stax, Hi, Goldwax, Atlantic, Chess and a few others at the start of the sixties was a natural progression from the blues. Once the Mississippi delta down-home acoustic singers had adopted electricity and moved their base up to Chicago the way forward was obvious. Secular testifying. God inspired rock and roll. Mix in rising black consciousness, civil rights and the end of segregation, and you have it. The sound of bling and black power. Soul Music. For around fifteen years until the emergence of funk and r&b disco if you listened to black music, young people's black music, then this was what you got. A world beater. Soul music snapped its fingers right round the world.

Could white men sing it? At Stax, other than for Delanie and Bonnie, no one tried. But elsewhere Joe Cocker, Stevie Winwood and Tom Jones made a fair fist. Cocker, if you don't know it's him, sounds remarkably similar to Ray Charles. In the sixties such things were important. Multi-racial bands were cool but as rare as hits by Billy Cotton. Otis Redding couldn't publically drink coffee with an Anglo anywhere in Memphis. But on the street everyone snapped their fingers and did the pimp walk. The white obsession with black culture was on the rise.

Memphis is almost as full of recording studios as Nashville. But while Music City attracted the majors Memphis had to manage with the innovative independents, the shoestring operators who, often as not, made up the business and how they worked as they went along. One such was Stax. It was begun in 1957 as Satellite Records by white brother and sister Jim Stewart and Estelle Axton. Their first two singles were white country. Neither was a hit.

But in 1961, in a rush of blood, Stewart discovered R&B and recorded first The Veltones and then Rufus and Carla Thomas. The line was set. The label's name was changed to Stax (drawn from the names of the two founders) and they hacked a distribution deal with Atlantic. In June they recorded an instrumental from a band they named The Mar-Keys. *Last Night*. It was their first huge hit.

Stax had studios and its own record shop on McLemore Avenue (Mack-Le-More Americans say), the premises of what was once the suburban Capitol Theatre in a district that was originally mixed-race but now heading black. Run by Estelle, the shop allowed the label to test market and gain immediate local response. The hits followed. William Bell, Rufus Thomas, Otis Redding, Sam & Dave, Eddie Floyd, Johnny Taylor. This was Commitments and Blues Brothers territory. The house band who played in one combination or other, and usually with a bank of added horns, were the MG's. Booker T. and the MG's. *Green Onions* was their 1962 smash, that ever so simple organ instrumental with its slicing guitar breaks from white musician Steve Cropper. On guitar he was everything Eric Clapton was not – simple, incisive, spare – solo over almost as soon as it had begun. Don Covay and Wilson Pickett recorded with the MG's at Stax although their records were released on the Atlantic label.

Booker T. Jones was so young it was impossible. Seventeen when he made *Green Onions*. He was barely older than the dancers who funked their way through his so simple three-note classic right across GB. The MG part of the band's name did not stand for Memphis Group as the radio told me. Instead the band was named in the style of The Triumphs who'd hit with an instrumental called *Burnt Biscuits*. Triumph was the British sports car their producer drove. When it came to Booker T. then his band had to be called after another British sports car. Obvious when you know. The MG[45].

The hits kept coming even if Stax management dropped the baton many times. In between world-wide smashes from Judy Clay, Isaac Hayes, The Staple Singers, Little Milton, Albert King, and Otis, time and again, the label managed to foul its distribution deals, alienate its national partners, get managed by gangsters, waste half its income on fur-lined offices with Blaxploitation-influenced bling and expense claims that gave staff pretty much anything they desired. After coming back from the financial brink at least twice, changing owners and losing its entire catalogue Stax finally went bankrupt in 1975.

Woman to Woman was a hit for Shirley Brown in 1974. After that there was nothing. Back catalogue, that which remained, and intellectual property was bought by Fantasy Records in 1977. Stax became little more than a reissue label for decades until Concord Records bought Fantasy and started to take on new artists and make releases on a revived Stax label in 2006. Booker T. Jones, still on the soul trail, was one of their early signings.

Memphis preserves the fabric of its history almost as well as Merthyr Tydfil does. Beale Street went through a period of butchery in the 1960s with buildings being demolished and others boarded up. In 1989 the new owners of the Stax studios on McLemore, the Church of God in Christ, tore the building down. It was as if the huge success of Elvis' Graceland mansion as a money-turning visitor attraction had not happened. The real world was clearly under the Church of God's radar. For a time a local entrepreneur sold bricks from the demolition by mail order. Memphis soul by post. But the Church of God in Christ did nothing.

History, however, like reissues themselves, often comes back for another crack at the present. The state put up an historical marker on the site in 1991 and then, at the turn of the millennium, a group of interested parties connected together enough public and private money to provide the wherewithal for a rebuild. In precisely the style of the Stax studios of old, and using the original architect's drawings, the whole 926 East McLemore operation returned to the street like Dr Who's tardis. This time the enterprise didn't make new music but celebrated what had already been achieved. Museum, store, community centre. New red bricks. Wide pavements. The Stax Museum even has a dance floor. A museum world first.

When I get there I haven't worked out that this isn't the original building. There's no sign telling this slippery truth. Things only become apparent when I get inside and find the building too clean and crisp and lacking the props and the detail that half a century of music making ought to have left. The Satellite Records store, founder Estelle Axton's research department, is in place and packed with just about every Stax soul reissue possible – including, I'm glad to say, that underrated gem from Booker T., *McLemore Avenue*. This was originally issued in September, 1970, only a few months after The Beatles had brought out their *Abbey Road* which Booker T. used as a source. He was audacious enough to record an album which consisted entirely of instrumental retakes of the British Beatles vocal originals: *Here Comes The Sun, Because, Polythene Pam, Come Together* and the rest, ditching *Maxwell's Silver Hammer*, The Beatles track most everybody hates. The songs are arranged in medleys and run for a good forty minutes. Booker's Hammond M3 couldn't be better suited, enhanced with Steve Cropper's typically scant guitar licks and with just the odd voice-over echoing what could be lyrics or most likely aren't. Just the sound of the band noodling.

Why did they make it? The band had always been fond of Beatles' tunes, dotting their earlier albums with organ–driven takes on *Lady Madonna, Michelle, Eleanor Rigby* and others. These errant tracks are re-collected as bonus cuts on the remastered Stax re-release I buy. Again. I've one CD already at home as well as the 12-inch vinyl original. On the cover the four MG's are photographed in line, straddling McLemore, in homage to the four Beatles on that zebra crossing outside the Abbey Road studios in London. No zebras in America. Just bewildered onlookers. Sue and I have already defied zooming Buicks and men with pickups getting ourselves photographed outside Stax doing the self-same thing. An imitation of an imitation. Duchamp would have loved it.

Highlight of the Museum might be the walls and walls of original album sleeves showing just how many the company made. The soul explosion made real. As many names I recognise as those I don't. 12-inch cover art which as a form has been in decline for years. Actually, though, it's the Hammond M3, sitting casually alone with a typed identifying label stuck to its top as if it might be an exhibit in some small town museum. The very instrument which Booker T. Jones used in the ground-breaking sessions of 1962.

They'd come into McLemore's studios to back Sun rockabilly hard-hitter Billy Lee Riley. Of all people. Riley had made the dance floor filler which introduced a whole generation to the words 'doodly squat' in 1957 – *Red Hot* – and was still living off the proceeds. Author Robert Gordon reports that on this occasion Riley was too drunk to do much and, rather than waste the session time, Booker T. recorded *Behave Yourself* for potential single release. This was the laid-back night time blues instrumental that for decades I'd imagined to be an authentic B-side filler rather than the proto A-side it actually was. As had happened with Cliff Richard's *Move It, Green Onions* – the original B – was laid down almost as an afterthought. A sinister-sounding groove which referenced *Peter Gunn* and was sliced across with that Cropper guitar. Radio DJs flipped the record leaving *Behave Yourself* in the wilderness. Booker T. broke big time.

In the UK it was there at the core of the emerging Mod sound. Every band there was had a version they'd play, and dozens recorded it. On the flip of The Rolling Stones' Lennon and McCartney composed, *I Wanna Be Your Man*, is something called *Stoned*, a Nanker Phlege (Jagger Richards) composition. It's *Green Onions* in all but name.

I'm out in the street again, humming it. In fact it's a number I, hopeless musician, can actually play. Piano, guitar, harmonica, spoons, penny whistle, anything. Defines an era. It's that simple, that memorable, that addictive.

On the way back to where we've left the car on College Street we pass a run-down, wooden-sided, tar-paper roofed two-story house with its porch collapsed like an earthquake had recently hit. Out front is a painted sign announcing this as 'The Historic Home of Memphis Slim – Renovations Coming Soon – Soulsville USA'. Slim, a jump blues pianist of the old school, had been born in Memphis and although he'd made his name in Chicago and later moved to Paris where he'd stayed for thirty years, it was in Memphis where he'd been laid to rest. To renovate, his home looked as if it would take knocking down and starting again. What they'd done with Stax, of course. According to plans this Historic Home would soon be a museum, recording studio, community facility, employment generator and long term memorial to a musician who, today, is about as unfashionable as it was possible to be.

Soul he never was. Blues with added electric guitar and drums and the piano leading. A musician who'd gone on a tour of Europe with Willie Dixon during the early 60s revival and stayed. He'd managed to release more than eighty albums. Slim, despite his girth, was no slouch. He'd recorded with everyone from Buddy Guy to Canned Heat, BB King to Alexis Korner and Matt Murphy to Lowell Fulson. In France he found acceptance and a response to his late-night blues that was missing back home. He married a French woman and died in her country in 1988. His grave is next to that of his Father in Galilee Memorial Gardens Cemetery just off the Isaac Hayes Memorial Highway. Twenty miles from where he began.

On Beale they are still rocking. You can do that 24/7 in this city. But I've got to lie down.

14 • Memphis – Where Sun Shines Everyday

Everyone knows this, I guess, but it's still worth restating. This city of the birth of the blues, Memphis, is also the place where rock and roll began. That's despite the rival claims of Cleveland[46], St Louis[47], New York[48], New Orleans[49] and distant Gilfach Goch[50]. The blues might be everywhere here, from Bobby Blue Bland to Buddy Guy; Memphis Minnie to Furry Lewis; and Doctor Ross to Joe Hill Louis; but so too are rocking boogie, rockabilly, and good old rock and roll.

I'm on a coach operated by Mojo Tours. This is a former jail bus, manufactured by Blue Bird, so the guide says, but it just looks battered to me. Howard is the driver. He's told us that so we can feel easier about tipping when we come to get off. There's a sign above his head showing where the Blue Bird Body Fluid Clean Up Kit is stored. It's right next to the Blue Bird First Aid box and the Blue Bird marker plate of Quality Control. The company are best known for manufacturing the ubiquitous all-yellow American school bus. But that's clearly not the only model they built.

The guide is Terry Tom the Tennessee Cat. He brandishes a steel mandolin. He wears a black and white two-tone shirt. On his head there's a short brimmed hat. Round his neck is a harmonica harness holding a kazoo. His day job, he tells me later, is working as a computer programmer. You can't live off the buses alone. He sings our way around the sites.

On the tour we mostly don't stop nor disembark too often (the tourists, once you've got them off you can't get them back on) but we

145

do pass by a lot of musical history. WC Handy's former house at the end of Beale. The teenage home of Elvis, an apartment in Lauderdale Courts on Winchester, one of about eight addresses the Presleys used before their son made enough to buy Graceland. We rise up the slow incline to skirt by the restored Levitt Shell in Overton Park. Here in July, 1954 the ever so young Elvis made his first public appearance. Getting it all in, but not necessarily in the right order, the Tennessee Cat is doing passable versions of John Sebastian and Gus Cannon jug numbers as we pass.

On the stage in front of the Levitt Shell[51], back at the dawn of what was to become rock, Elvis was an opening act for the then chart high-flyer Slim Whitman. Whitman was the man who brought yodelling to the charts and made pencil moustaches as desirable as cowboy boots. Elvis stole the show. He did *Blue Moon of Kentucky*, his brand new and very first Sun single. The Tennessee Cat does his version, complete with kazoo interlude and, in the bouncing traffic, a pretty good attempt at leg quivering. Elvis had been billed in newspaper adverts for the show, his first concert ever, as 'Ellis Presley'. Organisers thought he was a girl. Presley was nervous and kept on the move throughout his performance. Screaming began and didn't stop. Afterwards, he asked his guitarist Scotty Moore what the noise had all been about. "It was your leg man," Scotty told him. "It was the way you were shakin' your left leg." Legend begins.

We get the Cat's take on *Knock On Wood* as we pass down McLemore and the rebuilt Stax. Along the way are the Hi Studios. Cat points but doesn't do anything from Ann Peebles nor Al Green. For some reason we get *Rocking Robin* instead. Hi were Stax's great rival in the soul stakes, outclassed at the time but possessed of a longevity that Stax never had. Like Stax they began with rockabilly. Their first big hit was *Smokey, Part Two* from The Bill Black Combo. This was released in 1959 after manager Colonel Parker had fired bassist Bill from Elvis's backing band for too much clowning and for never turning up on time on time.

Bill Black had great early success as a solo artist. Between 1959 and 1962 he had eight hits in the US top 40. In 1962 he opened his own recording operation on Chelsea Avenue. These he called the Lyn Lou studios (named after his son and daughter) and were where lost rocker Billy Swann[52] recorded. They are a little too far north of McLemore for the Mojo bus to visit. Bill Black was a doomed man. Illness dogged him. His Combo got the job of opening for The Beatles on their thirteen date first US tour in 1964. Black himself, however, was in too bad health to lead. The band went round the screaming circuit without him. He died of a brain tumour at in 1965. He was 39.

Lincoln Chips Moman's American Sound Studios that once stood on Thomas Street are also unvisited. The building in any case has been flattened and replaced with the inevitable parking lot. This is a tradition of mine, visiting empty piece of air where things once were, but not, sadly, on this occasion. Here Moman, who began his career as a guitarist at Stax, recorded Elvis' 1969 late career flowering. *In The Ghetto, Suspicious Minds, Don't Cry Daddy, Kentucky Rain* and a raft of others were all cut when Moman took control from those members of Presley's ragged retinue who normally called the shots. With his house band, The Memphis Boys, Moman put 120 songs into the Billboard charts between 1967 and 1971. Wilson Pickett, BJ Thomas, Dusty Springfield, Neil Diamond, Joe Tex and others were all Moman stars. But historically that star has clearly faded. They don't get mentioned.

At Sun we stop. This is the place, after all, where rock and roll grew and bore fruit. That it's so small and so suburban amazes me. Sun could have been in a back street in Cardiff Docks for all the style we have on display here. The shop front looks like a hairdressers from half way up Rumney Hill. Domino's Pizzas and Premiere Kitchen Fitters are opposite. If it wasn't for the giant sun gold Gibson fixed on the wall above the door and the red Thunderbird, all chrome and 50s style, sitting outside then we could be in smalltown anytown anywhere. Junction of Union and Marshall Avenues. Then I spot it. Marshall Avenue had been renamed Sam Phillips Avenue in his honour. There are black and white photos of Roy Orbison, Elvis and Jerry Lee peering through the windows on the first floor.

Neon signs declare this to be the Memphis Recording Service, the business started by former Sound of Muscle Shoals WLAY radio dj Sam Phillips. Phillips recorded singers without contracts, people who walked in off the street, those attracted by his policy of having an ever open door. He drew in BB King, Junior Parker, Bobby Blue Bland, James Cotton, Rufus Thomas, Howlin' Wolf and others and sold the best of their recordings for single release to labels such as Chess and Modern. It was Sam Phillips who discovered sax player Jackie Brenston. Brenston and His Delta Cats recorded what for many was the very first rock and roll record, *Rocket 88*. The band were actually Ike Turner's Kings of Rhythm but as Brenston sang lead he got his name on the label. In 1951 Chess released it and it went to number one in the r&b charts.

In 1952 Phillips launched his own label. Sun. Because it rose every day and the world started again. It's the line current Sun label owners peddle and I guess it's good enough. His school friend Jay Parker designed the now world-famous logo. It's been seen on t-shirts in Aberdare, in Edinburgh, in London, New York, Moscow, Mumbai, Malawi and in Afghanistan. It's been reproduced on beer mats in use in bars built into suburban homes by men with seventies handle bar moustaches. It's been revived as a highly marketable item by the nostalgia industry in the new millennium. Sun, shining on clothing, bags, mouse mats, fridge magnets, badges, cigarette lighters, wall hangings, neon art, trousers, cases and on the labels of re-released records by the million. The permanently rising Sun in all its yellow rock and roll splendour. The world forever starting again.

Sun's early singles were mainly rhythm and blues. Black jump, harmonica boogie, barrelhouse blues, piano and sax, all with what was to become Phillips' distinctive Sun sound echo. Johnny London, Handy Jackson, Joe Hill Louis, Willie Nix, Walter Horton. Outside of Memphis none of these ten-inch shellac records went anywhere much. Listening to them today they sound like what they were – black bluesmen laying down not that distinguished late night bar room shuffles that The Rolling Stones and their 60s ilk would never find the time to imitate. But Phillips had an ear and an open mind. He hit it big with his recording of Rufus Thomas singing *Bear Cat*, a novelty rocking answer to Big Mama Thornton's *Hound Dog* (which used the same melody and for a time ran Phillips into copyright infringement difficulties – and would return later in the repertoire of his greatest discovery). He recorded hillbilly old-timer Harmonica Frank and Little Junior's Blue Flames doing *Mystery Train*, although with nothing like the rolling excitement that Elvis would later give it.

Presley walked into his studio in 1953 wanting to use Sun's make-your-own-record service to record a song for his mother. The singer of *My Happiness* caught Phillips' ear but it took him a full twelve months to do anything further.

Presley's first commercial recordings at Phillips' Sun studios in July, 1954 are shrouded in historical glitz and glory. This was the moment, many claim, that rock and roll was really born. The rest had merely been a trial run for the slap bass, slightly echoing[53], upbeat menace that Presley ended up laying down that day. Had he really walked into the studio a year before to please his mother or was it to get his voice heard by the label's boss? And was he back because Phillips wanted to record a white boy singing black songs or simply because he needed a new balladeer?

The two songs Presley recorded with Scotty Moore on guitar and Bill Black on bass are legend. Arthur Big Boy Crudup's black *That's Alright Mama* and Bill Monroe's bluegrass *Blue Moon of Kentucky*. Both songs were taken way out of their original comfort zones and made into something completely new. *Blue Moon of Kentucky* was a song as old as the Appalachian hills except it wasn't. It had been written by bluegrass pioneer Monroe as a 3/4 waltz and recorded by him in 1946. Presley changed the tempo and added a few histrionics. Fellow Sun label rockabilly singer Charlie Feathers, who Phillips never really regarded, claimed that it was he who'd given Elvis the arrangement but I doubt that. Feathers' own later recording of the number follows Elvis's style to a tee.

Crudup's *That's Alright Mama* also came from 1946. He was a minor delta bluesman, sometime field hand, and a bootlegger (moonshine, not albums) who would have vanished into the Mississippi mud if it hadn't been for Presley. As it was his sixties blues boom revived career went pretty much nowhere despite many attempts including a visit to the UK and a recording session with Bonnie Raitt. His playing sounds authentic but his blues somehow lacked the spark that would have put him up there with Elmore James or Sleepy John. Even *That's Alright* wasn't entirely his. The lyric lifts a chorus from a Blind Lemon Jefferson record made in 1926. Crudup had to wait until the 60s before his songwriter royalties were paid. If it hadn't been for those he would made more from his hooch running than he ever had as a singer. He died in 1974. I put the Crudup original into the player and check it, just to be sure. Was it really as exciting as Elvis must have thought it was? I listen. Proto rock. Yep, it still thrills.

The single Phillips released, Sun 209, as often as not got flipped by local djs. Both songs rose up the local Memphis charts, such as those were. Phillips lacked the financial muscle to make much more out of it than that. But with Presley he'd heard what the future sounded like and was determined to go there. The blues seams he'd been working were supplemented with a fresh and exciting stream of upbeat hillbilly country – rockabilly. The mixture, rock and roll, took over the world.

It's hard to underestimate the importance of Phillips and Sun. For a short period from the mid-fifties onwards Sun released a run of artists who were to become rock and roll's heartland core. Roy Orbison and The Roses, Jerry Lee Lewis & His Pumping Piano, Carl Perkins The Rocking Guitar Man, Johnny Cash and The Tennessee Two, Warren Smith, Billy Riley and His Little Green Men, Sonny Burgess, Charlie Feathers. And more Elvis. Twenty odd songs, five singles, a rush of mid-fifties rock and roll gold including some of the best music Presley ever recorded.

At the end of 1956 Phillips, short of capital, unable to reach the larger markets with his local distribution sold Presley's contract to RCA for $40,000. Elvis had become too big to handle. RCA got the rights to his entire Sun back catalogue.

The Sun studios today are an historical relic. A stop on the tourist trail, fronted by a store selling Sun merch, all you could ever want with that sunburst label reproduced on it. Inside I run into a crush of visitors, middle-aged and beyond mostly, old enough to have experienced this music when it was brand new. The studio itself is tiny, as studios often are. The ceiling is misshapen and covered with acoustic boards. There's a full drum kit and a long line of guitars on stands. Above the microphones are giant photos of the stars. There's atmosphere and the pungent memory of what was once laid down here.

The hand-out tells me that but I just can't feel it. It's a little like visiting Stonehenge with a surging mix of Danes, Americans, Germans, Spanish, and white boys up from Southend bubbling around you. Any power the stones have or had is dissipated by the security fence and the pointless chatter. I touch the end of an uncased Gibson. Might have been the one Scotty used for his pre-Steve Cropper angular solos? Who knows.

Presley was the world's first teenager. Or at least the person the world's first teenagers chose as their model. Who else, in Britain back them, could have filled the job? Jimmy Young, Jack Payne, The BBC Show Band, Mantovani? Elvis's Sun years never reached us until they were over. His first UK record took until May of 1956 to appear. It was the RCA-recorded *Heartbreak Hotel* released on a blue-labelled HMV 10" which turned at 78 rpm. A frighteningly amazing record with a hook that caught you, shook you, and wouldn't let you go. Menace was not the word. Its power has not dimmed through the decades. His British promoters knew they were onto a winner. During the next months they released a further five singles, none of them in the right order, but all of them hits.

The British fifties were mostly an extension of war time. Rationing had only ended in 1954. The streets were badly lit, most things were broken, the towns were still full of the wreckage caused by bombs. The trains, when they ran at all, rarely did so on time. There was no colour. Everything was dark. There was no gap between childhood and the responsibility of being an adult. You left school at fifteen. You worked pretty much like they did in the Mississippi fields, from dawn to dusk, from can see to can't. The pubs closed at 10.30 pm.

For me Elvis in this landscape was like a visitation by the spiders of Mars. Valhalla, Thule, Shambhala, rock and roll Avalon. That he was resented by our elders and our betters who all warned us against him and his shaking legs made him, his music, and what that stood for all the more desirable. It's hard to credit all that, now, in the new millennium sun filled Sun Studio Memphis streets.

Elvis was so important at Sun because there he sounded so authentic. You could hear the connection between what he did and the hillbilly bluegrass blues and boogie music that surrounded him. The guitars were electric, just, distortion played no part, you could hear the chords and the notes. The bass was upright. It slapped. Drums were a hardly ever employed. The songs could be followed back into the past from whence most of them had come.

We admire all that now. But back when Presley first appeared the only thing that was important was that the blood thundered and insurgence was in the air. Things went well, more than well, for Elvis right up until he went into the US army in 1958. By the time he came out in 1960 rock and roll and his part in that H-bomb explosion was pretty much done. 1960-62, a time of pap and soft-edges, until The Beatles arrived in 1962. Purists will say that the Sun years were never equalled by the more commercial material he created at RCA but that's being pedantic in the extreme. His early RCA recordings include classics such as *All Shook Up, Don't, Jailhouse Rock, Hard Headed Woman, One Night* and that world-buster *Heartbreak Hotel*.

Elvis made his millions quickly. And he spent them almost as fast. He first bought a house on Audubon Drive, a good six miles out from the Sun Studios but still in suburban Memphis. His rising fame attracted the fans and living at the residence became increasingly untenable. In 1957 he asked his parents to find him an out of town 'farmhouse' and they selected the former home of the Toof family who'd named it after their daughter, Grace. Back then Graceland was eight miles distant from downtown Memphis, out in fields where you could exercise horses and there were groves of pecan trees. The mansion was in colonial revival style, tall white Corinthian columns supporting a Southern States entrance portico, elaborate front door, two stories, evenly spaced windows.

Graceland sits on Highway 51. Bob Dylan, ever the completest, did a song for this one as well as the much more famous Highway 61. The song is on his first album, a retread of Curtis Jones' original *Highway 51 Blues*. The actual road is long, running from New Orleans to the Canadian border. The Graceland portion was known as Bellevue Boulevard until the city decide to rename it Elvis Presley Boulevard in the singer's honour.

The legends of Graceland are fuelled by music itself. "I'm going to Graceland" sang Paul Simon, backed by The Everlys, in 1986. Marc

Cohn, en route, saw the ghost of Elvis up on Union Avenue. Merle Haggard went there on his way to the promised land. No More Kings found themselves there alone. Richard Thompson went "From Galway to Graceland to be with the king". The place, now that Elvis has gone, has a life of its own.

If I'm doing it then I might as well do it well. We book into Heartbreak Hotel which, if it wasn't for the neon sign over the door, could be a warehouse in all its white featureless slab concrete facade. It's on one side of the football field sized parking lot opposite Graceland itself. Our room has photos of Elvis on the dresser and on the walls. There are three Elvis channels running on the cable TV – photos plus music, videos of the great man singing and movies – his entire recorded career rolling in a non-stop thirty year loop. Here's *Love Me Tender* and then, thirty-one pale, plastic and badly-acted dramas later, round it comes again.

Out of the window the car park speakers are playing a selection of the King's greatest hits. Uh huh huh. His voice follows you wherever you go. In the lobby there's a pink, fur covered phone and an old b&w cabineted TV showing, yes, more Elvis: *Stay Away Joe*, never one of his best. Elvis rounding up cattle in a Cadillac. Not a decent song anywhere.

At the rear is a heart-shaped swimming pool with no one in it. A man with tattoos like scribble up his arms smokes and stares. Dusk. Elvis dusk. Tourists drinking. *Suspicion* leaking through the walls.

In motel style breakfast is offered in a dark communal dining hall. Plastic plates and plastic food, long-life bagels, small sticky additive-ridden cakes, bowls of grits, packets of fruitless muesli, long-life milk, reconstituted orange juice with added sugar, flat white expanded polystyrene bread, toast machine in the corner, array of jelly (jam) in individual portions, hard as iron butter substitute, coffee like luke warm brown water.

Graceland is an enterprise that churns money. It's the major Memphis tourist attraction and, after the White House, number two of all visited houses in the USA. That it's down here alongside a roaringly busy industrial highway with boondocks cafes, diners and car repair operations strung along the road around it is something the

Graceland entrepreneurs never mention. You arrive by transport, it's impossible to walk, and the game is to relieve you of your not insignificant entrance money, get you through in the shortest time possible and then deposit you in the large Elvis merchandise mall where, overcome by what you've so far experienced, you will naturally spend even more.

Graceland itself is small. Maybe not by Cardiff town house standards but by expectation. After *Dallas* and the shots on TV of the Elvis mansion as a ranch-house that could have graced the Ewing's Southfork I expected more grandeur. What we have is a much extended playhouse that might have fitted the Presley 1960s film-star aspirations but doesn't quite hack it as a music world heritage site in 2015.

The surrounding outer walls have been graffitied into submission. There's not a space for a further mark among the myriad expressions of Elvis love and Elvis loss. Love Elvis Tender. Amelia Loves Elvis. Elvis forever. The dates go back no further than the start of 2015, evidence of unadvertised encouragement and curatorial care. Beyond the music note-embellished guitar player gates attendants in uniform check your ticket, dole you ill-fitting and barely working headphones (so the throughput can be swifter), divide you into large groups and roll you off. You shuffle, in your shorts and your t-shirt, cameras stowed, gawping in awe. The Graceland experience is all on the ground floor. Upstairs is closed 'out of respect'. The tackiness of the garish royal reds, pavilion blues, and Elvis-chosen fur and leopard skin embellishments begins immediately.

That the singer had no real taste should have been obvious from the word go. Gargantuan white furniture, sunburst clocks, carpet you can vanish into. The jungle room, where Elvis recorded *From Elvis Presley Boulevard, Memphis, Tennessee* in 1976, was the singer's den, his man room, the place horsed in with his gang of talentless hangers-on. The official line is that it has an Hawaiian 'wild look'. Shag carpet, carved wood furniture, faux fur, bright green ceiling and rock and roll yellow walls fit the latter-day Presley mind-set perfectly. Indulgent, poorly functional, obsessed.

Beyond is the Racquetball Trophy room. This houses Elvis's gold discs, his platinum albums and his jump suits. Here they are, the eagles and the Aztecs, the white and the rhinestoned. They stand there in cases, the shape of the ever-ballooning Elvis but with Elvis gone. Clothes for the invisible man.

I would love to have found the mansion filled with a great Presley record collection including the works of the delta bluesmen, the soul singers that found fame in Memphis, the jazz music that preceded them, the rocking rockabilly that Elvis was central to, the folk music and hillbilly old time tunes that were his bedrock. But in the event there was hardly anything. A few racks of singles and a low stack of 12 inch albums with *Mario Lanza Sings Opera* on top. It looked for all the world like the album dump at Oxfam.

Jerry Lee Lewis came to Graceland in the small hours of November, 1976. He drove his Lincoln Continental right up to the gates and got the guard on duty there to wake the King. "Tell Elvis I wanna visit with him. Who the hell does he think he is? Tell him the Killer's here to see him". He brandished a gun. Elvis was woken but refused to leave his bed. According to Linda Gail, Jerry's younger sister, the Killer had been partying and drinking and "was a little bit out of it". The cops were called and the world's greatest rock and roll pianist was taken away. In the police photos taken that night the Killer looks young and pale but menacing. He has a cut across the bridge of his nose. This was incurred, it seems, after he tried to jettison an empty champagne bottle through the still closed Lincoln Continental window. Jerry Lee clearly resented the success of Elvis[54]. They'd both started out at the same time. The Killer had stuck to his roots, Elvis had moved on.

Elvis at his peak weighed 165 pounds. When he died in 1977 he'd hit 260. That's eighteen and a half stone. Fast and bulbous for a six foot male. How did you get like this Elvis? By being weak willed, thinking it didn't apply to you, not bothering, eating whatever you wanted, mostly cheeseburgers and peanut butter, and then in inappropriate, self-indulgent, gargantuan quantities. And because of your circumstances not burning any of it off. Now that karate had been put back in the box there was no running. No lifting weights. No getting on your bike on cycling up the hill. Heroes don't do that. Instead there was dope. Loads of that. And thinking you could own the world and it wouldn't matter and it didn't, of course. Not for a fat, white-suited time. But then, in the end, it did.

Out the back at Graceland is the swimming pool and the graveyard. Vernon, Minnie Mae and Elvis Aaron. The family reunited. Wreaths on display still being sent from fans the world over. The Elvis Club of Finland. The Presley Fans from South Korea. The Official Elvis Presley Fan Club of Great Britain. In the hot sun tour members take photos of themselves with the bronze grave markers behind them. Me too.

The guide tells us that Elvis read a lot, read all the time in fact, never went anywhere without his books and even had a special case made for them on the plane. Little sign I can see. The atmosphere is non-intellectual, unstudied, guns, go-karts, goofing off, 1950s rather than 1960s, everything to excess.

Over the road the Elvis memorial exploitation machine is in full swing. You can tour the Presley collection of automobiles, eat Presley burgers, buy Presley clothes, admire Presley's self-designed TCB ("taking care of business") logo shining there like a remedial version of Pan-Am's on the tail fins of the Presley planes. Part with your cash to the accompaniment of the King's greatest hits. Buy your own Presley jump suit, made to measure, finest leather. Presley snow domes, toy pink Presley Cadillacs. Get his albums, they are all here, just in case you missed any. There's a single copy of *Elvis at Sun*, sunburst logo and the king in pink jacket thrashing his guitar. If you only buy one then get that. It's a recording that has a special place in my collection.

15 • Clarksdale

Leaving Graceland the road to Clarksdale is shining like a national guitar, just as Paul Simon sang. Tennessee is over, Mississippi has begun. The road, naturally, is something about as famous as it can be. Route 66? Nothing so old fashioned. This is Highway 61. I'm at the wheel of the big Nissan automatic Avis have rented me, black and bulging, filled now with Elvis paraphernalia and leaflets about places I should visit picked up from the lobby of the Heartbreak Hotel. Clarksdale, home of the blues, and then Tupelo, the Presley birthplace up, out of the delta, beyond.

Highway 61 is straight as a die. No bleachers but full of sun[55]. No sign yet of the next world war. Clarksdale in another hour, easily done. Then I see it, a sign to the left showing the old highway. So there's more than one. The 61 I'm on is the straightened, designated fast track south. The old road, snaking through the places that hover near the river, was the one the bluesmen used. They came up out of the delta making their way to new sophisticated lives in the north, leaving the sun.

Walls, Tunica, and Lake Cormorant are townships built right up against the levees. The wide river is beyond, its great bulk shifting the land as it chooses. There's a half moon of Arkansas stranded on the river's east bank now, all mud and grass, watched over by Tunica's Gold Strike Casino. That's what passes for relaxation in this part of Mississippi, slots, roulette, blackjack, money spinning fruit moving before your eyes. You can't drive alongside this mighty river. Best you can do is track down side roads then walk. From the top of levees, mud banks twice the size of the sea walls at Wentloog on the Cardiff coast, you can watch the river traffic. The tows pushing their barges. River buses. Pleasure boats. There are the sounds of trains in the distance. Further on there's a strip of Mississippi on the western Arkansas bank. This was abandoned last time the river flicked its arms. Compensation, perhaps, for the lost moon of Arkansas on the Mississippi side that I've just passed. State ownership here is decided not by commission but by the will of God. The Delta. It's a Christian land.

The Delta, such a famous place, turns out to be not a delta at all. Not in the conventional sense. There's no sea next to it, no outpouring of water from fresh to salt, and no fanning of the land as it grows oceanward, towards the south. Rather, the Delta is the diamond of territory between the Mississippi and Yazoo rivers. It's a plain, almost flat as a salt lake. Its alluvial soil is rich from centuries of flooding. Some say this is the most fertile land in the world. Driving across it you can see for miles. There are great cotton plantations with irrigation systems arcing across them like suspension bridges. No one bends their backs to harvest the bolls of cotton any more. Machines do it all. This land was once centre of the slave belt, full of black workers and their cotton sacks, mile after mile of bowed black backs and white gun carrying men in charge. You don't see anyone now. Just cars on the highway and the white lines of planes as they cross the enormous sky.

Tunica is currently gearing itself up to become the gaming capital of the Southern States. Casinos and resort hotels dot the landscape. As a money-turning obsession this far outclasses the Mississippi Blues Trail that begins in a restored train depot next to the old highway at the edge of town. But I'm not here for the slots. The travel councillors behind the bright new railway desk offer me stacks of southern accented information on just how to get to Clarksdale using the blues routes. The whole of the Delta has been done up with hundreds of markers. These are durable metal plaques set up on poles. They celebrate everything from the site of the Hi-Hat Club in Hattiesburg to the birthplace of James Cotton.

The Hi-Hat was a mainstream stop on the blues chitlin' circuit of blacks-only venues around which any blues player with an eye on making a dollar would revolve. Cotton was a harmonica player born on the Bonnie Blue Plantation just outside Tunica. He had done twelve years as harp player for Muddy Waters' band which was a significant enough achievement in itself. He'd also recorded for Sam Phillips in Memphis, played with Howlin' Wolf, and then forming his own band in 1965 signed with Bob Dylan's manager Albert Grossman who made a shed-load sending him round the European rock circuit during the sixties blues boom. Chris Barber, however, had got there first.

In 1961 Cotton had travelled to Britain at Barber's invitation. In addition to surprising white jazz audiences with his black harp playing he recorded two eps[56] in London using a local pick-up band. This included Barber on bass, Keith Scott on piano, and Alexis Korner, on guitar. I'd found *Chris Barber Presents Jimmy Cotton Vol 2*, abandoned by a destitute South Wales jazz fan, in a local church jumble sale. So this was what the blues sounded like. Cotton making squeaks that, on the evidence of these recordings, owed nothing to the work of his supposed mentor, Sonny Boy Williamson. However, he did cover a couple of numbers with which British blues bands were later to make their mark. *Good Morning Little Schoolgirl* (The Yardbirds, Ten Years After, Rod Stewart), and *Going Down Slow* (Manfred Mann). Unaccountably he had also recorded a blues version of *Polly Put The Kettle On*. How could anyone do that and remain an icon of cool? James Cotton, Mr Superharp. Born in the heat at the top end of the Delta in 1935, still active, just about.

The blues was the music of the white sixties. This was the quintessence of rebellion, of counter culture, of teenage angst, and long-haired guitar heroes. It was something the rest of the world saw as the wailings of a disreputable underclass. People in dinner suits abhorred it. It was not played on *Family Favourites*. You didn't hear it at the grand dances held at city hall.

Yet now, around a hundred years after they were first heard, Mississippi, blues birthplace, was offering full-on official government support to the music's furtherance. The Mississippi blues had been discovered as the state's great tourist salvation. This was the poorest place in the Union. It was full of dirt and unemployment. Now it was stacked about with tourists checking out all those blues stars they'd listened to in their unruly youth. Me included.

We shift west to pass the marker for Muddy Waters' Stovall plantation shack (site of – all that remains is a photograph taken in the 1990s,
the original is now in the Clarksdale Blues Museum). It was at the
Stovall shack in 1941, just as Britain was facing its darkest World War
II hour, that Muddy was first recorded. This was by Alan Lomax, out
collecting material in the field for the Library of Congress. The
pioneering work of John and Alan Lomax should not be underestimated. Without them a great deal of the blues from the rural South
would never have seen the light of day. On what's become known as
the Plantation Recordings acoustic Muddy sounds as down home and
authentic as Blind Willie Johnson. The blues world of distorted guitar
chords and high energy shouted vocals was yet to arrive.

Clarksdale grew to prominence as "the golden buckle on the
cotton belt", a small outpost of the Memphis cotton traders, a place
where former slaves would gather, through which the Louisville, New
Orleans and Texas Railway ran. Today, in Mississippi somnambulant
heat, it appears about as full of life as the drowned Welsh village of
Capel Celyn. We park on John Lee Hooker Lane right over from
Yazoo and Delta and find two blues records stores next door to each
other. We are about the only people on the sidewalk. A white farmer
drives past slowly in a bashed about pick-up, winds down his window,
smiles, and shouts out "Good to see ya, hope you like our town."

Son House cut a number with *Clarksdale* in the title, so did Charlie
Musslewhite and Mississippi Fred McDowell, as did John Dudley. Elvis
Costello came here to record and pick up the magic. Page and Plant
had a whole album named after the place (*Walking Into Clarksdale*).
Inside Gary W. Miller's[57] Bluesource shop the unshaven owner,
cigarette in hand, doesn't stop talking. It's a lonesome business, selling
the blues. I buy Peetie Wheatstraw's *Complete Recordings* (mainly
because this was a nickname of mine, rather than because I am a
particular Wheatstraw fan) and another John Estes set, *Broke and
Hungry*. All blues singers were once like this, broke, hungry. They've
been singing about it ever since. What I'm actually looking for is a
recording of Muddy and the organ-driven Earl Hooker Orchestra
doing *Little Brown Bird, You Shook Me* and, amazingly, *Muddy Waters
Twist*. These tracks were originally released on an ep in the 60s and

now appear lost. The owner can't help[58].

On the way to our booked over the internet accommodation on Commissary Circle, just south of town, we pass the blues' world's most famous crossroads. This is the spot where Highway 61 and Highway 49 meet. It's the place, as blues legend has it, where Robert Johnson sold his soul to the devil in exchange for the ability to create the best recordings the blues world has ever known[59]. Much has been mythologised about Johnson. His music is certainly an acquired taste – raw, primitive bottle slide under a harsh but highly inventive voice that was echoed by the notes he pulled out of his guitar. Johnson was born in Hazlehurst, Mississippi, well south of Clarksdale, in 1911. He died in the same state twenty-seven years later. He was knifed for messing with someone else's woman, he was poisoned, he died of syphilis. Take your pick. Where his body is buried is also subject to conflicting assertion. At least four sites in Mississippi have made claims. There are memorials at three, all asserting that the bones of the blues singer lie below. Johnson sang on street corners and performed for small change at juke joints. He recorded twenty-nine songs and had virtually no success while he was alive.

In 1961, at the start of the British blues boom, RCA issued a selection of Johnson songs on an album they prophetically titled *King of the Delta Blues Singers*. This was a fine use of promoter's hyperbole. Who, at that time, had even heard of him? Amazingly the album did go on to become the world's most important blues record. It influenced a whole host of white blues imitators and spawned a raft of electric guitar-driven hits based on Johnson material. Probably the most well-known of the dead singer's acolytes is Eric Clapton with his Cream recording of *Crossroads*. Everybody back then (1968) danced themselves flat to Clapton's soaring (and, it has to be said, never ending) interpretation. Others include just about every white British blues guitarist of the period – Robert Spence, Keith Richards, Alexis Korner, Peter Green. Both Green and Clapton recorded entire albums devoted to Robert Johnson material, as has American guitarist John Hammond. Bob Dylan claimed (in his autobiography *Chronicles Volume One*, 2004) that if he'd never heard Johnson he never would have felt the freedom to record material as he did.

At the crossroads there's a set of three interlocking guitars set atop a pole and a marker showing that this is where the 49 hits the 61. Beyond that pretty much nothing. This is suburban Clarksdale where little happens bar passing cars. We go into Abe's Bar-B-Q for pulled pork, coleslaw and beans. Founded by Abraham Davies in 1924 reads a sign. "We cater! Platters served. Sandwiches. Short Orders. Hot Tamales." The place is full of sticky Formica. Abe's not hot with the cloth.

Down the road apiece is Krosstown Liquor and since this is America where getting your hands on a drink can at times be difficult for those not in the know we enter. There's a sign reading YOU WONT BE SERVED WHEN YOU ARE ON YOUR PHONE but this doesn't stop the owner who is on his the entire time we are there. The store is split into two by a thick plastic screen. A much larger half, about 90% of the total area available, houses cash register, the stock and the owner. A second, wooden-floored slice about the size of a toilet is for the use of buyers. Business is done through a slot. There's a stream of customers while we are there. They all buy Jack Daniels. Each one is black. Not to stand out we buy JD too. The owner takes our dollars, still phone talking, and slips us the bottle shrouded in an alcoholic's brown paper bag.

Our accommodation, directly beyond the shunting yards, is the Shack Up Inn. A set of huts and other recycled material structures neatly surround an open green space. Dotted here and there in a studied replication of randomness are the ruins of 20s pick-up trucks and ancient rusted cotton farm machinery. There is a corrugated tin warehouse along one side. Shack Up, whose sales slogan is 'the Ritz we ain't', offer overnight stays at this, the Hopson Plantation, in refurbished sharecroppers shacks and rooms created inside a cotton gin. The emphasis is on the unpainted and the authentic, the hand-built and the falling apart.

Naturally we've rented the Crossroads Shack. Inside this has an out of tune piano with the front missing. Ten-inch shellacs of blues numbers are nailed to the walls. There's a functioning shower made from a perforated tin can connected to a hosepipe. There are slots in the wooden floor which allow the used shower water to fall directly outside. In addition I find a wind-up gramophone and muffled pre-war blues playing through a half-wrecked radio. Son House, I think. A notice at reception, a glitzy souvenir-selling desk housed in a tottering wooden structure at the corner of the site, informs us that a whole long list of famous blues players have performed at the Shack Inn. Tom Waits, Pinetop Perkins, John Mayall, Robert Plant, Charlie Musslewhite. "Anything on tonight?" No.

Back in town the blues appear to be pretty much all there are. We pass the Riverside Hotel, hang out of just about every blues singer passing this way and the place where Bessie Smith was taken to die after her fatal car crash in 1937. The building looks like a sprawling version of the kind of bungalow you see in Rhiwbina, slate roof, boxed eaves, low box hedge and garden chairs out front. According to author Elijah Wald both John Lee Hooker and Robert Nighthawk lived here for extended periods and Ike Turner used to rehearse his band in the basement. The place still rents rooms.

In a former freight depot on the Yazoo and Mississippi Valley Railroad stands the vaguely shambolic Delta Blues Museum. The displays have the community air of the Pontypridd Museum but with added flamboyance. They've got Muddy's hut, the one I went to see out on the edge of the Stovall Plantation. Here it is, rough-hewn wood, dry and mightily rustic. Museum saviour and financial angel Billy Gibbons from the band ZZ Top has had a plank taken out and made into a guitar. They've also got instruments from a number of other blues greats including Charlie Musslewhite, Big Joe Williams and BB King. Some of the displays are stuck up with sellotape. Others have information labels done on typewriters and altered in biro. It feels so much nearer the music it celebrates. There's a stage to the side, used to mount shows and festival concerts. The gift shop offers Crossroads hoodies, Hoochie Coochie man t-shirts and a whole section devoted to Muddy merch. Do they have Muddy backed by Earl Hooker? Not here.

The most famous man in Clarksdale today is Morgan Freeman, star of numerous Hollywood films and the voice you usually hear narrating TV programmes on the blues. He co-owns Clarksdale's best blues club, Ground Zero: catfish, pork barbeque, live blues and beer. Open Wednesday through Saturday. It's Tuesday. We try Freeman's fine-dining restaurant, Madidi's on East Second Street, where there are carpets and upholstered bar stools. The menu is upmarket and the bar serves Raspberry Kiss Cocktails and overpriced beer. The chef, slightly oiled but able to talk and still dressed as a chef, has deserted the kitchen to mingle with prospective diners. He's holding court on the subject of smoking. He loves it, hell he does.

Next door, where we escape, is Hambone, a sort of folk art, primitives gallery, music store (blues a speciality, what else?) and performance space. At the Cat Head Delta Blues & Folk Art Store earlier owner Roger Stolle, the town's main source of what's on information, had assured me that the Hambone would be the only place to hear live blues in Clarksdale on a Tuesday. "You've picked a bad day. Everyone's either resting or off at the Howlin' Wolf Blues Festival at West Point". West Point was where the Wolf was born. It's a hundred and fifty miles from here. "But the Hambone will have something. Give it a go."

We do. We get Davis Coen, an electric guitar blues singer who sounds so much better on his online mp3s. He's backed by Hambone owner Dixie Street on drums. They chunder through rather soulless versions of the blues standards. Dixie has spent the first part of the evening behind her makeshift bar selling cans of Coke and Bud for a dollar a go. They've spent $30 on a beer licence. "Well worth it," Dixie says. The chef turns up from next door, his kitchen deserted, still dressed as a chef and now somewhat more pissed than he was before. He sways and stumbles, banging into folk objects d'art, chairs and walls. So, too, does Gary Miller from Bluesource, still unshaven, still smoking. "Bet you guys are glad you've found this place," he shouts, banging into a line of empty chairs. He take a long pull on a hip flask. Clarksdale is a village on a Tuesday. I keep my eye out for Morgan Freeman.

After the break Davis Coen returns to shuffle through *Good Morning Little Schoolgirl*. The Chef has passed out. Gary Miller has slipped away as, apparently, have the rest of the small audience. There's just us, and Dixie. Davis does *Trouble In Mind*. I get the feeling I don't want to listen to more. We suck in breath, stand, and go, waving to lonely Dixie, nodding to Davis, leaving the Hambone to play the blues to its folky self. We head back to our Mississippi sharecropper's place, south of the tracks.

16 • Tupelo

Tupelo. Named after its black gum trees. Fought over in the civil war. And before that, a time before, fought over by the French, trying to enlarge their new world empire. Among the local street names – Coolidge, Lincoln, Hoover, Robert E Lee – not a trace of the French remains.

Getting to this glade of gum means driving east and up over the Tallahatchie River. "Tupelo, little country town in Mississippi, it rained and it rained and people got worried and they began to cry. Did you read about the flood? Wasn't that a mighty time?" That's John Lee Hooker singing about the Tupelo floods. Mississippi is a land of floods. It's a place where the rivers won't stay in their channels and the levees, the great mud bunds that hold the Mississippi, when the waters rise they break.

1927 was the worst. The levees were overwhelmed right along the river's length. The ensuing flood was a natural disaster of unprecedented scale. Memories of this time turn up again and again in the blues. "People lost everything they had, their crops and their livestock that means their horses, their mules, cows, goats, and everything they had on their farm". That's Big Bill Broonzy in *Joe Turner Blues*. In *Broken Levee Blues* Lonnie Johnson has "The water round my windows and backin' all up in my door". Charley Patton sees *High Water Everywhere*. Joe McCoy and Memphis Minnie tells us what happened *When the Levee Breaks*, reprised and revitalised half a century later and a world distant by the high electric power of Led Zeppelin in 1971.

There'd been months of heavy rain, end of 1926 and into 1927, without break. The river rose and rose. It topped its banks. First at

Carroll, Iowa. After that at Peoria, Illinois. Bridges and railroads were weakened and washed away. Down in the Mississippi valley the levee was breached at Mounds Landing just south of the Mississippi's junction with the Arkansas River. The levees then began to fail along the river's entire length. The floods were on a biblical scale. The Mississippi was suddenly eighty miles wide and towns were swamped with a hundred feet of water. The lower delta returned to the sea. It was a human, political and agricultural super-disaster. It changed the lives of everyone who lived and worked in the twenty-seven thousand square miles affected.

And it wasn't only the water that caused distress. Being the segregated Souththose in power chose to favour whites over blacks when it came to rescue campaigns. Thousands of black plantation workers were forced to work restoring the river's banks and cleaning out flooded municipalities. They were made to labour for poor or no wages. The distress of their own families and their waterlogged shacks could wait. When all was done financial losses, adjusted for inflation, were greater than $150 billion. You could have let off an atom bomb in Mississippi and damaged less.

Resentment was considerable, to say the least. It led to mass black migration north and a steady shift of black support from the Republican party to the Democrats. This realignment would reach its apogee with the assassination of Martin Luther King in Memphis in 1968 and the subsequent overturning of the Jim Crow segregation laws. Hard to think that this place was once a mirror of pre–Mandela South Africa. This blues land I'm travelling across has a terrible past.

On the 1927 Mississippi flood map when I call it up the reds and oranges indicating the depth and spread of the water do not extend quite as far as Tupelo. The land is higher there, one hundred and twenty miles east of the flood waters' epicentre. Maybe Hooker got it wrong. Memory is an imperfect vehicle. The blues have never been the most accurate repositories of history.

I've got none of this in my head, however, as we drive. Tupelo is half way out of Mississippi, on the road back to the Appalachians. It is known for making textiles and for having its Main Street Bank held up by Machine Gun Kelly in 1932, his last known robbery. A couple of minor Sun label rockabilly singers were born here. Ray Harris and Jumpin' Gene Simmons. Between them they're famous for *Juicy Fruit, Peroxide Blonde in a Hopped Up Model Ford* and *Come On, Little Mama*, each of which sounds exactly like something else. When you get right down there innovation was never a value at rockabilly's core.

Tupelo was, of course, where Elvis was born. 1935. His twin, Jessie Garon, died at birth. Presley, back then, had yet to add that second letter a to his middle name. He still was Elvis *Aron* Presley. *Aaron* came later on.

Times were hard. The family lived in Tupelo for twelve years before moving to Memphis. Vernon, Elvis' ne'er-do-well father, was sent to prison at Parchman Farm for cheque fraud. His mother couldn't keep up the payments on their shack out there on the unpaved streets of East Tupelo. They moved. They did this nine or ten times during Elvis' first decade[60]. Their peregrinations included a brief stay near Biloxi on the Gulf Coast, but mostly it was East Tupelo, all before a job in Memphis roped Vernon in. Shacks, rooms, wooden falling down places where the rent was low. Then Vernon would fail to pay the rent and they'd move again.

Before the war, Tupelo proper had yet to develop the creek-crossed, corn and cotton fields between it and what was to become its eastern suburb. That didn't happen until 1946. In the 30s East Tupelo was a separate town. It was a place with the reputation of being the roughest in North Mississippi. It had its own red light district. Among the population were bootleggers, poor white factory workers and unemployed blacks. The Presley birthplace was a wooden structure on an unpaved thoroughfare running up off Old Saltillo Road[61]. A shotgun shack. The family lived there from Elvis's birth at the start of 1935 until his father's imprisonment in 1938. Barely two years for the magic of the singer's young spirit to seep into today's no longer rocky ground.

Finding the Presley family one room country little shack isn't difficult. Downtown Tupelo is full of direction signs. The Presley birthplace brings in thousands of tourists annually. Get them there, take their dollars, send them filled with wonderment off on their way. The one room shack is actually two and a bit rooms, white painted so it gleams as it never did when Vernon Presley built it. It's surrounded by manicured lawns and well maintained driveways along with two fair-sized parking lots. The site has taken a leaf from the fearsome faux sophistication of Graceland and expanded from a single spot where the fan could commune with Elvis's spirit to a thirteen item tour around tree-filled grounds and with a 1939 green Plymouth sedan parked out front. This is a replica of the car the Presley family drove when leaving Tupelo for Memphis. It has been polished until its chrome gleams and is parked facing northwest, the geographic direction of Memphis. You can shake in your boots in Elvis shock and awe when you stand in front of it.

The house itself isn't much. Wooden floors, linoleum covered, check tablecloths, washboard and tub on open display, iron bedstead. On the stoop there's a swinging seat in which you can have your photo taken. Of rock and roll, if it was ever actually here, there's little trace.

Across the lawns from Presley's first home is the Elvis Childhood Church. This has been designated as a historical landmark by the State of Mississippi. It's the kind of place that, had it been in Wales, would have been rejected by CADW, the ancient monuments body, on the grounds that it had no unique qualities and was of far too recent origin to be of national concern. Little wonder our boy believed so strongly in the Lord, he could see his holy roller First Assembly of God Pentecostal praying place from his bedroom. The white clapboard church is barely larger than the Birthplace itself. Inside there's a multi-media display showing how services could have been with video of a respectful white choir belting out gospel numbers and the preacher waving his holy arms.

The church has actually been transported here. Its original site was several blocks distant where, in the depressed days of the lost thirties, a tent had once been erected on a vacant lot. The charismatic Christianity preached there caught the local spirit and the tent was replaced with wooden walls. In later years the Church built itself a bigger facility and the original was turned into a private house. It was saved from demolition by Guy Harris, who'd known Elvis as a child. He had the structure carried by low loader along the Tupelo streets to the site of the birthplace. There it was restored, rededicated and opened up for international glory. The spirit certainly still flies. While I'm in there fellow tourists join in with the recorded hymns. A number stand and shout subdued halleluiahs.

In sight of the church is the statue of Elvis as a child, guitar toting and wearing oversized dungarees. It's a sort of Capodimonte thing putting me in mind of Elvis as Superboy. "The statue is positioned with the chapel on his right and the museum to his left symbolizing the strong spiritual values Elvis learned in Tupelo and the challenge of materialism he would eventually face....". So runs the hand-out. Elvis will fly off in a moment, playing soft songs for his mother, and save the whole damn world.

At the Birthplace the very air is saccharine. Rather than filling me with warmth, fellowship and a sense of Elvis nearness I feel instead a rising sense of panic. There's nothing here of value, history has been sanitised, the crags and cuts and pains of even a mild person's reality have been airbrushed flat. Fiction foams and the memorials leer. At the Fountain of Life thirteen spouts (representing the years Elvis lived in Tupelo) spill water over granite "a very hard stone symbolizing the enduring power of strong values learned during Elvis's formative years." On the Walk of Life are dated granite blocks denoting each year of Elvis's life from 1935 to 1977. The first thirteen, the Tupelo ones, have markers offering important Elvis facts. Here's a spellbinding example: 1943 – Family reported income of $1232.88 and Paid $12.56 income tax. Three Germans in front of me, all wearing I love Elvis tees, are pouring over it in wonder. One of them is taking notes.

In the Museum, where the Birthplace version of reality is restrained by glass cases, I should at least be safe. But no. Here, in money-no-object splendour is the personal collection of Janelle McComb "a Tupelo resident and long-time family friend of Elvis". McComb is (or was, she died in 2005) head of the Elvis Fan Club. She's also a poet. Her *Memories of Graceland*, a work composed at the request of Jack Soden from Elvis Presley Enterprises and read out at the opening of Graceland to the public in 1982, is housed in its own spotlit case. "She reportedly composed *Memories of Graceland* in a matter of minutes" it says on the information panel as if this were something of which to be proud .

"I've stood aloft on the stately hill for lo, these many years
I've known the great joys of life and wept the saddest tears"

Ah, lo, lo, lo, we poets need more of that word. The TKB logo that so delighted Elvis on the tails of his planes and this slice of amateur verse are of a piece. Elvis of the limited imagination. And with a management too bowed in awe of the man to tell him.

Actually I have no idea what I'm doing here. It's not as if I'm a long term fan. In fact Elvis largely passed me by during my formative rock and roll years. Yes, I heard *Heartbreak Hotel* and *Tutti Frutti* out there in steam radio land. They played him at the funfair in Barry Island, Cardiff's nearest sandy seaside. But they were passing things. I was nine in 1956. *Sparky's Magic Piano* was more to my taste.

Elvis I discovered for real in later life. Hearing *Mystery Train* played in all its magnificent Sun period echo by a dj short of beat group singles might have done it. But it wasn't until the seventies that I actually got my hands on any. The RCA release in 1976 of the Presley *Sun Sessions* filled in all the details for me. The King he has certainly been.

Outside the Birthplace complex is the Mississippi Blues Trail Elvis marker which tells me that Presley continued to incorporate the blues into his music throughout his career. Not to my ears. Elvis Presley was no down home blues singer, despite his Sun label origins. Check the back catalogue. Not much Mississippi delta in there.

Presley would sell records but the edges would be smoothed. The interests of the buying public would be paramount. Even his country collections, and there were quite a number of these, sound like countrypolitan Nashville where turning a buck was all there was. In fact Nashville was where Elvis recorded much of this material with stalwarts Chet Atkins and pianist Floyd Cramer appearing on his discs. Over the years Elvis appears to have abandoned any real interest in music itself. He never followed the careers of others, ignored his roots, and broke new ground not at all.

If he'd lived and Rick Rubin had got hold of him just imagine. Rick Rubin was the producer who saved Johnny Cash, in his final years giving us the stripped back sound of the American Recordings.

Rubin could do wonders with even the least promising of material. Check his Neil Diamond career-salvaging *12 Songs* and the equally engaging *Home Before Dark*.

Elvis was Elvis. Apart from the 1968 *Comeback Special* on TV and those American Studios sidesteps in 1969 everything would be santised and smooth. This was down to Colonel Parker, his mind-controlling manager, and his relentless pursuit of movie dollars. That rock and roll rebel, the one he was that Sun made him, that singer was never to return. There'd be no *Elvis the Sessions Recorded in London*, no *Elvis Returns to His Roots*, nor *Elvis meets The Rolling Stones*. Could have been, so easily. The Beatles went to see him at Graceland at the height of their career. Elvis had no idea what to make of this band of Liverpool jokers. Rapport was low, despite John Lennon admitting to Elvis's significant influence on his early work. Presley stayed contained, manicured, managed to the last crease in his white flared trousers. Elvis was never an innovator.

Not to say that in his extensive output there are not decent sounds. Among his hundreds of sides there are any number of great hit records, songs that endure. Despite the British Invasion and the rise of alternative culture Presley records continued to sell. His low budget films, however, did not. But hell, if you've ever tried any of those last dozen then you'll know only too well why.

What can't be denied is Elvis' place in the culture itself. All you need to do is look back at the photos of him at the start of his career. He's all snarl lip insolence, mouth half open. What you looking at me for? Pimp walking, jeans, hair slicked, intelligence replaced with threat. I can get there, give me a beer, give me a burger, give me dope and let me enjoy myself. The white Anglo Saxon work ethic and belief in self-denial ain't for me, boy, despite the church I go to, despite the God I love.

The fans have collected together and, with no contribution from the millions turned over annually by the Presley Estate, have funded the Tupelo Elvis Presley Memorial Chapel. "A place of meditation at the Elvis Presley Birthplace Park". Inside is the original pulpit lifted from the First Assembly of God white clapboard church just across the lawn. On it rests Elvis' original Bible, his holy hands have turned its holy pages. If he had been a Catholic then deification wouldn't have been far off.

We leave and drive on east taking the Natchez Trace Parkway[62]. Slow and easy, billboard free, endless sky.

17 • The Death of Elvis in Wales

Elvis is on UK TV. It's 1968. He's dressed in all black leather like a motorbike rider, or a male Cathy Gale out of *The Avengers*. He's come back. His sound is good, chilled then ripping up hot and rocking. But we don't need him now. The man had his chance. We've got Led Zep and Jimi and Clapton. A rock journalist somewhere says that Elvis ought to get on a plane and come over here. That's the spirit of the age. But he never does.

That NBC Christmas Show was a creation designed to make Elvis relevant again, to put the King back on his throne. His myriad fans never countenanced that he'd left it. But the for the rest of us this jokey throwback looking like he ought to be out there manning rides at the funfair no longer held any kind of relevance. Good, yeah. But in the same way that Joan Baez's run of great folk albums was completely capped by her wonderful *Farewell, Angelina*. This was released too late, late 1965, into a cold world where roots were giving way to fuzz fretboard pyrotechnics and the soaring, dope-driven extremities of guitar-driven rock.

Did Elvis have anyone there on wah-wah? Not really. He had Scotty Moore and Charlie Hodge in there on electric guitars but they played it straight.

By the time Elvis died in August 1977 the world had changed again. The convoluted depths of over-produced adult orientated rock had turned players back towards self-sufficiency. The working class had regained the upper hand. Three chord anthems once again dominated. Punk was on the streets. Despite his origins as a blue collar rocker Elvis was now, other than to his fans, about as relevant as Fred Astaire.

Not that Elvis fandom should be discounted. There were millions, still are. The diehards who had locked into the music of the King at some early point in their lives and were staying the course. Those graffiti-scrawled walls outside Graceland are testament. Elvis's death is well documented. The hysteria. The copper casket. The miles of mourning fans in line each side of Graceland's gates. Caroline Kennedy arriving to view the body. 80,000 fans lining the route up to Forrest Hills Cemetery. Fans killed in the crush to see the coffin, to touch the King. The misinformation. The sales opportunities. The Colonel's onward plan. Then there's the enduring legacy, mounting record sales and, even now, almost forty years later, a presence that won't go away. There are conspiracy theories by the dozen. He did not die. He was abducted by aliens. He's been seen working in a garage out west; in a tyre shop in Merthyr Tydfil; he's retired and living as an old man on the warm west coast.

In Wales, you might have imagined his presence would have had a hold stronger than most. The South Wales valleys were still behind the fashion head by about ten years. They retained a love of Teddy Boy gear and the seat-ripping, flick knife wielding rock and roll that went with it. But it wasn't quite like that. On the 16th of August, 1977 I was standing, browsing the lp racks at Buffalo Records on the Hayes in Cardiff. Buffalo was the place. For a record store it was large and it sold the sound of the seventies in its entirety. There were American imports and then bootlegs if you knew where to look. There was an atmosphere of youthful counter culture tempered by trade. Moving out of the racks were The Eagles and The Stranglers and Bob Marley.

The store was owned by David Marley and David Bassington and one of them turned off the slice of guitar rock that was playing as background to tell us that he'd heard it, Elvis Presley, he wasn't making records anymore, he was sorry to announce but the king was dead. There was a moment of silence and then some gangly kid in spike hair and tartan bum flap shouted "Old fart" and the world's bustle resumed. The music started up again and the death of one of the greatest in rock and roll was passed over as if it didn't matter.

And he didn't matter, either. Out there at music's cutting edge. Old guards never do. But that didn't stop the Colonel's almost instant my boy's gone but we're going to capitalise like fury marketing campaign from putting *Elvis' 40 Greatest* into the UK number one slot a month later.

In the UK Elvis was huge. In his day he was as big as The Beatles who were as big as Christ. The world, Kennedys, Khrushchevs, Thatchers and Reagans notwithstanding, remained a rocking place. There was plenty of room for imitators and fellow travellers, the singers who had moulded themselves in his image: Ral Donner, Sonny James, Ronnie McDowell, Jack Scott, Cliff Richard, Fabian, Conway Twitty, and there were dozens more. These guys, or their managers, could see the money Elvis's record sales were making and in the true pop music tradition engaged in imitation, recording songs the King might have made himself, just so they could earn a slice. The choice of repertoire was important. These singers did not record their versions of existing Elvis successes. They sought out songs that, had he heard them, might have got past the Colonel's hard-handed repertoire control and been cut by Elvis himself. Fabian's *Turn Me Loose*. Cliff Richard's *Move It*. Conway Twitty's *Lonely Blue Boy* and, for my money the best of all, Ral Donner with *You Don't Know What You've Got*. That one was so Elvis-like you needed to double-check the label just to make sure who it actually was. When fashion changed these singers either faded or they shifted style. Cliff became elder statesman of British Christian pop. Fabian a teen idol film star. Conway Twitty the High Priest of Country Music.

But sounding like him wasn't enough. For some singers they had to be the King. While he lived a small industry had grown up featuring several dozen Elvis impersonators. These ranged from Carl Nelson from Texarkana, Arkansas, who'd begun singing *That's Alright Mama* pretty soon after Elvis had recorded it and built up a local following to a glut of Elvis sound and look-alikes who'd risen to fame after winning small town talent contents. In 1970, well before Presley died, the much troubled folk protest singer Phil Ochs had appeared at Carnegie Hall done up in a gold lame suit made for him by Nudie Cohn who had fashioned the Elvis original. In an attempt to be "part Elvis Presley part Che Guevara[63]" utterly unexpectedly he included an extended Elvis medley as a component of this new in your face Ochs[64] act.

These duplicate Elvises gained work filling-in on the circuit playing those places Elvis might have gone too had he been able to replicate himself. These were precursors to the Bootleg Beatles and the Stolling Rones, you knew that it wasn't actually Elvis but you could dream.

After the 1977 death the world of Elvis impersonators significantly altered course. There was an immediate glut of work for those already on the circuit. Ral Donner narrated Presley's voice for Malcolm Leo and Andrew Solt's 1980s biopic *This Is Elvis*. Ronnie McDowell doubled as the singer for John Carpenter's 1979 TV film *Elvis*. And the concert work also ramped up. Suddenly the world again wanted a slice of the King, sight of him, a touch of how he had been, a piece of his magic.

Impersonation was already stylised with performers selecting from a whole range of Presley periods and adopting the appropriate costume: the gold lame suit, the drape jacket, the jumpsuits, the American eagle cape, the Hawaii shirts, and, to new millennium eyes, the inordinately flared trousers. After the King's death costume wearing went into overdrive and has pretty much remained so for the nearly forty years that have passed since he left.

Presley costume is a fancy dress and stag party staple. Check the range of garb available at Amazon. Black Elvis bouffant wigs, white capes, great jewel-studded belts and full gold lamé suits (made from plastic) can all be purchased for less than the price of a *Best Of Elvis* reissue.

Out on the circuit Elvis imitation began to change its character. It was no longer enough to make yourself look like the King. You had to become the man. Associations were formed, contests run, shows mounted. Impersonation became the realm of the amateur. Elvis Tribute Acts (ETAs) filled the paying stages.

Leslie Rubinkowski, who in 1996 spent a year trailing around America studying ETAs for her book *Impersonating Elvis* (Faber, 1997), reckons there to be 5000 out there in the USA pretending to be Elvis. Centrepiece of ETA activity is the long-running Images of the King contest staged in Memphis during Elvis week, August 10-16, the week of the fans' Graceland candle-lit vigil, the week during which Elvis died.

Rubinkowski identifies a number of ETA characteristics. Performers are obsessives. They try to both dress and sound like the King. They study the films and adopt Elvis's mannerisms, his walk, the way he stands. They mimic his facial expressions. If they can get there then they try to weigh just the same as he did in whichever period they have chosen to follow. They sing the songs. She reckons that she's heard *Polk Salad Annie* more times that any decent human being should. The music becomes a sort of photocopy.

Why do they do it? Academic Eric Lott who has researched the phenomenon, believes Elvis Presley impersonation to be almost exclusively an unstudied working class activity. If you can't be black and hip then you can be a white negro, you can be Elvis. "Like Elvis, I think I am a black man wrapped in white skin," said Chicago impersonator John Paul Rossi. Lott calls it a "retro fantasy in postmodern garb[65]".

Most ETAs stick to the standard repertoire, but a small number transcend it. Listen to Robert Lopez who performs as ElVez and melds Elvis material with that of Mexico. The results can sometimes be astonishing. After a while of listening to this material and occupying its world the pleasures of reality can really beckon. The cutting excitement of those early Elvis Sun sides is so hard to replicate. You can sound just like it but generally you end up doing so minus the magic. Beyond is an Elvis world of increasing schmaltz, off message vocalising and instantly forgettable money-making songs that have survived only because the King once recorded them. You need to escape, get home and stick on some Beethoven or, better, the cutting tremble of Bukka White's primitive vocal roar and his stinging slide guitar. *Fixin' To Die*, yes.

I'm in Porthcawl now. That small town on Wales' Glamorgan Heritage Coast which rose to prominence as a nineteenth-century coal port but is now a shabby seaside day out full of b&bs and cafes. This was the place where once the miners from the entire Welsh coalfield vacationed. That was back when coal was King and Benidorm was still to be discovered. There's a fair, Coney Beach Pleasure Park, well there was. Today the place is undergoing a period of redevelopment. Around the site extend great fields of caravans linked by sand-filled roads. There are gift shops and bars and eateries and an enormous stretch of waste land now doubling as a car park. Glamorgan Heritage Coast be damned. Porthcawl is Caerphilly unbuttoned, Tonypandy on sea, the Rhondda with some sand but even more beer.

The Porthcawl Elvis Festival 2014 is now in its eleventh year. It is supported by a couple of local firms, Ace Taxis and Harris Printers, and is fronted by the founder of the Argentine Welsh Football Society, the distinctly non-Elvis look-a-like Peter Phillips. Without foreknowledge you might imagine the weekend to be one of musical reflection and historical recollection. An Elvis lecture perhaps. A session on Elvis' blues roots. Stalls selling back catalogue and compilations of obscure b sides. Wall to wall showings of the King's, with one or two notable exceptions, uniformly dreadful musical films. Not a bit of it.

As Eric Lott has suggested, Elvis imitation is almost entirely blue collar. And so, too, is Porthcawl, despite the golf links just along the coast. The women of a certain age who line dance in pink feather boas outside Dolly Parton concerts in Cardiff (see Chapter 25) are all here. So too, it feels, are the rest of what's left of the middle-aged in the South Wales valley hinterland. As you walk around you pick up that valley buzz. Not a single accent seems to be anything else. The poet Robert Minhinnick whom I bump into on James Street outside the Sustainable Wales café, Sussed, which he helps run reckons the Elvis festival to be a "magnificent working class eisteddfod[66]". "It's an excuse for drinking," he tells me. "Same sort of thing as international rugby. You should see them go at it down around the Hi Tide, front of the amusement park, on Saturday night. Elvis staggering. They all are."

Everyone is also dressed as Elvis. It's hard to take in at first but every second person you look at is either wearing the full gold lame kit or sports enormous sideburns plus black bouffant hairpiece in imitation of the King at the height of his sartorial powers. And you don't just dress as Elvis here if you are performing. The audience kit themselves out in tribute as well. Women dress in US Army uniform circa *GI Blues* or wear fifties style dresses, great flurries of petticoats and a rampage of polka dots. The men are often Elvis tribute t-shirted with false sideburns hanging from the arms of their fifties-style shades and with maybe a *Blue Hawaii* necklace of flowers draped round their necks. There are platoons of infantrymen in neatly pressed and considerably convincing US Army uniforms. And there are hosts of white-caped Elvis replicas. There are also a multitude of wigs. Real hair, synthetic bristle, some resembling pieces of carpet and loads in full plastic extrusion like shiny black helmets.

In one afternoon rambling the not yet quite autumn air of the seafront I spot Elvis singing on most corners and with further versions tributing the King inside bars, hotels and cafes. His fans are legion. I see female Elvises, smoking Elvises, overweight double the original at his worst Elvises, Elvis on a skateboard, pogoing Elvis, Elvis phoning home, Elvis on crutches, Welsh speaking Elvises[67], Elvis carrying three pints, Elvis fishing, Elvis at 80, Elvis in a wheel chair, junior Elvises, two of them trampolining in full caped regalia, Elvis surfing, Elvis as Lord Mayor wearing chains around his neck.

In fact the real mayor of Porthcawl, Phil Rixon, once asked the organisers what he could do to help the festival and ended up arriving by pink Cadillac and renewing his wedding vows in full *Blue Hawaii* dress at the film's wedding scene recreation on the seafront.

Amid all this Elvis hoopla what I didn't see, even once, was anyone actually playing a musical instrument. I discount here the Gilgal Baptist Elvis preachers from the local evangelical church at the top of John Street who did have guitars but were singing Neil Sedaka numbers. They've got a white board mounted on a stand with the words "Is anyone greater than Elvis?" written across the top. They want passers-by to add "Jesus" and while the son of man does make an appearance he's outnumbered by rival claims: Billy Fury, Bono, Morrissey, Barry Manilow.

Porthcawl's Elvises are almost without exception karaoke men. There are a few ETAs who have made it through the heats and will appear in front of a full band in the who is best Elvis grand finale at the now distinctly ungrand Grand Pavilion. On the streets and in the bars, however, you look like the King, you sound like him, but you do it solo to backing tapes.

At the Hi Tide bar and diner complex at the beach edge there are four stages which offer a revolving display of ETAs. Audiences are huge and even at eleven in the morning well on the way to being rumbustiously pissed. We get Jimmy Elvis, Jamie Elvis, Karl Memphis,

Ben Presley, Memphis Morgan, Elvis Melvis, Johnny Be Goode and Ponty Presley all doing their best. After a time the sheer weight of Elvis musical thump begins to deaden the mind. I've heard *One Night* so many times now that I can no longer tell it from *Suspicion*. I never want to hear *Wooden Heart* ever again.

On the sea front a pretty passable Elvis dressed in white drape and suntan has set himself up with laptop and amp driven speaker system. He's asking for requests and after running through a few of the expected Elvis smashes, *Ready Teddy* and *Guitar Man*, a drinker in the crowd asks him to do something by Dion. "Dion? You mean *Runaround Sue*? That's not Elvis. I can't do that." "Well sing it like Elvis would," shouts the drinker. There's no reply. We get *It's Now Or Never* instead.

Would all of this have been going on if Elvis had not died when he did? I doubt it. There's something about youth being taken away that parallels the King's life with the lives of his fans. There's also something about the way that Elvis didn't write his own songs and wasn't anything remotely near being termed an intellectual that appeals to his Porthcawl working class once coal mining fans. They remember the good times and want them back. Is that musical form, rock and roll, that drove itself up a side alley beyond which no progression was possible actually now be dead here in South Wales? By the Porthcawl evidence, certainly not.

18 • The Alabama Music Hall of Fame

U p beyond Tupelo the land is unexplored country. I guess that's the music, or the memory of it, playing its inevitable part. There are no significant songs I can recall that mention the Joe Wheeler State Park, Athens, Moulton or Decatur[68]. Not yet. You say De-KAY-tur, by the way. Been told that at a truck stop. Not the French way I first pronounced it. There are Decaturs right across America, from Michigan to Nebraska. They are all named after Stephen Decatur (1779-1820). He was a Commodore in the Revolutionary American Navy, a Yankee Nelson whose became a hero of the new Republic and was celebrated in every new township that couldn't think what else to call itself. Decatur, Alabama, was originally known as Rhodes Ferry Landing but name-changed by order of President Monroe in 1820 after the Commodore had been killed in a duel. Americans have largely forgotten him now. His ships were modest and made of wood. Theirs today are indulgent, all-metal structures the size of football fields, that extend American soil to the far reaches of blue water earth.

Alabama, the place, has stuck in my head since I heard it celebrated as a child. Up you came, from Alabama, with a banjo on your knee. Uncle Mac[69] played it every week on the BBC. This was *Oh! Susanna*, Stephen Foster's minstrel song of 1868. Originally it had been sung right across the Southern States by white men blacking-up to look just like the former slaves they had working in their fields. The minstrel shows were full of songs that sounded like they might have been sung by blacks but never actually were. A sort of pasteurised black songbook created for white folk. How these creations were really viewed by the people who inspired them is anyone's guess. Much, I suppose, as

American blues singers viewed the British blues bands of the 60s – with a mixture of suspicion and derision. "These boys want to play the blues badly and that's how they play the blues … very badly[70]", as harmonica legend Sonny Boy Williamson is reported as saying when he first heard The Yardbirds.

But the minstrel shows were not supposed to be authentic and neither was *Oh! Susanna*. Although by the time I heard it the song had acquired its own patina of legitimacy[71]. Part of the Great American Songbook, that place where fiction and reality mix and the result dominated the Western world.

Most of Alabama is flat, a rich alluvial plain that descends to both the Mississippi River and the Gulf of Mexico. The part I'm crossing, where the state butts up against Tennessee, is more mountainous. It's full of lakes, rivers and creeks, forest and sun. The bands with the state's name in their titles are legion: Alabama Shakes, The Alabama 3, Alabama Thunderpussy, The Alabama Jug Band, The Alabama Sacred Harp Singers, The Blind Boys of Alabama, and the best sellers by several million, Alabama themselves. I turn up the radio and hunt the local wavebands. Hearing Alabama in Alabama would make a nice circle. But all I get is urban rap bracketed with southern Gospel. "Brother, will your weaknesses keep you from being used mightily by God? Time is short, the Enemy is real. Turn to Jesus now."

The place we are heading for is Tuscumbia, a town of barely 10,000 that was once called Big Spring until Native Americans got it renamed after the chief rainmaker of the local tribe, the Chickasaws. It's here that the State Legislature have built their own Alabama Music Hall of Fame. Situated just back from Highway 72, it's the expected out of town shopping mall replica, endless parking lot, impossible to fill even if Madonna was in attendance, a structure of flat roofed slab with arched doorways and vaulted water cascades out front. You'd think in the pressing heat they'd be welcoming but today they're off. Site of a fountain, pond drained, concrete showing dry grey, visible settlement cracks.

The Hall was opened in 1990 after a state-wide search for a suitable venue. Huntsville architects Smith, Kranert and Tomblin turned in credible plans for a structure that would never be land-locked by the structures of others. Leave space for your own expansion was the rule of the day. Music can only get bigger.

Music Halls of Fame, it turns out, exist as a sort of twentieth century rash right across America. Unlike in Wales, land of song, where we have precisely none the Americans have realised that as music is part of their world-dominating culture it should be celebrated as such. We have a tradition going back a thousand years and we hide it in the bowels of our museum of folk life and resited buildings, St Fagans. The Americans invented theirs somewhere in the middle of the nineteenth century and have been celebrating it with bells, whistles and constant dollar investment ever since.

There are examples of Music Halls of Fame in almost every state and for as many types of music as there are genres. The Jazz Hall of Fame in Oklahoma. The Folk Music Hall of Fame, New York. The Classical Music Hall of Fame, Cincinnati. The Country Music Hall of Fame, Nashville. The State Music Hall of Fame in Oregon, Memphis, Minnesota, Louisiana, Hawaii, and just about everywhere else that music runs the game. Here in Alabama, a state pretty involved in the music business when you get down to it, the Hall of Fame opened in 1987. It has 12,500 square feet of exhibition space with plans to open wings devoted to southern music research and a huge audio-visual theatre capable of mounting actual concerts before too long. The future is always a bigger and more sparkly place, even in America.

Music Halls of Fame seem to do two main things. Firstly they display and interpret artefacts connected with music and musicians important to their area of interest. And second, and perhaps more significantly, they induct lucky individuals. You get nominated, you agree, there's a ceremony of sorts, and then there you are, an inductee with your portrait on the wall and your cv housed forever in the files. In a sense it's a bit like that thing they do for poets. Once you've reached a certain point in your career, usually determined by age, your fellows and the institutions and publishers around you hold a night of celebration. This centres on your work and features a stream of individuals taking the stage to talk about you and your place in the literary firmament and to read out examples of what you've done. This happened to the Welsh poet Herbert Williams several years ago when he reached 70. "It's a great thing and all that," he told me, "but what's next? The end I suppose."

Inside the Alabama Music Hall of Fame we are the only visitors. Admission is $10 and there's no guidebook. In fact the whole merchandising thing, normally a feature of just about any American institution, is sadly lacking here. If they come then you can sell things to them. But not in Tuscumbia. There's an excuse for a stall retailing kids colouring books and pens plus a few stickers, t-shirts and mugs but that's about it. Not that there's anyone manning the desk should I have wished to buy.

We cross the bronze stars in the floor that form the Alabama Walk of Fame – Percy Sledge, Jim Nabors, Tammy Wynette, The Temptations, Hank Williams Jnr. Dozens more. There's supposed to be a music-controlled colour chandelier bouncing a light show around the place here but, like the fountain out front, it's not functioning today. Beyond is the Hall of Fame Gallery stuffed with portraits of inductees. These are all done by self-taught Tuskegee artist Ronald McDowell. As portraits they are unsettling. There's something leery and two dimensional about the look of these singers. Their hands are too large and their eyes focus somewhere towards the back of your head. There are hundreds of them too. Testament to both McDowell's dogged tenacity and the sheer number of musical achievers who have a connection with Alabama soil.

McDowell is a local hero in the Michael Jackson mould. In fact word is he advised Jackson on the cover of his *Thriller* album. Stare at that portrait of the lounging King of Pop for a while, one awkward hand visible and the other not, and you can see McDowell's style. Celebrated for his God-given gifts and his African-American heritage he's the man in this part of the world. Public sculpture, portraits of the governor, commissions for the African-American rich. "He's the best artist in the universe" runs a comment on his web site. You've been warned.

If it hasn't produced more painters than you can easily count, Alabama certainly makes up when it comes to music. The state is one of the beating hearts of American song. Nat King Cole, The Commodores, Martha Reeves, WC Handy, The Louvin Brothers, Dan

Penn, Jimmie Rodgers, Hank Williams, Dinah Washington, Arthur Alexander, Hank Ballard, Emmylou Harris, Lionel Hampton, Eddie Floyd, Lionel Richie, Wilson Pickett, Big Momma Thornton, Candi Staton, and dozens more were all born in this state. The Hall of Fame is determined to acquaint me with them all.

Geographically-based music museums like this one make the assumption that the visitor is interested in any and all musics, every-thing from kazoo virtuosi to composers of military marches, from guitar eccentrics to cello masters and from collectors of early music to street rappers. Lucky for me, though, Alabama is in the south. It's the home of back-country bluegrass, sacred harp singing, blues with attitude and rock that twists and shouts. What I came for. News is that this year new inductees will include Hank Locklin, Dan Penn and Sun Ra. My taste completely.

Beyond the Gallery lies the main exhibit hall with more excite-ment than I'd expected along with a few things that I'm sure I've also recently seen in Nashville[72]. Recording equipment from Sam Phillips' Memphis Recording Service, otherwise known as Sun, for example. But in a case there's the Elvis contract Phillips sold to RCA in late 1955. One of the music world's most significant documents.

There are the clothes of country stars, their guitars, their rhinestone jackets, their bootlace ties. You expect to see all this and I've certainly come across similar displays elsewhere. There are cases full of songwriter's manuscripts. A wax figure of Nat King Cole at his piano. Erskine Hawkins' trumpet. The gold discs of Wilson Pickett and Percy Sledge. A replica of the great Muscle Shoals studio. Juke boxes every-where, amps, video monitors, speakers in stacks. Everything leaks sound into the echoing hall.

The most eye-catching exhibit could well be the 1960 Pontiac Bonneville Convertible sitting there with more than five hundred silver dollars stuck onto its paintwork. There are rifles and a batch of silver six-shooters mounted on its sides. On the front are a pair of Texas longhorns, just to make sure you know this is a country car. It was owned by Happy Hal Burns, one of the earliest singing cowboys, a man clearly given to displays of Alabama excess.

Centrepiece both physically and in terms of importance is actually a bus. On the front it says Alabama. It's that band's Southern Star tour bus. Alabama, the million selling rock band who dominated the American charts during the 1980s, majoring on Confederate flag-waving and making the south their home. What did they mean in the UK? Not that much. Like them we'd been brought up on the slick and smooth 1970s sanitised country of The Eagles, as well as the bar room rock and resolutely red neck sound of boogie bands such as The Doobies and Lynyrd Skynyrd. Skynyrd's *Sweet Home Alabama* from 1974 was something you rocked to in the clubs in Cardiff Docks. It became so popular that there were confederate flags flying from allotments in Pontypridd. Blokes I knew had the Dixie Flag tattooed on their arms and painted on the back of their cars. It was a symbol of rebellion, an essentially white male activity that involved trucker horseshoe moustaches, cheroots, bourbon drinking and drunken dancing to The Doobies' *Listen To The Music* time after time.

By the end of the American seventies The Doobies were in hibernation and most of Lynyrd Skynyrd had lost their lives in a 1977 falling plane. The band Alabama, known in their formative, Doobie-tracking years as Wildcountry, were listening as closely as they could to the million-selling Eagles. They changed their name to that of their state and signed what was to turn out to be a 75 million album selling deal with RCA. America does this. It has styles and players who sell into the stratosphere but end up meaning not that much over here. Dion was such a singer. Capitalising on his teenage successes with The Belmonts he was a hit on both sides of the Atlantic with two late rock and roll triumphs – *Runaround Sue* and *The Wanderer*. His equally on the button follow-ups, a whole string of them running from *I Was Born To Cry* to *Little Diane*, and *Ruby Baby* to *Drip Drop*, all sold a million in the USA but pretty much sank without a trace here.

While we were exploring Punk and the spiky eighties the Americans were revamping heavy metal. They had dozens of bands: sexist, bare-chested, high voiced derivatives of something that might have begun with Led Zeppelin but by now had severely lost its way. Bands like Kiss, Van Halen, and Mötley Crüe lead directly to the distinctly US phenomenon of hair metal. This was where the excessive hair styles of band members were just as important as their lead guitar licks. Lyrics were vapid nonsense and tunes all sounded the same. Bands like Kix, Night Rangers, Quiet Riot, Cinderella, and Faster Pussycat cycled and recycled their videos on MTV. They dominated the US Billboard charts. But with the exception of Bon Jovi and Guns N' Roses almost all these highly successful outfits failed to make progress in the UK.

Not that Alabama were a metal derivative. Far from it. They were a country rock outfit. Probably the most successful one there was. They occupied that place where bands like the *Sweetheart of the Rodeo* Byrds, Poco, The Flying Burrito Brothers, New Riders of the Purple Sage, The Nitty Gritty Dirt Band and Bob Dylan with his out and out country turnaround album *Nashville Skyline* (1969) had all been pointing. They took the pedal steel big-hat country music hardcore sound, stripped it of any folk meanderings or authentic backwoods voices, added drums and electric lead and blew. They made inoffensive, rebel-sounding music. They wore beads, beards and long hair, and branded themselves as country boys to the core.

If they'd stuck to delivering three-part vocal harmony Creedence-derivative material like *Mountain Music* and *Tennessee River* their music might have retained some sort of connection with the authentic. They would even have been acceptable if they'd stayed sub-Willie Nelson meets Crosby, Stills and Nash as they did with *My Home's In Alabama*, their greatest hit. At least then we'd have been able to enjoy it all as inoffensive, easy-going country with the sort of rhythm you can tap your feet to without feeling a schmuck. But they didn't. They added rising stings and removed anything that could possibly make you think of Hank Williams or Ernest Tubb. They were branded[73] "squeaky clean, safe and germ free", by country writer Kurt Wolf. A description that fits them to a tee.

Guided by their record company cousins Randy Owen, Jeff Cook and Teddy Gentry, the creative core of Alabama, saw success out there in radio land. Rather than cleaving to the soil beneath their tooled cowboy boots their music was massaged and smoothed until it could no longer offend anyone. It was all easy-going, sentimental, and family-friendly. It was slick and it was overproduced. There was not a single jangle or rough corner present. Nothing was out of place, everything was calculated to sell and sell again. Hang originality, forget authenticity, avoid the real, pop music is there to turn a buck. Let's turn them. Aided by the slickest of promotional operations, the advent of FM radio and then MTV, Alabama sold more records during the eighties than any country act before them ever had. They stayed on top, moving effort-lessly through dozens of similar-sounding albums and twenty-one #1 equally similar-sounding hit singles. They were the sound of America in the Eighties. But they didn't travel. Round the bars and clubs of South Wales did you ever hear Alabama? Not a chance. They would have been perfect as background music for life-style stores and fashion boutiques. Instead all we heard when we went shopping were the Gipsy Kings.

Beyond Alabama what is there? In a sense the music they made and the success they had with it pretty much sealed up everything I wanted to hear until the rise of alt-country and the revival of folk and bluegrass music a decade of more later. Looking at their empty tour bus with its bars and beds and over-plush joint smoking interior I feel nothing but depression. This is where the music I love should never have gone. It was better up in the mountains. Where they knew what to do with it. Where I'm heading next.

The remainder of the museum blossoms out with a disparate mixture of Martha Reeves' stage outfit, an effigy of Hank Williams in full country-singer suit, a Wurlitzer juke playing songs written by Alabama composers, dioramas displaying the costumes worn by the likes of famous Alabama gospel acts Jake Hess, Gold City, and The Speer Family, the original control desk on which Rick Hall recorded Arthur Alexander's hit *You Better Move On*, and all manner of memora-bilia, pens, ashtrays, recording contracts, tie pins, cuff links, rings, from stars you know and stars you don't. Country detritus. Famous guff.

Alabama's new music isn't here yet. None of the new bands are on show. No Banditos, Dead Fingers, Doc Dailey & Magnolia Devil, Fire Mountain, The Great Book of John, Lee Bains and The Glory Fires, St Paul and The Broken Bones, or The Pollies. The material they play – country punk, soul revived, melodic roots rock, big bearded Americana, folk retrodden – has put Alabama back on its lively feet again. It's on the radio as we drive out onto the highway. Music in this state is as vital as the air.

19 • The Shoals

Hunting for the Shoals turns out to be easier than I think. Turns out I'm already here. Tuscumbia, that outpost of the once hard-line segregated and eternally southern state of Alabama, is one of the four cities that are collectively known as Muscle Shoals. You've got to look hard at the map to work this out and even harder out of the limo window. Despite being called cities these are not places of great urban density. In fact the whole district has a sleepy rural feel. At the last census the total population of the Quad Cities, Sheffield, Florence, Tuscumbia and Muscle Shoals, was 12K. There are more people living in Penarth.

This is a place where there's heat in the trees and the cattle move slowly in their fields. Where electricity came late and you expect the ploughs to be pulled by mules. The cotton still grows and there are fields of it within the city limits. To the east the Tennessee River around which the Quad Cities cluster has been blocked by the Wilson Dam. This many-arched show stopper was built by Woodrow Wilson in 1924 to power the nitrate plants on the eastern edge of Muscle Shoals. The ensuing lake has widened the river's shores. The shoals of mussel, if they ever existed, have now moved on.

Collectively the Shoals could be small town most anywhere down here in the still sticky south. They are famous for being the birthplace of WC Handy, and of DJ turned record producer Sam Phillips. Phillips got out smartly, moving the few hundred miles west to Memphis to begin his world-changing storm. George Jones lived in the Shoals at the height of his career. They are also the place where John Paul White, formerly half of the duo The Civil Wars, currently resides. But he's not dead nor famous enough yet to warrant a plaque. I'm here looking for a studio. In fact two studios. Rick Hall's Fame, the one that started it, and his house band, The Swampers', break-away operation, the Muscle Shoals Sound Studio on Jackson Highway.

How it was that this river settlement on the way to Huntsville should have become the world's best at laying down tight, chunky funk and filling a white world's hit parades with a non-stop stream of black smashes remains one of those much discussed mysteries. In the film *Muscle Shoals* Jimmy Cliff, wearing a jacket that resembles a leather cheese-grater, suggests that some places on earth just have that magic. There are flickers and breaks in the space/time continuum. Paris had one filled with modernist painters. East Anglia with left field poets. Muscle Shoals has recording engineers producing pulsing, world beating, sanctified soul.

The enigma is how such black-sounding stuff should, with the obvious exception of the singer, be designed, controlled and made almost entirely by whites. Rick Hall, the man in Muscle Shoals at the start, had a background in country music. So, too, did Jim Stewart at Stax. How did these guys become front runners in the production of blues, soul and r&b? A bit of research among what Iain Sinclair calls Google Slurry soon pulls up a few more apparent anomalies. I check out some of the other great black music labels and their attendant studios – Atlantic, Aladdin, Modern, Kent, Hi, Speciality, Goldwax, Chess. All turn out to have been founded by Hungarian Jews, Polish immigrants or white southern Baptists. Going further to track the down home blues specialists – such as Arhoolie, Folkways and Delmark – I discover all to have been established by whites. The great field recorders and collectors – John and Alan Lomax, Chris Strachwitz – were white too. Pretty much the only blacks who'd set up independent labels I could find were former DJ Vivian Carter at Vee-Jay in Indiana and Berry Gordy at Motown, Detroit's Hitsville USA.

In America, land of the free, a monied black middle class had been slow to emerge. In the pre-war south, African Americans with money to invest were rare. The achieving of socioeconomic parity appeared to be impossible. The order of black workers and white owners prevailed. Even today with segregation gone and the world, apparently, a clear and loveable place, the disparity in income between black and white Americans remains stark. Little wonder that the post-war record industry with its fixation on black music should be powered by the only people with any kind of available financial resource – the whites.

Things, however, have shifted considerably in the sixty or so years since Howlin' Wolf first walked into the Sun studio in Memphis. Today producers, engineers and label owners are as likely to be as black as the music they sell. But that was not so when Rick Hall first set himself up running the Fame studio precursor – Spar Music – 'Commercial Recordings, Songs Published' – above a drugstore in Florence. That was at the end of the 1950s and although there was little success with the actual recordings made here some of the songs Hall wrote went on to be cut by George Jones, Brenda Lee, Roy Orbison and Clyde McPhatter. For Rick Hall song writing was the income earner. Record producing, which turned out to be his enormous talent, came second.

In the way of things Hall and his first business partners, Tom Stafford and Billy Sherill, fell out. Money, the business's direction, working out who was boss. In response Hall established his own operation, what was to become the first Fame studio, in a former candy and tobacco warehouse on the edge of town. Wilson Dam Road. This was a cobbled-together place with egg boxes and second hand drapes on the wall for soundproofing and sheets of ancient carpet salvaged from a local theatre to cover the floors. Here he recorded Arthur Alexander, a local boy, singing *You Better Move On*. Hall used his first Fame Rhythm Section, a collection of local musicians, all white and all able to follow direction. The sound was sparse, precise, close. A future trademark. The recording was a hit. Big enough to power Hall on to establish a larger operation, the present Fame studios, on Avalon Avenue.

Much has been made of Alexander. His first record was cut at Spar Music in 1961 and released on Judd Records. It failed to do a thing. A year later he made *You Better Move On* in the studios on Wilson Dam Road. The Rolling Stones liked it so much the put their version on their first ep. Alexander's *Anna (Go To Him)* was then covered by The Beatles on their album, *Please Please Me*. Word was that this singer was a source, a genius with direct access to a deep seam of Mod-era r&b. With supporters like he had his work should have soared to the top. But it never did. Somehow Fame failed to make him famous. There were no world beating long players nor roarings up the world wide national charts. Alexander kept on. He switched labels. He tried his hand at country. He lost direction. He became a bus driver. In 1990 he was rediscovered. But it was too late. He died of a heart attack in 1993.

Rick Hall is a man made good who comes from the most destitute of rural backgrounds. His parents were sharecroppers. His first wife died in a car crash. His father had a fatal accident with a tractor. Hall's story is one of succeeding against these odds, of overcoming tragedy, of being let down by those around him, and then bouncing right on back. It would make a great TC Boyle novel or a marvellously melodramatic mid-century Hollywood film. Greg Carmalier did almost that when he directed a big screen doc telling the whole Rick Hall story in 2013. Hall, by this time in his 80s, appears as the person-ification of slightly overweight cool – earing, locks flowing, overgrown moustache with tips that point heavenward. Just like Salvador Dali's.

The Florence Alabama Music Enterprises (FAME) Studio on 603 East Avalon is situated near a road junction and next to a car parts reseller and a chain pharmacy. It looks a little like a bunker. It became one of those lacunae in space/time where wonder bleeds through. With his first rhythm section mostly moved onto more remunerative work in Nashville, Hall established a second. The Swampers, as they were unofficially named. This was Barry Beckett (keyboards), Roger Hawkins (drums), Jimmy Johnson (guitar) and David Hood (bass) sometimes supplemented by Spooner Oldham on piano. White locals, all of them. They might have looked as if they worked as shelf stackers but they were able to deliver the crispest, sparest of black sounds.

Although Hall reckoned he could record any kind of music (and early on actually produced a hit for Buddy Holly sound-alike Tommy Roe) it was for the emerging black sounds that he enthused. Rivalling, and sometimes trouncing, Hi and Stax in Memphis, Fame was the studio that brought black America to self-awareness through soul music. Never as bombastic or as bling-ridden as rival operations, Fame tightly, and to funky perfection, turned out the hits. Hall could do this. He was director, musician, engineer, businessman, and visionary all rolled into one.

The Tams, Jimmy Hughes, Joe Tex, Joe Simon, James and Bobby Purify, Arthur Conley, Etta James, Irma Thomas, Clarence Carter, Wilson Pickett, Don Covay and once, just the once, Aretha Franklin. These were his stars. There was an actual Fame label on which Rick Hall would launch local singers who might not have made it otherwise. But mainly Hall used his expertise to record product which others would go on to sell. Jerry Wexler at Atlantic was an early enthusiast. Amazed at how such a black sound could emerge from a bunch of southern whites he brought down the argumentative and confrontational Wilson Pickett. Pickett had already recorded *In The Midnight Hour* at Stax, upsetting everyone in the process, and was now on a roll. At Fame where tolerance was greater he cut *Land of a Thousand Dances* and *Mustang Sally*. Both were huge hits. Duane Allman, hippie locks flowing, showed Pickett what could be done with a Beatles song. Together they recorded a searing version of *Hey Jude*. Fame could do no wrong.

The Aretha falling-out of 1967 is well documented. The black queen of soul, a clear rival in the regal stakes for Bessie Smith, had spent years with Columbia. There she'd recorded nine albums of soft-edged jazz numbers and well-meaning pop – all without much success. When her contract ran out Jerry Wexler at Atlantic signed her and brought her west not to Stax but to Fame. At the East Avalon studios The Swampers provided the inspirational and mould-creating backing for the world's best soul record ever – *I Never Loved A Man (The Way I love You)*. Nothing before (or since) quite equals this for passion, power, brooding suspense, rising excitement and, yep, sweet soul music. Rick Hall was the total control freak who directed Aretha's every move. And he delivered the goods.

The session was not without tension. Hall and Aretha's then husband, Ted White, fell out after a drunken racial argument. In despair Aretha flew back to New York having recorded just the one song. She was never to return. An upset Jerry Wexler withdrew his Atlantic custom. This left Hall bereft but he didn't let it slow him down.

Neither did the simultaneous departure of Fame's brilliant and now pretty famous Swampers rhythm section to set up their own studios across town. Wexler took his business there – to the new Muscle Shoals Sound Studios at 3614 Jackson Highway.

Undeterred Hall went out and found himself a new set of backing musicians – these he called The Fame Gang. This time the house band was multi-racial and had resident rather than brought in horns. Hall copyrighted the words "Home of the Muscle Shoals Sound" and emblazoned them across his studio walls. He went to Chess and took on Etta James. His first recording with her produced *Tell Mama*. Not quite Aretha but still ground-shakingly good. He had a new deal with Capitol. And the hits kept coming.

Soul produced some of the great crossover hits of the period. Music that set the white-dominated hit parade on both sides of the Atlantic afire. On the dance floor at Cardiff's sixties Top Rank the numbers that tingled the blood were led by Otis Redding, Wilson Pickett and Aretha Franklin. Out there where women rocked round their handbags and blokes, for the first time for hundreds of years, began to enjoy the pleasure of dancing by themselves. I witnessed it. The electric excitement of *Land of a Thousand Dances*. The crying thrill of Aretha with *I Never Loved A Man*. The total addiction of listening to Otis, pounding, praying, making the spirit rise up right inside you. Material recorded mainly at Fame. Suddenly we all wanted to be able to slide and slip like African Americans, to play horns, to honk and parp, to rip and ride. White Negros? Heavens, almost everyone there, from Tonypandy to Tremorfa, thought they were now black.

And then it all went wrong. For me anyway. Otis died in a plane crash. Pickett went off the boil. And James Brown, sweating, and Little Richard screaming, brought us Funk. He told us once and then he told us again. He felt good. I never did. The line went off to where I didn't want to see it go. Drowned out the blues, took them out of the hit parade and made them old people's music. Ancient songs. Made them a minority interest. Put them in the museum. The world stopped grooving to it. Out on the white again dance-floors you were either disco or else you were punk.

But at The Swampers' new studios the stars were queuing. That chink in the space/time continuum through which it all flows was still there. It embraced the whole of Muscle Shoals. Who came? The Rolling Stones, Paul Simon, Canned Heat, Rod Stewart, Bob Seger, Cat Stevens, Santana, Traffic, Joe Cocker, Lynyrd Skynyrd, Boz Scaggs, JJ Cale, Dire Straits, Bob Dylan. Skynyrd sang about The Swampers on their world maker *Sweet Home Alabama*. Cher recorded a whole album which she titled *3614 Jackson Highway*.

At Fame, with his new gang of backing musicians delivering as good a sound as The Swampers, Hall recorded Lou Rawls, King Curtis, Little Richard, Joe Simon, Bobby Womack, Paul Anka, Tom Jones and, for the money if not the musical style, The Osmonds. The grass didn't grow.

The signs aren't up yet, directing the tourist cars on in. The Shoals streets are crossed by telegraph wires and traffic lights at the intersections hang from poles. It's easy enough to drive around this place and find yourself first on Avalon then on Jackson Highway. Both studios are still in place, prefabs, industrial huts, in the full Alabama light. They are both shut when I drive past. Wrong day again, wrong time. The state has put the Jackson studios on the Alabama Register of Landmarks and Heritage as it has the still working Fame Studios on Avalon. The Swampers have opened a new and larger operation on Alabama Avenue although still record at Jackson Highway. Or did when I passed. The studios have now been sold on to the Muscle Shoals Music Foundation who will turn them into a museum and tourist pull. Music as magnet once again.

20 • I'm In Love With A Knoxville Girl

We're driving into Knoxville along the 75 on the way up from Chattanooga. Apart from the minor diversion to look at Muscle Shoals we've been on this highway pretty much since Tuscumbia's Alabama Music Hall of Fame. The road is long. All American roads are long. They are full of traffic that slips and changes, rises and rolls: high-sided artics, great silver rigs that own the world, limousines like space ships, chrome encrusted constructs as large as dustcarts that blimp across the lanes like rolling balloons. There's not much that moves with zip. In America you just don't. Jap cars do their best. There's the occasional European, a BMW, a Merc, but nothing from Britain, nothing at all.

America is all road, connected by songs that name the places the highways pass. The turnpikes, the freeways, the black tops, the blue highways, the corduroy roads, the endless routes. The 66, the 61, the 49. *Twenty-Four Hours From Tulsa, I've Been Everywhere, Hit The Road Jack, On The Road Again.* They come out of the car's multiple speakers as we roar. Today it's *Don't Give Your Heart To A Knoxville Girl,* The Cherryholmes' rocking, banjo-driven bluegrass piece, a mass of high energy. It keeps pace perfectly with the car's rolling thunder. Composed by Cia Cherryholmes, last heard on stage at Pontypridd, this is a perfect new millennium addition to the bluegrass canon. Except that when you listen to the lyrics closely you can hear the echoes in there of earlier songs.

The one the town is famous for is *Knoxville Girl.* "I met a little girl in Knoxville, a town we all know well...", recorded originally by Arthur Tanner and His Blue Ridge Corn Shuckers in 1925 and revitalised by succeeding generations of mountain music players and others ever since. The Blue Sky Boys made their version in 1937. The Osborne Brothers did it in 1972. There's a great rockabilly version by Charlie Feathers from 1973, complete with spoken introduction, growls, drums and twangy guitar. Nick Cave and The Bad Seeds recorded the song in the 1990s. Billy Bob Thornton made a country rock version with his band The Boxmasters in 2007. The definitive version remains The Louvin Brothers from 1956, reprised in 2007 by Charlie Louvin, his brother Ira long dead, using Will Oldham as the second voice. The Louvins somehow make their harmonies ache and soar. The Everlys must have heard them because they did the same.

The Everly Brothers should have recorded this song. They actually lived in Knoxville for a few years back in the mid-fifties before their fame hit. It's ideal material for their seminal *Songs Our Daddy Taught Us* from 1958. I check again. It isn't there.

Journalist Paul Slade is a *Knoxville Girl* obsessive. Actually he's a murder ballad obsessive, and has set up a blog[74] which details his research into many famous songs of violent death – *Stagger Lee, Frankie & Johnny, Tom Dooley, The Lonesome Death of Hattie Carroll* – although it's the *Knoxville Girl* who takes up most of his time. He tracks the song back through a variety of Appalachian, Irish and English versions deciding that the song's early DNA is contained in sung references to a bloody nose. This is how coming home with blood all over your tunic has, for centuries, been explained away. No, I haven't been in a fight. This happened when I suffered bleeding from my nose. Every time Paul Slade spots this in a lyric he's sure the song in question comes from a common source.

Here's the line in 1685's *The Bloody Miller*:

How came you by that blood upon
Your trembling hands and clothes?
I presently to him replied
By bleeding at the nose.

And now how it's sung by The Louvin Brothers in 1956's *Knoxville Girl*:

Saying, "Dear son, what have you done
To bloody your clothes so?"
I told my anxious mother
I was bleeding at my nose

The Wexford Girl, *The Oxford Girl*, *The Bloody Miller*, *Hanged I shall Be*, *The Berkshire Tragedy*, *The Cruel Miller*, *The Wexford Murder*, *The Lexington Miller*, *The Oxford Tragedy*, *The Noel Girl*, they all talk of bloody noses.

This is the way traditional music works. It's transferred from hand to hand, voice to voice, fiddle to accordion, crumhorn to squeeze box and back again. Before the advent of recording, which means pretty much everything before the early twentieth century teens, the only way to hear anything traditional was to do so in person. Little was written down, most musicians couldn't read nor write anyway. Almost everything relied on memory. Performers would hear someone else singing, try to memorise the lyrics and how they went, and then recreate versions of their own. Melodies would alter, lyrics would be misremembered, misunderstood, forgotten. Changes would be made, bits added, bits taken away.

This process continued well after the advent of recorded music and mass literacy should have made the practice irrelevant. As late as the 1960s folk boom older songs were still being cannibalised to create new ones. Check the early work of Bob Dylan, for example, where new lyrics are bolted onto much older tunes[75]. Or the British genius guitarist Davy Graham who would mash together multiple melodies taken from a variety of sources, sometimes acknowledging them and at others not. Were these his songs or those of others? Did he put (*trad – arr. Graham*) on the label? Or simply (*Graham*)? He did both. In cases where Bob Dylan had put new lyrics onto earlier melodies he always claimed them as entirely his own.

So what is the song *The Knoxville Girl* about? A man returns home, takes his loving girl for a walk, by the river, along a garden path, discovers she has a roving eye, has been unfaithful, is about to be unfaithful, did him wrong, is too brazen for his taste, is somehow at lascivious fault. So he kills her. Takes up a stick and does her violently down. He goes home. There's blood all over his clothes. He blames a nose bleed. The traditional excuse. But he's caught, in the end, and imprisoned for his crime. In his cell he awaits the scaffold. And he pines for his Oxford, Wexford, Ekefield, Lexington, Pineville, Knoxville girl, the girl he loved so well.

Samuel Pepys had a copy. He was a collector of printed broadsheet ballads and had amassed more than eighteen hundred. Many were about murders including a version of 1685's *The Bloody Miller* containing a reference to what could be the song's real origin – the death by violence of one Anne Nichols, pregnant, at the hands of Francis Cooper, Miller's servant, of Hocstow, near Shrewsbury.

Slade, true to his journalist calling, tracks this event to the church where the murdered woman is buried and finds her name in the parish records of St Mary's Church, Westbury, Shropshire. *The Knoxville Girl* in all its variants runs in a bloody, five hundred year arc. Rural England to outback Appalachia, green and farm-filled Shropshire to Knoxville, a frontier town in Tennessee with a rough and ready reputation. It has been sung by everyone from Britain's Norma Waterson and Martin Carthy to Cleburne County Arkansas's primitive, broken-voice acapella vocalist Almeda Riddle.

I have to see the churchyard, naturally, to put myself inside the Knoxville girl's orbit. We drive there. Westbury is twenty minutes south-west of Shrewsbury. It's across flat Shropshire countryside, full of cold, dry air in the lee of the Welsh hills. St Mary's parish church goes back to at least the twelfth century. It's ancient structure has been given to falling down and being repaired, again and again. Spires have tumbled, roofs collapsed, doorways been blocked and unblocked, buttresses added, whole extensions created, windows broken and then restored. If this were a town house you wouldn't buy it for fear of subsidence or internal collapse.

Time here is held in a sort of fractured rural vortice. The churchyard, showing evidence of having once been totally round, is full of crumbling memorials. A hand out, sellotape-edged and bearing the legend "not to be taken away" is on a table inside. It tells me that they held wakes in the graveyard until 1283. Wakes were formally a celebration of the church's saint which involved much prayer and reverence.

Informally there was drinking, dancing, bull baiting and revelry.

Hard to imagine now, in the cemetery silence of the bereaved, stones all around. There's nothing here, either, earlier than about 1750. Nothing to show where the Knoxville Girl would have lain. Her 1693 burial is recorded only in the parish register. "Anne Nichols, truculenter occisa" i.e. violent death. Her grave marker was cleared in one of the Georgian reconstructions. Her murderer, Francis Cooper, would have been interred not here but elsewhere, in unhallowed ground. I walk the space to pick up the spirit, low sun striking through leaves. What do I expect? A shimmering of the air or great electric currents? There's nothing.

I return the church key to the village post office where it is held as a defence against random vandalism or village drunks and abusers sheltering inside from the rain. I hunt the car's meagre supply of music for Anne's song. Left it at home. Nearest I can discover is Oscar Isaac's reworking of Dave Van Ronk's traditional *Hang Me, Oh Hang Me* out of the Coen Brothers film *Inside Llewyn Davis*. "I wouldn't mind the hanging, but the laying in the grave so long…". Another traditional number bent by age and multiple transmission. Fits the spirit of what I'm tracking.

When that's done I put on The Everly Brothers' album, *Songs Our Daddy Taught Us*. This has been played so many times now that the in-car CD player can do it without a disc. Up comes *Down In The Willow Garden*, a song about the death of yet another lover with a roving eye. Murdered, this time, by knife wound with the body thrown in the river. The singer is there on the hangman's scaffold, still in love with his dear little girl, full of Appalachian mountain regret and remorse. Same source? Who can be sure?

Knoxville is a town of around 200,000 built at the confluence of three rivers. It was a Confederate town and is replete with Civil War sites. It's the largest place in East Tennessee. It houses the State University and in 1982 hosted the World's Fair, a thirty-year old victory that still resonates.

I'm travelling here because Knoxville is a choke point on the route up from the South to the clean, clear, green reaches of Appalachia. I've been through before, except you don't go through you go past – a spinning ring road that joyfully skirts the town, a sort of American take on Birmingham's spaghetti junction. Hurtling vehicles, high sides, hardly a gap between them, carriageways arriving and leaving on both sides with dazzling frequency.

Only this time I'm biting the bullet and entering the city itself to visit the Welsh writer Jon Manchip White. White has lived here for decades. One of his ancestors was the martyr Rawlins White, fisherman, ship captain, burned to death for his beliefs in St John's Square, Cardiff.

In his long life White has published upwards of thirty books but he's by no means the most famous of Knoxville's literary sons. That honour has to go novelist of horses, outcasts, apocalyptic vision and venomous heat Cormac McCarthy. McCarthy's books have been turned into films (*The Road, No Country For Old Men*) and been declared by the *New York Times* as among the greatest novels of the past quarter of a century (*Blood Meridian* in 2006).

In Market Square, Knoxville's civilised Jemma el-Fnaa, there's a McCarthy slab which extracts from his 1979 novel *Suttree*. This describes the square as it was in 1951. Full of blind singers, psalmists, street preachers "haranguing a lost world with a vigour unknown to the sane", farm trucks, the smell of feed everywhere, flower ladies in bonnets, "underlips swollen with snuff", fish sellers, gutters clogged with greenstuff. It's not like that now. There are men with wide street brushes, litter pickers, crisp clothed outside café tables, and air of civilised calm.

McCarthy no longer lives in Knoxville. After an early start he retreated, in true writer style, to a cabin in the Smoky Mountain foothills. He then moved on, fame pushed him, to New Mexico and the land described in that greatest of his works, *The Border Trilogy*. The first of these is a stunning novel of loss and wisdom and a vanished American age. *All The Pretty Horses*. Billy Bob Thornton directed the film of the same name in 2000. That same Billy Bob who recorded *Knoxville Girl* with The Boxmasters (see earlier). America is so vast and so full of serendipity.

Jon Manchip White was born in the Welsh capital, appropriately given his ancestry, to a family of ship captains and ship owners. He moved to America in the Sixties to become writer in residence at the University of Texas in El Paso and later to teach English as a Professor at the University of Tennessee in Knoxville. He married, took American citizenship and settled.

We meet at the top of the steps. Jon is tall with a white Hemmingway style moustache. He wears old man gabardine trousers with a belt which avoids half the loops, and sags round the waist. The legs end just that bit short over his brown and shiny shoes. His eyes are failing and he wears all-encompassing shades which make him look more like a land speed record attempter than Roy Orbison.

Despite thirty years as an American Jon has not adopted any kind of southern accent. And you'd think he would. "You get along better", he tells me, "if you sound European". We get the full Knoxville tour. The downtown, the outskirts, Indian Park along the Tennessee River, the University district, the civil war sites, the battlefields, who died, who shot whom, where they fell. Jon is an expert and we get detail in abundance including gingerly executed performances of how Brig. General William P Sanders died and pointings to just where artillery shells fell.

News headlines are everywhere. Earl is threatening. Hurricane Earl Empties Outer Banks. This Storm Is Going To Be The Big One. Take Care and Take Cover. "Should we be worried?" I ask. Jon shakes his head. "They exaggerate," he's sure.

At the East Tennessee Museum there's an exhibition of photographs of early Appalachia, its backwoods, wood huts, preachers and banjo players. All in faded, fractured sepia. There's a splendid photograph of Pastor Jimmy Morrow from Cooke County brandishing a poisonous snake. This has an extract from Mark 16:18 underneath – "Jesus said they shall take up serpents". But centrepiece of the show is a full-sized motorbike made from wood, carved by James Bunch from Monroe County with a pen-knife in 1996.

Outside on Market Square we watch the stage being rigged for that evening's concert. The Knoxville Jazz Orchestra will be there in full glory, a dinner-suited sixteen-piece in the Stan Kenton mould. They will swing with vigour and invention. Bluegrass would have held me or rockabilly made me stay but adding jazz to the mix of my adventures right now will simply complicate things. This music is, however, pretty much Jon's style. There he is in the heart of the bluegrass world, right on the main line that runs from banjo-picking Appalachia through countrified Nashville and on to the ends of rockabilly Tennessee and what music turns him on? New Orleans. Not that he's actually suggesting that we come back later to listen.

"I've got a great jazz collection," he tells me, "nothing later than Dizzy Gillespie. I like the stuff Philip Larkin did. Armstrong, King Oliver, Fats Waller, Sidney Bechet, and Bix. But I've no time to play any of it anymore and no place to store it, come to that. I'm putting it all on e-Bay. Slowly. Bit by bit. But it doesn't sell. Does anyone listen to real jazz anymore?"

Earl has been downgraded to a tropical storm, the radio informs us. But we may get some rain. The trees around us sway slowly. But the rain doesn't come.

Jon died in 2013. His final novel, *Rawlins White, Patriot to Heaven*, appeared in 2011.

21 • Asheville

The car is full of rising sun. There's western swing on the radio and the great open spaces of America are rolling past the windows. I'm travelling again. Who am I? Hugo Williams looking for Chuck Berry in *No Particular Place to Go*. Duncan McLean searching for Bob Wills in *Lone Star Swing*. Dos Passos on a freight car in *USA* looking for easier times. Kerouac chasing Cody Pomeroy. Everyone heading for Denver, for San Francisco, for Seattle, for Big Sur, for New Orleans. The road always moving. The fluid, shifting, American state of mind.

The radio is WKSF, Asheville's Kiss Country, broadcasting from Mount Pisgah, an almost 6000 feet eminence in the Blue Ridge Mountains and one I've actually been up, in another life, in an earlier time. I'm at the edge of WKSF's reach and the signal comes and goes with that fuzzy Doppler that makes it sound like Radio Luxembourg once did. The dj is playing a contemporary band called The Hot Club of Cowtown. Through the reception's crackle and fade, they sound just like Bob Wills.

Wills is the man who made dance music in that place where cowboys polka and gypsy jazz turns into *mariachi el Mexicano*. He added Stetsons and steel guitar and made it big in Texas. There was a time in America's pre-war years (and they had more of those than we did) when out west this up-tempo fiddle-driven house was pretty much all you heard. Duncan McLean spent a whole season in the nineties hunting across Texas. He was looking for traces of his hero, the long-dead purveyor of marimba blues with a western beat, Bob Wills, the King of Western Swing.

Wills died in 1975 but some of his band members and former

associates still hung on. Decrepit, aged beyond belief, worn by the sun and the past in equal measure they met with McLean. Reluctantly, eagerly, Alzheimer's leaking from their hands. They dragged out their ancient fiddle cases, found their pedal steels, cleared the ornaments off the pianos in their front rooms and gave our man a taste of how it once sounded, creaky old music with dust in its grooves. Swing swung. Like New Orleans Jazz sounded to my ears when I heard it first. That on my pensioner neighbour's 78-spinning wind-up gramophone when I was 8. He was keen to spark an interest in a boy who thought Rosemary Clooney singing *Mambo Italiano* on the radio was how it rocked, daddy-o.

Western Swing never had a UK high spot. Relegated to background parts in the occasional black and white western showing at the local suburban fleapit we were rarely exposed to this music's charms. It began in the hands of fiddle player Bob Wills and vocalist Milton Brown. Both were band leaders in the thirties. They took the Texas sounds of the singing cowboy and mixed them with hot jazz, southern blues and rocking Cajun. Dance drove the music. Jive, lindy hop, bop, jump. At times it can sound surprisingly like Benny Goodman[76] or one of the other kings of big band swing. At others it resembles Stephan Grappelli, Django Reinhardt and the Hot Club de Paris. Western swing had drums and horns, electric rhythm, steel guitars and clarinets. But up front were always the fiddles. Brown, who died young, might have rivalled Wills as the king but his absence left the founder of The Texas Playboys to wear the crown. And he did. This was good time music, easy to listen to, with plenty of finger snapping, foot tapping and throwing your partner around and around.

When The Texas Playboys tackle the tradition, on *Corrine, Corrina*, for example, what you get is swing beat rather than soulful blues. Their version is as far from Bob Dylan's folk recreation as you can possibly go. They did it first. Except when you delve you find they didn't. Bo Carter recorded the song in 1928, The Mississippi Sheiks in 1930. And they both would have heard it someplace before. By the time Milton Brown and His Musical Brownies took it on in 1934 the lyrics had changed but the melody, its tempo boosted, lingered. Wills revamped it again in 1940. Twenty years later Bob Dylan returned the song to its folk origins, mashing it up with other blues and, as Bob is wont to, changing parts of the melody and slowing it right down. But it was still basically the same song. *Corrina* hasn't yet the four hundred year reach of the *Knoxville Girl* (see Chapter 20) but it's on the right track.

The 40 crosses Douglas Lake and pushes on towards Newport. A port, up here where the Pigeon River and the French Broad have their headwaters? It seems just so. In the nineteenth century flat boats would ply their dangerous ways downstream and negotiate the Tennessee River (into which the Pigeon and the French Broad both empty) all the way to New Orleans. Newport, as small towns go, lacks the wide streets of Middle America. But it does have the telegraph poles with cable everywhere on show. There's a railtrack running right up East Main Street with a depot that has no platforms. At Dollar General there's plenty of root beer, shucked corn and cheese in spray-on cans. But no alcohol. Not even a can of lager. Sorry, son, we're a dry county. That one again.

Further on the land rises and the road narrows, even this one, the superfast interstate. It's the US A470[77] really, bending and turning its way through hillsides of rock and mile after mile of standing trees. The Hot Club of Cowtown, playing earlier, have gone to be replaced by Wills himself. Between messages from the sponsor, a dentist with an Asheville practise offering painless root canal, porcelain veneers and wisdom tooth extraction without fear, Wills does *The Waltz You Saved Me For* with sliding steel like this were Hawaii. I want him to yodel, to sound like Slim Whitman but he doesn't. Actually Wills doesn't sing either. He's old fashioned, he leads his band like Ted Heath did. With added yelps and ah-has. The singer is Tommy Duncan, Wills' employee. They put this record out as a single in 1947, year of my birth. It was unplayed by the BBC, why would they?

Asheville – if you live there you know this is North Carolina and the capital of the mountains. But if you come from another country then you mix it with Nashville, a place that is certainly not the same. Asheville clocks are an hour on or an hour back from where we've been. We crossed the timeline somewhere. A kink in the continuum. I recall seeing a sign but can't remember just where and in a place this vast it hardly matters when.

The town is clean and clear. The glaring swelter of the Tennessee plains have vanished to be replaced with dapple and soft glow. Asheville, the downtown of which isn't really that much larger than Pontypridd, has a reputation as a sort of American Glastonbury. A hippie high place in the east where the head shop flourishes and the zodiac still commands. Walking down Lexington Avenue I translate this place to Camden High Street circa 1970. Used goods stores, antique shops, bookstores, record dumps. There could be a Compendium Bookstore[78] here where I'd go in and Nick would buy from me by the dozen the latest *second aeon*. Outside reggae would leak from doorways and rastas would drift on dope's magic smoke. End walls would light with murals. Sun rises, psychedelically swirled. The Buddha emblazoned. *International Times*' doe-eyed girl, bandana holding back her locks, shining like gold.

In cheese cloth shirts and worn to thread jeans new millennium passers recall what once was, and up here clearly still is. Asheville holds on to the other way of seeing things, of alternatives, joss stick knick-knackery, pyramid future telling, I-Ching decisions, thonged leather, dark glasses against capitalism's secret glow. Two guys with battered guitars (and here I mean battered – banged to hell and then emblazoned with marijuana-leaf stickers surrounded by right on man slogans in bright primary colours) strum on a street corner. Incredible String Band? Nope. Bluegrass, old tyme mountain music, what else?

We're staying at a B&B. But unlike those establishments in, say, south Devon, where there's never any sauce to go with your bacon, and you've got to be out on the street by 9.30 am and not return until 5.00, the American equivalent is of a different order. Joe and LaDonna welcome us to their grand colonial revival mansion on East Chestnut Street with a swirl of chocolate. Chocolate is in the driving seat here. It's everywhere. There's not a bowl, a surface, a bed pillow, a chair arm nor shelf that is not replete with packed and wrapped choco delights, all strewn in abundance for b&b guests.

We get the Wall Street Room which has a four poster bed plus canopy. Plastic flowers wind up the corner pillars. Velvet drapes and hanging curtains soften every edge. Downstairs LaDonna, wearing the sort of expensive high fashion that only women of a certain age ever manage, serves breakfast. This is advertised as a Candle Light Gourmet Southern Breakfast and is accompanied by southern piano muzak drifting in from speakers out there hidden behind the choco mountains. We get three-cheese frittatas, pumpkin waffles with orange walnut butter and French toast doused with apricots. The guy opposite me sitting with his overlarge wife says he's a marine, here for a break. He repairs Harriers. "You Brits certainly invented a real good one there".

I'm asked what I do. If I say I'm a writer then they'll all want to know what it is I'm currently working on. Dangerous territory. Never talk about the present project for fear of infection. Talk it up and you'll never get it down. Writing is full of quarks. They go quietly about their business but ask them what they are up to and they get resentful and change. I could tell the assembled company that I'm a poet. This usually silences people. On the other hand some simply draw breath and start talking about Dylan Thomas and say they, too, knew a Thomas someplace but that person never wrote a thing. I end up saying that I'm in publishing. As usual this diverts the conversation into a discussion about e-books and how easy it is to read great literature these days and to do so without paying a thing. Not paying. How the middle class get on.

Out on the street I discover that Asheville could pretty easily make claim to be the second hand record capital of the western world. I'd always thought that our surplus vinyl twelve inchers had all been shipped to reclamation dumps in the third world. There have to be abandoned millions of these vinyl dinner plates now that the CD has replaced them and, indeed, has itself been replaced by various sorts of digital download approximations. I imagined, in fact I'm pretty sure I didn't imagine but I actually read, that there are villages in Africa consisting almost entirely of vinyl. LP sleeve walls, vinyl roofs, albums burned on stoves for cooking, men searching through the stacks outside, hunting for the picture disc rarity that might turn them a USD on eBay.

Instead they are here. Filling the entire basement of a store back of Main Street, unopened crates by the hundred, topped with boxes with their ends ripped and removed. These reveal the massed black plastic music inside. I scrabble a bit, struck in awe by the sheer size of the operation. I feel like I felt when I first entered the Hermitage in St Petersburg (then Leningrad, God that was so long ago). There was so much on offer, so many wonders, that I couldn't cope. Instead I blanked. Stopped. Turned round and went back outside where I could at least breathe. I feel like that now. Touch a box, see inside pretty much everything from your musical life in twelve inch slices. Lonnie Donegan, The Rolling Stones, John Cage, Dion, Terry Riley, Lou Reed, Gene Clark, Gram Parsons, The Mothers of Invention, Commander Cody, Tiny Tim, Bo Diddley is a Gunslinger, Mario Lanza sings. And sings. And sings. There's one assistant drinking coffee. He's sitting behind what looks like an unfolded wallpaper pasting table with a cash box and a newspaper. There's no background music playing. I'm the only customer.

I can't handle this. If I gathered wonders to me what would I do with them? Lug them round north America for the rest of the trip then pay extra air weight to get them home? I was never ever resolute enough to be a real collector, one who'd go after complete runs of a single artist or seek out specific rare items – gold label, special edition sleeve, misnumbered advance copy – things like that. The Beatles *White Album* on white vinyl with "Whil My Guitar Gently Weeps" misprinted; Frank Ballard's *R&B Party* on Phillips International; a first pressing of the *Great White Wonder* bootleg, with no stamp on the label. These things were here, no doubt, but I'd never find them because it would take me weeks.

Instead I buy a single item, souvenir of the occasion, something to get me back out on the street without losing face. I choose *Root Boy Slim and The Sex Change Band*. This is an album I once owned back in the early psychedelic boogie-driven seventies but have long lost. Root Boy was actually Foster McKenzie III, born here in Asheville and a permanent thorn in the side of whatever system he happened to be engaged with at the time – scholarship, employment, friendship, the market for dope. He made a clutch of heavyish psychedelic rock albums during the seventies, including this 1978 classic, and then died of overdose in 1993 at the age of forty-seven. His success, even in the land of his birth, was highly limited. He's buried in Fletcher, just south of Asheville on the 26.

A little further on, Root Boy under my arm, I find more. Record stores on corners offering bluegrass and hillbilly roots, Ricky Skaggs, Del McCoury, The Steep Canyon Rangers, Creek Dippers, Blue Highway. Asheville might be the Height Ashbery of the mountains but it certainly hasn't bought into the swirling of psychedelia. In fact the town seems to dislike the new – even the old new – preferring music you make like you did decades before. String driven, pick and strum.

At Jack Of The Wood, a self-styled Celtic Pub that, with no irony whatsoever, offers a full range of English ales, Hillbilly and Irish music mix pretty much as they do right across Appalachia. We get Mrs Doyle from Macon County sitting in a circle with her accompanists offering old tyme done on double bass, banjo, guitar and harmonica. She's followed by Timberwinds, a local bluegrass outfit who up the tempo but still don't offer drums. Round me in the large rustic bar people who most of the time never drink beer at all have great yawning pints in front of them. It's what you do when you are on holiday. This is a visitors town.

Asheville is known for its music festivals. The sadly defunct Belle Chere. Shindig on the Green. The Mountain Dance and Folk Festival. Long weekends of roots music that fill the mountain air. But not while I'm here. Story of my unplanned life.

On the street again I check if there's anyone famous I've missed. Doc Watson's accompanist David Holt is a resident. Robert Moog who invented the world changing synthesiser was born here. But Asheville's most famous son is the novelist Thomas Wolfe. The first one. He's more or less the inventor of autobiographical fiction and one of the towering giants of American twentieth century lit. He was brought up in a rambling wooden house owned by his parents on Spruce Street. There he wrote *Look Homeward Angel*. In this work he styled Asheville as Altamont and the house itself as Dixieland. The book sprawled its way through forty chapters. *Look Homeward Angel* inspired, among many, the young Jack Kerouac. He used its impetus and lightly shrouded fictional style as a basis for his own early prose works, *The Sea Is My Brother* and *The Town and the City*. Little wonder that Kerouac, master of speed (user of speed), the man who wrote his best known novel on a single roll of teletype paper, could never be described as brief. Even his haiku, the three line Japanese form, were rolled out in great sequences that seemed never to end[79].

The Wolfe house, the Old Kentucky Home, where Wolfe lived among the boarders his mother took in to pay their way is now a museum. It was one third burned down in 1998 with fifteen per cent of the contents lost. Arson. Someone threw a fire bomb through a window and the ensuing conflagration managed to damage every single room. Fifteen years on and still no one has been caught. There's a significant reward held in escrow for information leading to a conviction. Thomas Wolfe hater, how can that be?

But they've done the restoration. The men in white coats moved in and did the walls with Zissner Bullseye, an odour-blocking primer paint, and wiped every surface with deodorising cloth. New timbers, new linens. Raised the cash by selling Thomas Wolfe souvenirs. I buy a yo-yo with his name on it. Check the programme to see upcoming readings and talks in profusion. A house of literature. Dylan Thomas's Boat House without the writing shed.

Wolfe's main productive period largely co-incided with the great depression. In a short career he wrote four novels and dozens of short stories, novellas, and plays. His problem was always length. He overwrote and his first editor, Maxwell Perkins, at Scribner worked hard to reduce him to manageable size. So hard, in fact, that Wolfe switched publishers in 1936 resenting the way his work had been, to his mind, inappropriately cut. The submitted script for his first book was 1100 pages. The published version was half that. Despite this his new editor at Harper Brothers, Bernard DeVoto, received a million word manuscript from an unrepentant author in 1938. An average novel runs to about a sixth of that. This was just before Wolfe headed west on a tour of the national parks. He never returned. While visiting Seattle he was diagnosed with miliary tuberculosis of the brain. Unfixable. He died a few months before his thirty-eighth birthday. He's buried in Asheville, up the road from Root Boy Slim.

Back at LaDonna's I try out the yo-yo. It has a picture of the writer on one side and the address of the house on the other. I used to be able to make these things spin out sideways, shoot up above me and then roll, walking the dog, across the floor. Learned as a kid. The Wolfe model unwinds slowly towards the carpet and then falls and disappears under the bed. I'm left holding a piece of string. Luckily I've also bought *Look Homeward, Angel* as a large format paperback. Only edition they had. I read instead. Later I stuff it in the back of my case where it takes up the space of at least furteen albums. It's what we do for great lit.

22 • The Blue Ridge Mountains

Higher up in the hills it becomes harder and harder to work out just where we are. The roads bend and turn along lines of least resistance, lacing themselves through places with names as utilitarian as the settlers who left them. Groundhog Creek, Carolina Prong, Barnes Hollow, Rocky Bottom. These are hard lands where staying alive itself is a challenge. You succeed by farming the hollows, logging, hunting, moonshining your way through prohibition or by hacking out coal in the region's mines. For a long time Appalachia was where the frontier was. It was an untrammelled wilderness up beyond the fertile lowlands. It was a place where you expected the harshness, the rugged difficulty, and that schizophrenia associated with those who could manage a life which daily mixed destitution with lonely joy.

The myths of this country are almost as large as the country itself. You can see Davy Crocket in his coonskin hat sliding through the undergrowth. The *Beverly Hillbillies'* Jed Clampett is there again with a mad look in his eye, hauling moonshine from the still. Men in half-mast pants and check shirts clog dance solo on a single spot. Behind every tree stands an Indian with a bow or a musket or a knife. Shawnee, Cherokee, Mingo. There are no real ghosts for this is and always was protestant country. But the rolling mist among the trees, the smoke of the Blue Ridge Mountains, leavens the air with unease.

Today Appalachia has found a new purpose. Like much of Britain the land is now a museum. It's a tourist attraction, a multi-state national park full of hiking trails, hunting runs, white-water rafting and silver rivers stuffed with fish. Visitors to what was once called the Alleghenies but is now universally known as Appalachia come to find what traces they can of the old mountain life, of the banjos being plucked amid the greenness and shucked corn sold hot and buttered, on sticks.

The music itself has been tamed. Those songs and tunes which came from Ireland, Scotland, Wales and England have all been categorised and recorded over and over. They now belong to the world. Today practitioners do not need to live anywhere near the Appalachians. There is no requirement for them to have met Doc Watson, Samantha Bumgarner or Frank Proffitt or to know anything really about their lives. How they made their music. How they came to sing and play as they did. Appalachian Mountain Music revivalists can come from places right outside the Union. They can sit in their circles in distant Europe or Australasia and play just like Lester Flatt, note for note.

Appalachian mountain music has a touch of the history of the Cornish language about it. That Welsh-like tongue had a last speaker in fish-seller Dolly Pentreath. She died in 1777 and took the language with her. Centuries later cultural activists brought the whole semantic apparatus back from the grave. They picked up its dusty DNA from books and letters and began speaking the language again. Their revival enthused a stream of fans. In the 2011 census 557 people, a proportion living well outside the county of Cornwall itself, declared Cornish to be their main tongue. Several thousand other enthusiasts claimed an ability to use simple phrases. Cornish, if not quite world-beating, is certain once again alive. The whole edifice, however, creaks with artifice. It is based on supposition and memory, on cultural fanaticism and a desire to be different. No bad thing in an increasingly Starbucks-on-every-corner homogenous world.

No Starbucks here in the mountains however. The only coffee you get is that pale brown gloop they keep in pots on the stoop at cheap motels. If you can find one of those. In Appalachia, if you want a drink, you bring your own.

We're on the Blue Ridge Parkway now. This is a tourist highway where multi-axle vehicles are banned. There are no sales of Gatorade along the roadside, no advertising hoardings or turn offs for motels and fuel and all that fried chicken super-sized fast food that dominates the interstates. The Parkway is a 500-mile stretch of simple two-lane blacktop. It has no intersection cross-traffic and barely any directional signs. It runs through Virginia and North Carolina following the ridge of the Blue Ridge Mountains, after which it is named.

And on that Ridge, driving up near the sky, you get a different sort of local, the Harley-riding silver surfers. All smoothness and style. No oil or frayed denim – everything is expensive perfection. Tooled-leather panniers, Range-Rider Indian fringed jackets, headbands, shades. They don't buzz you, these ancients. At their age they've nothing left to prove. With the eagles they glide. I pull in at an overlook, a lay-by with a view. Deep Gap Overlook stares down on a cavernous hollow that's full of trees. In the distance little moves. I listen hard for the spooky sound of claw-hammer plucked banjos but don't hear a thing.

The town we reach, if it is a town, is called Hot Springs. Clutched in the confluence of the French Broad River and Spring Creek it's the only place with spa waters in the whole of North Carolina and only the second in the entire Eastern States. In 1791 William Nelson bought the springs for "two hundred pounds in Virginia currency[80]" and began catering for visitors. In 1837 Asheville entrepreneur James Patton built the first hotel and encouraged a rush of health seekers up from the cities looking for relief from their ailments. He had 350 rooms and a dining hall that could seat 600. They called it Patton's White House. It was big enough. The springs fixed anything, if you read the literature. Pretty much as they did at the Victorian-era Welsh spa towns of Llandrindod, Llangammarch or Llanwrtyd. The lame, the halt, the cancerous, the bad-skinned, the infirm, the poor of breath and weak of mind. Those suffering from depression, from frailty of any kind.

The hotel burned down in 1884. Conflagration would be a future feature of this place. At that time the town was known only as Warm Springs. In 1886 a surfacing aquifer of higher temperature was discovered prompting a town rebrand further up the thermometer. Hot Springs it became, a much more marketable place. The hotel was rebuilt, known in this iteration as the Mountain Park. A mere two hundred rooms but of high quality the brochure assured. The cures it offered were extensive[81]. But in the new century it fell on hard times.

It unaccountably burned to the ground again. Two further hotels were built and for a time both traded well enough but eventually both succumbed to the Hot Spring's curse: conflagration and insurance claim.

By the time I arrive in the new millennium all that's left are the baths themselves. These are set out along the riverside in rickety but freshly-painted compartments. They are operated by a young woman in a doctor-style white cotton coat who smiles non-stop. You can take a Jacuzzi filled with water rich in calcium, radium and lithium, get your batteries recharged, and mop yourself down next to the French Broad. I try and emerge after 30 mins of swirling exposure a new man. No more general physical debility and mental exhaustion for me. I'm cured.

Cecil Sharp came to Hot Springs. There's a sign commemorating the fact near the Post Office. "Balladry. English folklorist Cecil Sharp in 1916 collected ballads in the 'Laurel Country'. Jane Gentry, who supplied many of the songs, lived here." It says all this atop a pole. Sharp was the founder of the English Folk Dance and Song Society and an avid collector and transcriber of folk tunes. His method, like many others in these days before tape and digital recorders, was to write down what he heard, lyric and melody, and eventually publish the results. What he was interested in – at least as far as his American adventures went – was tracking the transition of song and melody from original Irish, Scottish and English sources to their new homes in the high Appalachians.

Sharp was, and still is, a controversial figure. He began his lifelong interest in folk song and dance after witnessing morris dancing in action in a village outside Oxford, in 1899. At the time the morris tradition was fading and traditional English folk tunes were rarely played. Sharp began to collect, to notate both music and dance and to publish his results. His work led to a revival among new enthusiasts. Morris dancing and its accompanying music began to be heard in towns and places where it had never been heard before.

The controversy lay in Sharp's approach to education. For the newly emerging state school system Sharp published versions of his collected traditional English folk music bowdlerised so as not to offend to ears of the young. He also set his songs for piano and added parts to allow for choral singing. Traditional English folk music at the time was almost always performed unaccompanied. Sharp's interference had lasting effect. As late as the 1950s British schools still included what they imagined to be traditional songs in their curricula. These were arranged bizarrely for dozens of pupils to dismally sing together while their teachers plonked accompaniment on their slightly out of tune pianos. No fingers were ever stuck in anyone's ears. No bloody murders were recalled, there were no double entendres, no loves desperately lost or won. All was sweetness and artificially bright.

Sharp's visits to America, and he came more than once, trailed this controversy with him. Was he a genuine preserver of tradition or, for ideological reasons, a manipulator of what he found? He toured Appalachia at the time of the Great War in the company of his collaborator Maud Karpeles. What he discovered amazed him. Not only did he find the traces of traditional songs he had first encountered in his collecting tours of England but he also recorded variants, some of them wild variants, in both lyric and melody. English, Irish and Scottish folk was indeed a basis of Appalachian Mountain Music, but one that had been thoroughly mashed in the processes. Nothing changes traditional music like the oral tradition.

The significance of his work and its enormous achievement was eventually established in 1932 (Sharp died in 1924) when Maud Karpeles published *English Folk Songs From The Southern Appalachians*. It contained 325 songs drawn from 968 variants. In Hot Springs Sharp had met Jane Gentry who had given him 64 songs, the most he collected from any single singer. *Lord Randal, Little Musgrave, Barbara Allen, The Wagoner's Lad, Pretty Saro, Come All Ye Fair And Tender Ladies, Black Is The Colour, John Hardy, Pretty Peggy O* – they are all in his book.

Sharp's work is a towering achievement. This despite his negative views of blacks encountered on his journeys, his expurgation of the English tradition and his right wing leanings in an increasingly left orientated world. The British musicologist Michael Yates has written extensively about Sharp in America in *Collecting In The Appalachians* for the periodical *Folk Music Journal*[82].

Five miles up the road is the cabin. A place to take stock and to write up my notes. It's on the edge of a clearing, full of heat and burned grass and made entirely of wood. These hills are thick with such cabins. You can buy them off the peg and erect them in a long day. But the ones that command the higher rentals are those that seem made from the trees that surrounded them, the ones the owner has built himself. Two rooms, balcony, barbeque, TV that won't get a signal, small library containing works by Eric Newby, Jonathan Raban and Bill Bryson. And out front a two person Jacuzzi, watch the green with a drink in hand, our own personal hot spring. I'll be superman by the time I get home. I pull down *A Walk In The Woods*, and, bourbon in hand, immerse myself. Above me the sky is a dome.

The Appalachian Trail is a long distance path like no other. Longer than Pembrokeshire (186 miles), the Wales Coastal (870), even Land's End to John O'Groats (1200). This one is a mind-zapping 2150 and people walk it. They do the whole thing. Trail through walkers who stride the whole path. Not in one go, obviously, but they do it. For some it's an American national obsession.

The trail winds its way from Springer Mountain in Georgia to Mount Hatahdin in Maine. It was the idea of Benton Mackaye, a forester. The trail opened in 1937. It took the Brits a few more years to replicate the idea. The Pennine Way opened in 1965. At 267 miles this track along England's back isn't exactly a walk in the park but set against the Appalachian Trail it certainly pales. And the AT passes right through Hot Springs.

Walking it, well sampling it might be a better term, puts into stark contrast the differences between the USA and the UK. Access back home is climb on pretty much anywhere you want. Look up the walk on the OS map and then drive up the nearest lane, park on the verge and go. Here access is via sparsely scattered trail heads where you leave a written record of your departure. Just in case you're never seen again, leg broken, fallen into some gully, killed by hornets, eaten by bears, abducted by aliens.

Bryson's plan was to walk it all. The whole two thousand mile deal. He'd do it in order to learn about himself and about America, to become self-reliant and with that much walking going on he'd also become svelte and strong. He'd do it south to north, start in the

Georgia springtime and always be just ahead of the weather. He'd go well equipped with, as he puts it, a whole wardrobe in a pack on his back. He'd have high-tech wearables, mountain trousers replete with "70-denier high-density abrasion-resistant fly with a ripstop weave". Not only that but he'd also travel with a companion. His friend Stephen Katz, an overweight recovering alcoholic.

The pair begin in good spirit but it's obvious that they might well have overreached themselves. Katz has brought with him everything any wilderness walker could ever need, plus spares. The weight is excessive. As they go he reduces his by abandoning articles at first by leaving them carefully behind bushes and eventually simply by throwing them away. Anything to cut down the red-faced exhausted burn that comes from an unfit person slogging mile after mile under unceasing leaves.

They do well, nonetheless, and get themselves right out of Georgia and well into North Carolina. But there distress and desperation overcome them. They cop out. Right there at Clingman's Dome, the highest peak in the whole of Appalachia. They slip off the trail and slink down the blacktop to sample the pleasures of the nearest town, Gatlinburg.

Gatlinburg. Once you've been there you never forget. Bryson reports that it's a much more popular destination than the park itself, a place that provides everything the Smoky Mountains do not – crazy golf, bad cheeseburgers, overpriced sodas, the Elvis Presley Hall of Fame, Gatlinburg Space Needle, a Hillbilly Village, a Mysterious Mansion, a place doing country music, poorly, I could go on. Bryson does.

And where do I access the trail, to walk in the great man's footsteps? Newfound Gap, right on the state line. Eight miles up from Clingman's Dome, the place from which Bryson and Katz slunk. I'm there walking the trail he did on pretty much the only section around here that he didn't actually cover[83] in his book.

Walking the AT is not the same as, say, the Cotswold Way, although these two walks in the woods have one thing in common – trees. That's all you see. Trees above you, by your sides and their debris under your boots. Green and then green again. Nothing else to look at, no views of anything much other than further branches. Only in the Cotswolds there are gaps. Through these you can glimpse long barrows, iron age forts, golf clubs, castellated follies, butterfly reserves and monumental stone needles. The historical detritus of civilisation.

On the AT there is none of this. Best you'll get is an oak in a run of pine or a handbill tacked to a poll warning against lighting fires. A slog it might be but it delivers enormous satisfaction. I'm nearer the sun here than anywhere in the UK. This is the new world where everything is similar but nothing is quite the same. Leaf shape, small animals, birds. Things here have shifted slightly, there are variations in multiple form, much like the Appalachian ballads Sharp so diligently collected.

I slip on the headphones and listen to my chosen route soundtrack. Makes the journey cinematic. Round the corner will be monsters, the English in red coats, coon hunters, madmen with bowie knives, wolves, eagles, snakes. I've chosen Harry Smith's *Anthology of American Folk Music*, a collection of field and ancient backwoods recordings that for many of us offered our first glimpse of the extent of all this new world ancient material. Sister Clara Hudson's *Stand By Me*, Uncle Dave Macon's *Wreck of the Tennessee Gravy Train*, and then, with beautiful synchronicity The Hackberry Ramblers doing *In The Forest*, (actually *Jolie Blonde* with different words, recorded in New Orleans in 1938, but I don't let that worry me.)

When the set is done I ramble on in silence. Insects. Sound of the sun above me somewhere, heating up the leaves. Walking is indeed tai chi's total meditation, a place where the head clears simply because the world transiting around it sucks the mind's dross away. You become transparent. You are in a place where breath understands every single thing.

Going up the trail under the trees I let the mind compose. There are flakes of light falling through the leaves, like leaves themselves. Below the boots are mud and roots.

Walking the trail vs thinking about it. Sweating vs reading Bryson on the stoop. Being part of the world vs watching from the distance. No contest is there? And that Jacuzzi will be waiting for me when I get back.

23 • Pigeon Forge

Walking the road I'm on is not the safest thing to do. Given the city propensity for the lording of the car over any other form of locomotion walking can become a suicidal act. I have exited Big Dogs and stand in the parking lot with my purchase in my hand. An eight-inch bowie knife and half a dozen plastic harmonicas in various keys all housed in a cheap presentation box. The ideal gift. Stab and wail. $4. The knife turns out to be blunt and the harmonicas, the reason I made the purchase, are all hopelessly out of tune. The deal was closed by a man in a check shirt who said how y'all and smiled through tobacco-stained teeth. Pigeon Forge, city of the brash, a commercialised strip along the Smoky Mountain highway, cheap enough to brighten the lives of the poorest vacationer. It's a rolling sprawl of badly decorated prefabs, erected without the aid of architects. These are structures imagined by owners on jotter-pads and handed to companies of jobbing builders, Marlborough men with their orange boots and belted tool pouches, drills and hammers rather than guns.

Pigeon Forge by the Little Pigeon River. When I first saw the name on the map it had a resonance which has been totally belied by the reality. You are expecting old time banjo player Frank Profitt, you get larger than life Noddy Holder. The birds once here were passenger pigeons. Huge swarms that darkened the sky. Across the plains they flew in flocks that contained millions. They clustered in the valley cut by the Little Pigeon River. Nineteenth century wonders. Hunted to extinction by settlers.

The Forge made iron. Isaac Love started one here in the early years of the nineteenth century. It produced sponge iron and, on the wild frontier where the Cherokee still raided, made its operator a good enough living. Before that all there'd been was a stockade and a bunch of trappers and fur traders, men brave enough to seek a life where the devil held the upper hand and the Cherokee took full advantage. It was Cherokee land, after all. Their trails and warpaths criss-crossed the forests and their towns and camps clustered among the trees. What did the marauding Europeans expect? A welcome?

No sign of Indians now. Although there's a Christian dating operation that offers enquirers the chance to find God's Match and meet suitable Native American singles. Right here in Pigeon Forge. Non-denominational, Pentecostal, Southern Baptist. You choose.

The parking lot is one I've reached by chance or, actually, leaped into as a respite from the bumper to bumper autos cruising the main artery. That highway stuffed with gawpers, mom and pop, kids in baseball hats, teens fingering their smart phones, all checking for the next big, artificial sensation. Big Dogs offers all I'd want if I were a sportsman with an eye for never taking part. Graphic tees are a speciality. "I started out with nothing & I still have most of it left". "When I read about the evils of drinking I gave up reading". "I totally agree with myself". Along with a whole raft of further scholarly wonders. $18 a crack, offered in almost any colour you'd ever want.

In a sense the tees signal the flavour of this place. They are flags for an enfranchised but hopeless elite. For those with enough wherewithal to get themselves here in their cruisers but intellectually challenged after that. On the other hand this lurid township has to be something everyone should experience. Even if that's just to see how money can be made. Never underestimate the depths to which taste can fall. Never oversell anything when lukewarm, pale brown, caffeineless and served in a paper cup will do.

Nothing much happened here for almost a hundred and fifty years after Isaac Love established that fortuitous foundry where the Pigeon Forge Old Mill now stands. There were exchanges with the Native Americans. A few houses were constructed. Easteners up from the civilised coast arrived to take the waters. In a nineteenth century age when medicine was not that far from believing in blood, phlegm and bile the prospect of a wade in the Little Pigeon River curing your ailments was hard to resist. An all-embracing God arrived in the form of the Methodists who held revivals which went on for weeks.

As late as the 1950s Pigeon Forge was still a backwater on the way to pretty much nowhere. Despite President Coolidge having established the Great Smoky Mountains National Park in 1934 it took much longer for the town to get up to speed. It wasn't until new access roads were constructed and nearby Gatlinburg and Sevierville had ballooned as far as their geography would allow them that the expansion of Pigeon Forge was begun.

The place has the feel of a seaside resort with no salt water, no coast, and no place to promenade. Just roads and inland sprawl. It's a low density cluster that rolls the highway almost as far as the valley goes. After the mill with its wheel strutting its stuff in the river there's no history. No piles of stones, old walls, sites of. Not a single mark on the ground. What's here that anyone, just anyone, might want?

The Tomb Egyptian Adventures, The Smoky Mountain Shaggers (shag music from 7.00 am until late), Ripley's Aquarium of the Smokies, Parrot Mountain Garden of Eden, Professor Hacker's Lost Treasure Golf, The Titanic (yes, it's here, almost full size, and sinks daily), Cupid's Romantic Gifts, Southern Belle Lid'l Dolly's Dresses and Matching Accessories Factory Shop, Adventure Park Ziplines (fly over the city on a piece of wire), The Lumberjack Feud Dinner Show (watch them fight with hatchets and saws while you eat), Jurassic Jungle Boat Ride, Hollywood Wax Museum (open 365 days a year, meet Santa on Christmas day itself, such unbounded thrills), Elvis Museum and Gift Shops (what you didn't see in Memphis and Tupelo then you can certainly see here), The Rockin' Raceway, Wonderworks (a house built completely upside down), The Great Smoky Mountain Wheel (as big as the London Eye), plus any number of diners, outlet stores, remainder shops, candy stores, coke retailers, burger bars, Western apparel stores, and train, car, plane and boat rides for all and any ages. Hard to imagine what's missing. You can feel the blood rising as you gaze upon it. Pigeon Forge keep me from getting bored with life. You will.

Central Pigeon Forge, if the town can be said to have a definable centre, hosts at least thirty churches. The greater Pigeon Forge area has more than 160. That's a quantity of pews but then we are in the Bible Belt, heart of, with nearby Nashville as the buckle. God is in the soil. I should have known this, recognising the signs as I drove myself among the attractions spread out along the four lanes of the US 441 scenic highway that defines the town. There's the Gospel Magic Shop which sells a spiked coin that delivers you from evil, a forgiving God's rope that gets cut and then returns whole, mystic gospel beads that keep you free from sin, and the Which Way Card Deck which proves with certainty that God can turn you round. This whole retail operation is supported by the Emerald City Ministries. That should have been a hint. So too should the Smoky Mountain Christian Village which offers wholesome sacred spaces, football tables and hot tubs just off Goldrush Road. I might also have noticed the outrageously vast Christian Book Outlet Centre on the 441 itself. This warehouse around the size of an average British branch of B&Q offers more books about the Bible than there are words in the Bible itself. Feel the printed spirit here in the Smokies. Branches also at nearby Sevierville, Gatlinburg, Knoxville and other surrounding towns. Shedloads. Who, out there, is buying this stock?

The branch I ambled into, attracted by the surrealist sight of such an intellectual activity as literature here among the glare and gash of the Pigeons, lured me with out-front shelves of remaindered pop fiction at knock down prices. The monumentally huge Christian core stock was racked behind. Among the cheapo front of store magnets were hard-backed copies of my Cardiff neighbour, poet and sailor Gwyneth Lewis's *Two In A Boat*. Offered at a dollar and half. A tale of Wales and the watery world beached here in evangelical inland Tennessee. Spotting it I felt as if I had come upon a cut price version of the Mandan Indians[84]. Although, as everybody knows now, America was actually discovered by Islamic explorers three centuries before Columbus[85].

Why is this such a Christian land? Given America's history of native removal, rebellion, revolution and whole world-embracing immigration it all seems unlikely. Yet here it is and I'm at its teeming heart: the Southern Bible Belt that runs throughout the Dixie states. Texas, Oklahoma, Kansas, Georgia, Alabama, Virginia, the Carolinas,

Kentucky and beyond. This isn't Catholic or hard-faced mainline Protestant but hot Baptist, Methodist and Revivalist evangelical country. God counts but so does charisma. Here the things that lead are the literalness of the Bible, the need to find faith and not have it thrust upon you, to be baptised by immersion in water (being christened as a baby doesn't count), plus, naturally, the requirement to tell the whole world the truth, to seek converts, to celebrate the Lord by singing his praises as loudly and as often as you can. It's old fashioned Republican country. Conservative, moral, a place where you follow the rules. On Sunday you wear a tie even if that's cowboy bootlace. In fact it's pretty often cowboy bootlace. Ah God, he loves such things.

The history of Southern Protestantism is a vast subject and I'm intrigued. I usually am in places where God or his fellow travellers come near to the surface. Why here where there's slowness and heat? What does this deity propose to save and/or change in the world? And ultimately, in a place where darkness drifts and the future is a sea where the atoms have ceased to move, does any of this actually matter?

Like many other Western democracies, countries where Catholicism no longer holds sway (or is under threat), the Bible Belt has gone through a number of great renewals. Great restorations. Great resumptions. There have been times of mass redemption and fervour led by protestant evangelicals who could drug colossal crowds simply by the sound of their own voices and the power of their conviction. Across the Bible Belt there have been at least four such awakenings. The first were the Frontier Revivals of around 1730. These were led by Jonathan Edwards and preached to the already Godly. The most recent were the Charismatic outpourings of the 1960s. These took on the saved and the unchurched in equal number. They were fronted by Billy Graham, Oral Roberts, Jimmy Swaggart, Jerry Falwell and other media and money-aided larger than life preacher men.

For a long time the South has been a land of tented revivals, hysteria-driven declarations of belief before great crowds, fainting, speaking in tongues, receiving the fire of faith as it flowed through the very air. There's a pattern. Economic boom leads to excess. Excess breeds those things society finds hardest to deal with – the familiar targets of churches down the ages – intemperance, impropriety, immorality.

"Whiskey and women", as John Lee Hooker encapsulates it. Such things have to be resisted and the world once again put right.

This is a place where the Church flourishes. There are more per head of population in this area than anywhere else in America. They range from clapboard, hillside huts large enough for 30 or so to gather to the super-churches of the cities where congregations can reach tens of thousands. The South was once the stronghold of slavery and also a believer in the Confederacy rather than the Republic. In the civil war they lost. Some have never forgotten.

For all the differences there are between southern blacks and southern whites this region of former settlers and slaves is profoundly religiously homogenous when compared to the rest of North America. The Indians were cleared early and there were few mass immigrations from Catholic Europe and further afield, as there was, for example, in the mid-west and in the north. As historian of American religion Randall Stephens explains "Though Judaism has long had a presence in the South, it never thrived as it did in the urban North. Catholicism, too, remained isolated to certain quarters. That homogeneity lent itself to the evangelical surge or the creation of the Bible Belt[86]".

White and black do not today use the same churches. They might have begun together in the times of the original plantations. Both, then, followed a mainstream version of the religion of the colonizer: Anglicanism. But the rising Baptist evangelical tide saw separation. Following emancipation black Christians viewed their religion as a component part of the black exodus from slavery. They wanted black pastors in their pulpits, speaking their language. Same Christian beliefs, different shades. Today there are approximately eight million Black American Baptists and the religion flourishes.

In the UK, a country that was once the heart of religious conformity and where once Christianity drove all aspects of daily life it's hard to comprehend American belief now that our own is diminished. While we see churches attended by handfuls of the elderly America sees God in all things. Seventy-three per cent of the American population have declared themselves Christian. While crossing the South and trying to understand what I see and hear I need to remember this.

Religious belief surfaces in American roots music constantly. God-fearing country singers are legion. In fact, given the local demographic, it's pretty much the case that your career will not go anywhere unless you have let God into what you sing. Faith Hill, Keith Urban, George Strait, Dolly Parton, Randy Travis, Johnny Cash, Willie Nelson, Vince Gill, LeAnn Rimes, The Judds along with just about everyone else who has ever recorded in Nashville has at some point allowed God to surface in their work. Some country gospel singers record little else and have established for themselves a niche market of growing size.

Then there are the slightly more fervent bluegrass practitioners and their mountain gospel-singing fellows. You'd be hard to find a bluegrass singer who did not rejoice in the love of God somewhere in the repertoire. Analysing the trends Neil V Rosenberg has concluded that religious songs constitute around thirty per cent of the recorded output of the most influential bluegrass singers[87]. Bluegrass Gospel has become a way of celebrating religion in a secular context. You needn't attend church to express your faith, God comes directly to the stage and the street corner. Gospel bands are everywhere – Dale Lawson & Quicksilver, Canaan's Crossing, The Lewis Family, The Easter Brothers – and they appear on the programmes of all festivals.

Christian impact is greatest, however, in black music. It's impossible to imagine blues and soul without the sounds of devotion underlining them. Negro spirituals and black gospel music, replete as they are with call and response, shouted interjections and ever-building chanted fervour, are the cornerstones of both the blues and of soul music. Without the preacher's sermon and the congregation's heart-felt chanted reply there'd be no Ray Charles, nor Sam Cooke, Aretha Franklin, Otis Redding or Solomon Burke.

Ray Charles, the blind genius who started all this, took the black gospel tradition and made it secular. During the 1950s the impact of Brother Ray and The Raelettes hollering *I Got A Woman* and *What'd I Say,* both numbers based directly on gospel precursors, cannot be underestimated. The songs may seem commonplace and much imitated now but at the time they were nothing short of revolutionary. Charles was there with Sam Cooke at the birth of what became black soul music. Unlike its bluegrass counterpart this was at first a music of the ghetto, of the black parts of cities rather than the comparatively white mountains. Next, and again unlike bluegrass, soul music virtually abandoned God. Gospel might have been the music's template but it was little present in the final product. Religion and the love of the Lord turns up often in the recordings of, for example, bluegrass pioneer Bill Monroe. However, God appears far less frequently in the stage shows and albums of soul maestros James Brown, Wilson Pickett and Joe Tex. The transition acts here are Sam Cooke, who actually began as a gospel singer with The Soul Stirrers and then found huge success as a pop singer, and Solomon Burke who, as a sort of sideline, was also a preacher. Both men began near to God but as their careers progressed drop him from the act.

Some singers managed the mix better than others. The Rev Gary Davis, the blues and ragtime guitarist, was born in South Carolina on the way up to the mountains. He spent a life on the blues and folk circuit where fellow guitarists watched his fingers with awe. Compositionally he was of the old school but unlike many around him could play with a dexterity and invention that was stunning. He also preached a form of primitive evangelical Christianity and was wont to include on his albums slices of his store front sermons, along with his black congregation's response. Try *The Rev Gary Davis At Home & Church (1962-1967)*, or *The Sun Of Our Life – Solos, Songs, a Sermon 1955-1957* for the full flavour. Details can be found in the discography at the end of the book. On *The Sun of Our Life* sermon Brother Davis tells the tale of Jonah. This generates the expected ecstatic chants of *oh yeah right Lord* agreement from the congregation along with a sister singing softly "spurring Davis to a plateau of ecstatic song-like preaching (often in the same key as her humming)", as the liner note explains it.

Out on the highway again, cruising slowly from one Pigeon Forge excess to the next, the good Lord fades back into the background. Like Godzilla in jeans Mammon returns. In the area of good vs evil the Forge has seen plenty of battles. Most recently that has been over the demon drink. Tennessee is a dry state by default which, unlike Wales where 'dry' used to mean no drink on Sunday but okay any other day of the week, here means no drink, period. Unlike the nearby Sodom and Gomorrah townships of Gatlinburg and Sevierville, Pigeon Forge traditionally opted to stay dry. In 2009 and 2011 referenda held among the small permanent local population pulled in a result that opted again for the status quo. The selling of alcohol by the glass, to use the quaint American term, would remain a thing that happened elsewhere. However the vote of 2012 seemed to show that drink had at last triumphed, albeit only by a 100 vote margin. But when scrutinisers looked more closely they discovered that the total votes cast were significantly greater than the number of those actually on the electoral roll. Foul play somewhere. Men wearing white southern suits loading the ballot boxes. Interested parties slipping brown envelopes to those doing the counting. Something like that. A new vote was ordered. In 2013, despite strong representation from religious purists, things went the way of big business and dry Pigeon Forge became a place of memory.

Not that alcohol is in the hands of street revellers. No one is swaying down the parking lots bearing cans of lager and shouting. The sale of liquor by the glass means just that. Jack Daniels by the shot can be purchased at restaurants. If you want to buy a bottle then you still need to drive to Sevierville.

At the south eastern end of town Patriot Park is home to a half mile walk that displays the flags of all fifty US states along with memorials to a number of Tennessee veterans. It's the only park I've ever been in that is guarded by its own Patriot Missile battery. It's there at the edge, looking fierce and full of power. Pigeon Forge's premier park, full of patriots. There's an annual Smoky Mountain Cornhole Toss Tournament here in memory of Sergeant Brett Benton, a local killed by an IED in Afghanistan. Cornhole tossing is actually throwing bean bags at holes cut into planks of wood. Much in the style of that onetime staple, the horse shoe toss, but less dangerous. The beanbags don't fly as far and won't break your bones if they hit you.

Patriot Park is also home to the annual bluegrass and mountain music Stringtime in the Smokies fest. This is an entirely free, bring your own seat, typically Appalachian affair. There are side stalls offering chips and root beer. Residents bring home baked cakes to sell. It all seems out of character with cut price, mass market Pigeon Forge. On the half mile patriot walk a woman in long hair and a cheesecloth dress rolls a hula hoop through the air like this were the hippie seventies. Locals sunbathe, corndogs in hand, cans of coke settled into the arms of their collapsible chairs.

On stage is Shawn Camp, a cowboy attired country singersongwriter with a penchant for bluegrass styling. His claim to fame is writing Billboard number one songs for Garth Brooks (*One Pina Colada*) as well as hits for a whole raft of other Nashville singers including Brooks & Dunn, Josh Turner and Blake Shelton. Today, though, he's channelling Elvis, taking him back to his bluegrass origins. Not a great distance, given Presley's use of Bill Monroe as a launch pad. Camp has made a record[88] with Billy Burnette, son of Dorsey, a leading third of the incendiary Rock and Roll Trio. Between them they've restructuring the King in the image of Lester Scruggs or Frank Stanley. *Good Rocking Tonight* and then *Mystery Train* come picking down the line as if this were Clingman's Dome and we were there, sweet potato biscuits in our hands.

The idea is far more original than at first seems. Taking Bill Monroe that further step and then bringing him and some of the cornerstones of rock and roll remade in his image back again takes energy. And here's Shawn Camp, a front-on Nashville man, doing all that on his own. With his band he rocks on through *Hound Dog* with the mandolin flying. Country music is a broader church than many think. Looking him up later I discover that Camp is now right at the centre of a band called The Earls of Leicester[89] recreating the music of Lester Flatt, Earl Scruggs and The Foggy Mountain Boys. Once bluegrass gets into your blood it stays.

We're settled in our deluxe folding Ozark Trail armchairs bought from Walmart. You can't do the mountain circuit standing up. On stage are Timberwinds, old time country last heard in Asheville. They are followed by Boogertown Gap, David Grisman's Bluegrass Experience (with Grisman looking like an escapee from ZZ Top), and then Jack Lawrence and The Hackensaw Boys. For free admission you certainly get your money's worth. Nothing new but the present in full glory. If revolution comes to America again then it'll be disguised as a string band.

The sky curves west towards Nashville. The mountains are

backdrop with their history still pretty much intact. I'm aware of just how unfashionable this concert would appear back in my post-industrial backwater homeland. Our past is an earlier one and our present full of house rap and electro jive.

The Tennessee Mafia Jug Band are a six-piece who describe themselves as "Five Guys and a Scrubboard with roots like wisdom teeth." They're in hats and hayseed overalls. Upfront is Leroy Troy who plays a washboard embellished with bells, horns, and duck calls. With a hat half over his face but a force five tenor voice Lonesome Lester Armistead take most of the spotlight. The band come over like Cardiff's Railroad Bill with added authenticity and spectacular Smoky Mountain colour. We get *Howdy from Hickman County, Rabbit in a Log* followed by *Wrinkled, Crinkled, Wadded Dollar Bill*. There are any number of hee haws, howdy folks and corny country jokes. The energy is unstoppable.

We fingersnap back to the dark Pigeon Forge trolley that'll drive right along that four lane highway and deposit us at our motel at the other end of town. Music has been the Forge's salvation.

24 • Slick Fisher Road

Water sells. The sight of it does. Anything with a view of the river, the lake or the sea charges more. If your windows gaze down on shimmering blue then the rental will be prime. Construct a balcony which would enable the occupant to get nearer the shining water then the lease can double. I see it daily perambulating the bay of my native Cardiff. Apartments clustering in towers, glistening like the superstructures of ships, glass and wood, portal windows, silvered rails that form a hundred balconies. The whole residential edifice is like a moored cruise liner. Inland there's little new. It's only here where the millennium money flows that the build has rolled.

It's not new, this idea of taming the tide fields, the snaking water courses and the seeping swamps and then selling them on. At the height of Victoria's Empire when the Marquis of Bute held sway over most of Cardiff he munificently donated to the people a tract of his holdings that surrounded the Nant Brook north of the Fairoak farm. This was a bog of snaking stream with a reputation as a malarial swamp. With the connivance of the Council an earthen dam was constructed and what became the lake at Roath Park Pleasure Gardens was formed. It was a thirty-two acre stretch of clear water, dotted with islands, and occupied by swan and duck.

But the Marquis still owned land near the edges, real estate on which he constructed great houses, embellished with balconies and all with a view of water. Sales were brisk. The Marquis stood back and smiled. A generous, socially engaged and now much richer man.

Up here in the mountains the same tale has been playing. In the distance is a rugged, mountainous terrain with no highways and almost everything higher than 3000 feet. But first is Slick Fisher Road and at its lowest edge a spiky 640 acre stretch of glistening water: Lake Toxaway.

Before 1890, and like the Marquis's apparently useless Cardiff swamp, this place was a great sheet of inaccessible tree and fractured rock. It was criss-crossed by creeks and outfalls that twisted and turned, gathering eventually into the winding, white water of Toxaway River. America's Switzerland it wasn't although that was what it would become. A group of Pittsburgh businessmen, attracted to the area's potential wealth as a source of minerals and aided by the newly arrived railroads bought a great tract of the land. Their original mining proposals soon gave way to the provision of leisure. Lakes with hotels around them would bring in the wealthy crowds looking for a summer inland resort. Here hunting would be on tap and the health bringing qualities of the waters and the landscape would be a bonus. Led by their largest shareholder, Pittsburgh banker Edward H Jennings, they set about the audacious operation of damming the Toxaway with a 60 foot tall and 500 feet wide earthen bank. The result was a lake three miles long. Along the side of this Jennings and his partners constructed a golf course and the great five storey, five star Toxaway Inn. 500 rooms with accommodation for more than a thousand well-heeled vacation guests.

The dam was completed in 1903. Jennings refined the development by adding electric power and a lake encircling road. But the money making dream fell over in 1916 when the rains came, as they do so often in these Southern States. The whole of Western North Carolina suffered flooding. The River Toxaway brought down so much water that the new lake with a mud blocked end couldn't cope. In August a hurricane came ashore in Mississippi and moved up inland. The dam gave with a roar of fury, as contemporary newspapers had it, and poured its wall of water for 16 miles carving a great gouge in the land. With no lake and litigation in place against the dam's owners' guests vanished into the air. The Inn did not reopen the following season and the whole venture lay dormant for forty years.

When I arrive, a century on, the gouge is still partially visible. Sitting in the Chestnut Café high above the spillway with a brand new dam engineered safe and solid behind me the route of the rushing

1916 water is still clearly visible. There are tree stands that have never quite recovered, stranded boulders, and rips and runs in the under lying rock.

Following the disaster a group of Christians had bought up pieces of Edward H Jennings' land with a view to establishing a residential Lord-praising choral camp. Somehow their ideas failed to gel and they eventually sold on their real estate. Their buyers were the newly formed Lake Toxaway Estates Inc., property developers in the modern style. Toxaway Estates rebuilt the dam, filled the lake again with water and resold the land in small parcels. 1100 homes tastefully scattered along the new lake edge's 14 miles of roads were the result. This was a private and gated community with a country club at its heart.

It's a JG Ballard dreamscape. Manicured lawns. Shrubberies under iron control. A golf course played by retirees in soft shoes and pastel-shaded clothes. A marina where the rarely used pleasure boats rock gently in the sun. The Greystone Inn, a relic from the early days, stands exclusive and massaged of all hard edges. The monied residents are silent as they drift like automatons from the delights of their serviced townhouses to lunch in the country club at $50 a time. We circle the lake in our rented auto, posing as potential buyers, copy of the Lake Toxaway Company development plan in hand. I'd like to see lawns being mowed, children playing or residents, drinks beside them, relaxing on their lawns. But there's nothing. Ahead the world might be on course to dissolve into violence, burn, turn to crystal, or drown beneath rising tides. But unlike that Ballard fiction Lake Toxaway won't. In this place money has lobotomised the soul.

At the exit, beyond which Appalachia returns, the Toxaway sales Administrator accepts the returned map. "Not for you then," he says. I guess I've still got too much sparkle in my eyes. Our great zig-zag across these Appalachian Mountains, North Carolina to Tennessee and back, has at last delivered. I've got a growing familiarity now with both the landscape and the music. It's a Pavlovian sensation. I see a deck of rising trees or a road that bends itself round like a curling willow and the banjos rattle in the back of my head. To reach Toxaway we've driven through Waynesville – home of Soco Gap Bluegrass clogging – and on down towards the South Carolina State line. Ahead is the

Pisgah Forest, and the Shining Rock Wilderness with Cold Mountain at its heart.

Cold Mountain is known to the world largely through Anthony Minghella's 2003 Civil War masterpiece. It was actually filmed not here but in Romania where modern life, the director insisted, intruded less in the landscape. But looking around here at the trees and then the trees you wonder.

There's a place on Slick Fisher at which we're staying. The road slides up above the lake in a long gentle curve. It's getting dark. Enough to rattle me. Lost in a wilderness where lights don't exist and even in daytime habitations are hard to see, crushed up behind their shields of green. What do the directions say? "On the left there's a wooden sign". And by some miracle we see it, nestling in the shrubbery. Can't be too soon. Down behind us another lone vehicle is tail gating with its lights playing on our rear fender like one of those haunted and murderous trucks in Stephen King's *Maximum Overdrive*. We slow and it roars off into the distance, defeated, having to face the dark wilds now entirely on its own.

The local town is Brevard. Home of the Brevard White Squirrel Festival a sign announces. Small town America, wide streets, traffic lights that take eternity to change, telegraph poles, benches along the sidewalks. The local chamber of commerce promotes the place as a walkable community where main street meets the mountains and have a brochure that lists insurance brokers, the fire department, financial advisors and the court house in a handy list for visitors. On the cover is a photograph of a woman with a baby in a stroller gazing at a knick knack shop selling glass rabbits and ceramic fish. There's the atmosphere here of Builth Wells or Llanidloes, locals casually dressed in country clothes, jackets with elbow patches, cheesecloth shirts, bandanas, leather pouches attached to their belts.

On the road in, driving below the Toxaway Dam and not even noticing that it was there, we passed Eddy Hoots who makes a buck carving bears and owls from tree trunks with a chain saw. His slice of roadside theatre is a shower of sawdust and machine-driven roar. Cars go by. Mostly they do not stop. Nestled on a patch of rough highway edge overlooking the Toxaway spillway is Jack Owen's Boiled Peanut concession. "Toxaway Falls Stand" reads the sign. It's lost among a welter of notices offering Amish butter, jams, jellies, relish and fresh eggs. Inside among the age-bent postcards, guidebooks with their corners curled, sun hats, pens and jars of sourwood honey stands eighty-two year old Jack. Despite his name he recalls no connection with Wales. "My daddy he come from Georgia. He built this hut in nineteen and forty seven before they built [bee-ilt] that thar dam. When they did they gave him some money and he moved it right here. Same hut. Been here ever since. I don't do much. I'm just a dollar checker." His family cemetery is up the road. There are memorials there to Elijah D Owen, Bettie and Rebecca Owen. Could be Penrhyndeudraeth but the racoons let it down.

Sitting in Dee Dee and Jimmy's Rocky's Soda Fountain (est. 1947), all fifties Coke signs and offerings of Sinkers and Suds (donuts and coffee) and Pigs Between Two Blankets (ham sandwiches) I read the local paper. There's a campaign running to re-elect David Mahoney as Sheriff. There'll be a spaghetti supper fundraiser next week at the Brevard High School Cafeteria. And if you can spot the images of twenty fire extinguishers dotted throughout the publication then you are in line for a free pedicure at the Brevard Spa and Salon. I try my best but can only manage one.

Brevard is named after Dr. Ephraim Brevard, a Revolutionary War colonel and surgeon. He didn't come from here, didn't practice here, and is buried in an unmarked grave in Hopewell, more than three hundred miles to the south. The only industry to speak of is the Ecusta paper mill on the Davidson River. Wikipedia describes Brevard as a notable retirement centre. Seems for once Wiki have got it right.

Yet despite this, or maybe actually because of it, Brevard is home to one of the best of the new wave of young bluegrass bands operating out of the Appalachians – The Steep Canyon Rangers. Woody Platt, Rangers front man, has made Brevard his powerbase. It's here that he organises the annual Mountain Song Festival at the Brevard Music Center, just on the edge of town. The Music Center is actually a university facility designed for classical concerts but in the high summer it opens its sides (which come off a bit like a giant plastic toy), adds a string of stalls retailing the expected corndogs, soft drinks, t-shirts, and other bluegrass merch and plays roots music non-stop.

High spot, and the one we came for, are The Rangers themselves. They got their name from a bottle of Steep Canyon Stout. Substituting Rangers was simple. They are a new generation bluegrass band of considerable accomplishment and operating with a hell of a lot of style. Their lead instruments flicker into each other as they rock – mandolin, banjo, fiddle – joining, pulling apart, soloing, mixing again. The music, in this version of the band, is without percussion. This will arrive when Michael Ashworth joins the band later playing among other things, Cajon drums – boxes with holes in them to harden up the sound. They do *The Road To Knoxville*, a band-composed instrumental that comes over more like the Road to Lisdoonvarna than anything this side of the water. Irish dancing and bluegrass clogs close in on each other once again.

The Rangers mainly work their own original material. There are bursts of Merle Haggard and Huddie Leadbetter and a number written by Shawn Camp[90], last encountered in Pigeon Forge. But mainly the material is band-composed. Not that it ever moves far from the real bluegrass roots of death by drowning, rambling, drinking, loving pretty women, not going down the mines anymore, and climbing the mountains to look for the Lord. What's gripping is the way that The Steep's music stays entirely together and the voices transcend it, climbing in harmony, diving out unaccompanied, tenor and baritone woven together with that high and rising bluegrass soprano over the top.

Woody Platt's vision is that The Rangers' mix of the sacred and the profane, their maintenance of tradition without slavishly following it, and their willingness to play bluegrass no matter if alcohol is present or not (a big mountain divide, that one) will take them to the top. And it does.

The Rangers bring on their special guest. Steve Martin. This is the film star and comedian who has made bluegrass banjo playing his second career. The Steep Canyon Rangers are his chosen backing band. It's easy to forget, amongst all the glamour and reflected stardom, that The Rangers can actually outplay Martin any day they choose. But what we get instead is no battle but a genuine melding. Martin playing his own self-composed numbers as if they were Rangers' originals or traditional songs.

Martin has had a long association with the banjo. It was a staple of his early 70s stand-up days where the instrument was a comedic prop. He learned by playing 33 rpm discs at half-speed and listening closely to how the famous picked their notes. He was taught one to one by Nitty Gritty Dirt Band member John McEuen and, being the star he is, has experienced none of the blockages on the way up encountered by most other bluegrass practitioners. He's done the Opry, recorded with Dolly Parton and remade *Foggy Mountain Breakdown* with Earl Scruggs. Not that any of this should detract. This banjo player has talent and he has style.

In 2010, and order to put something back, he established the Steve Martin Prize for Excellence in Banjo and Bluegrass. $50K, a bronze statue and a pile of TV coverage – so no paper tiger. Jens Kruger from The Swiss Kruger Brothers won in 2013 and former Bill Monroe accompanist and Country Gentlemen player Eddie Adcock in 2014.

On stage Martin tells a few jokes and seems awkward for such an accomplished star. Around him The Rangers create a cocoon of contemporary bluegrass rhythm. The music, full of claw hammered runs and Martin's own slightly off-key vocal interjections, rocks off into the night.

25 • Dollywood

If the 2015 Elvis is a creation of the musically neutered and the eternally nostalgic then Dolly, equally fabricated, is one that keeps life bright and still has a musical future. Like Joan Collins, Barbara Cartland and Danielle Steele before her Parton appears entirely manufactured. She is enduringly unblemished. She glows and she twinkles. She is super real. While the King returns in multiple variety, anything from black leathered rocker to white diamanté hero, Parton exists in only one form. Diminutive. Lipsticked. Make up embalmed. She is a beehived, cigarettes on the bar, car-keys next to them blonde. She can touch men whose youths sat anywhere from 1960 to 1999. She's possessed of nails and eyes that cost a Rolex to keep up. She resonates perfectly with just about anyone who has sat in a pub somewhere and watched the party girls arrive.

How is she famous? For a bluegrass singer from Sevier County who started out singing duets with a diamanté-encrusted cowboy called Porter Wagoner she's come a terrific distance. All the elements that should keep a Southern States American singer well and truly out of the British consciousness were there. For the British Porter was a dark Irish beer and country was a place where the Royals went when they wanted to let off their guns. The nearest we got to the music was cardiganed Val Doonican smiling and crooning to us from his rocking chair.

Parton was totally countrified in her home American market. She spent six years appearing on Wagoner's TV show and stacked up the country chart hits in a series of solos she recorded with him. Elsewhere, however, she made no mark. Her upbringing was as alien to us as that of Ghandi. Parton was born one of twelve children in a dirt poor share-cropper family living severely out in the sticks on the Tennessee Smoky Mountains. Her grandfather was a holy roller preacher. Her father was a tobacco farmer. They lived in a "one room country little shack", that place again, where grindingly hard work, deprivation and thanking the Lord for how it all was seemed to be the totality of daily life.

In Britain, all that stuff with its dirt and its life among the trees, struck no chords. The UK equivalent was life among the Catholic working classes of Liverpool. Those gave us Cilla Black. Not quite the same thing at all.

After a number of false starts Dolly Parton hit the UK charts and entered her permanent position in the race memory with a 1973 song *Jolene*. No shrill voices, no steel guitars, no banjo plucking, no barn dancing fiddles. Not marketed as country music either. It was a UK no 7 hit and a great song. Almost anyone you meet today could hum it. Her UK follow up single was *I Will Always Love You* and it didn't do a thing[91]. Parton, the enigma.

Today she's the world stage super-star everyone recognises. She's starred in films and TV series and sung a hundred countrified, poppy songs that wash in and out of FM radio without leaving a trace. She became a disco diva when she needed to in the 80s. She dueted with Kenny Rodgers. She made albums with Emmylou and Linda Ronstadt. As a product she's the singer rather than the songs. Dolly. You don't recognise her voice (as you certainly would with Elvis) but her image. A six decade old glam queen, still toting giant hair, giant heels and giant breasts. As she said herself in one of her many self-disparaging slices of stage repartee, "it takes a lot of money to look this cheap".

The Parton enigma glows on. In 2014 she's so famous that in South Wales she can fill the 7500 capacity Cardiff Motorpoint Arena two nights running. Tickets are exchanging hands at more than twice their cover price. The whole deal is a victory for the British black market which, according to the *Daily Mail*, local trading standards, and UK post-war collective memory shouldn't exist at all. You can chance your arm on line at £180 for a side seat at the back and you might just get a ticket sent to you. Or, this being a world dense with scams, you might not. In the area around the Motorpoint's recently refurbished 1980s presence there are many dark recesses. In them men in coats stand offering stubs of paper for huge sums of money. They say these are genuine tickets and they look the part. They also might have been run up that afternoon in a back room above a chip shop. It's a lottery getting in.

On the streets are swirling hoards. Most of them are no longer young. Traders offer enormous stacks of black Stetsons with pink fur around the rims. £15 a go. They cost £20 inside. Business is brisk. They are accompanied by pink feather boas not seen in such density since the hippie age. In the local bars are lines of women of a certain age all clad in their own versions of Dolly's glitter, gold shoes and twinkling tops that slide around their wearers' bulbous frames. Spirits are high. Lipstick is applied. Cocktails are drunk. This is the UK standard now that Del Boy has made big glasses full of fruit, sugar, alcohol and paper umbrellas a thing of the working class.

Getting into the Motorpoint is a civilised stroll. Dolly does not attract bombers, dope dealers, men with guns and knives in the way other concerts clearly do. Security is a matter of having your ticket scrutinised. The full body searches, shoes off, bags upended, pockets fumbled through like at Jake Bugg's performance are absent. Inside, in Opry-style but perhaps lacking that operation's caché, the merchandisers are in full-frontal attack. The Dolly brand can be bought but you'll need a full wallet. Beyond the booze, coffee and hot dog concessions you can buy Dolly scarves, hats that twinkle from the lines of LEDs laced around their brims, and t-shirts with giant portraits of the aged superstar. There are pink hoodies with the word Dolly on the front at £60 a go. Portrait bandanas at £15, ties and mugs at £12. The new double album which combines a Dolly greatest hits with a second CD of the show itself, *Blue Smoke*, goes for £20. I saw it earlier at HMV for half that. This isn't stopping the buyers who are carrying it away by the ton.

Among the well-behaved expectant audience it's spot the young person. This is the Ynysybwl Line Dancing club writ large. A valleys audience aided and abetted by the inner suburbs of Cardiff. There are heavyweights everywhere. Great tattooed blobs in short dresses, men with trousers that could engulf a motorcycle and sidecar, baseball caps, Stetsons, women with pink roses in their hair, flash and shimmer, mothers and daughters now and then but mostly gaggles of timeworn goodtimers, oiled and getting oilier, still rocking in their own sweet way.

What I can't figure is where this southern Welsh love of pop country has come from. We've never been a nation of steel guitar players and in normal society, i.e. Cardiff anything goes Queen Street on a Saturday afternoon, you are unlikely to encounter a broad brimmed American hat nor find cowboys busking outside Boots. Somewhere back among the dross of Barry Manilow, Richard Chamberlain and Engelbert Humperdinck, Dolly managed to slide herself into pop consciousness. I missed that.

Her set is long. Two and a half hours with one twenty minute break, no support. Dolly is in full glitter mode, hair and breasts both stunning in their endurance. Early comes *Jolene* so we can get plugged into her soundtrack with something we know. She rolls through the hits mixing them with numbers taken from *Blue Smoke*, the new album. This is, after all, the *Blue Smoke* Tour. There's a light show with violent red and bright whites that flashes and turns itself on the audience, illuminating us like this was wartime. The backdrop is an oversize screen that alternates between showing giant live Dolly close-ups with scenes of trees, mountains, rivers, old-time communities and trains that smoke and steam. She's making sure we recognise her roots.

She does the hits. She sings *Rockytop* and blends it into a version of Boots Randolph's *Yakaty Sax* and then tells us in her softened southern drawl "Ah do like Benny Hill." She sings an acapella *Little Sparrow*, a take on *Don't Think Twice, It's Alright* and what should be a soaring version of *Banks of the Ohio* but isn't quite, although the crowd are with her for every second.

The self-deprecating jokes fill the slots between songs. "People ask me how long does it take you to keep your hair looking as good as that and I tell them I don't know I've never been there while it's being done." Zipping smartly across stage in her white cat suit she switches through a blitz of Appalachian instruments – harmonica, pipe, dulcimer, violin, sax, and then a rhinestone encrusted banjo worthy of the Museum of Appalachia's back room. It's a slick and stylish performance from someone at the top of their game. We get sentiment by the soup ladle. The audience love her. We've got lives like that, it's great to be with someone who has had it tough, yup, done without. Dolly smiles benignly. Her show is a triumph.

She does the same thing a day or two later from the Pyramid Stage at Glastonbury. Worthy Farm hosts the queen of country pop. She unites the entire muddy festival, all 80,000. Those who've been up all night, the gays, the straights, the politicos, the grizzled, the left field fans, the kids, they all sway to what she does and, for that moment, they really love her.

Knowing this does not untangle the Parton myth for me. The Brits are not by upbringing a nation of soft-centred country music fans. They do not relish the old time much. Plucked string breakdowns went out with Norrie Paramour's Big Ben Banjo Band. Yet here we are whooping for Dolly and her country ways. That's what happens with a nation that has mainlined on Americana, from the old west to big city street trash, for more than sixty years. The essence enters the bloodstream. It flows around us, mixing with music hall and industrial darkness so well that when we hear it we imagine it's our own.

That Parton is an icon for the gay community merely clouds the waters. She's spent a decade denying rumours of a lesbian relationship with a long term female friend. The rumours have been driven by the fact that Parton's husband of 46 years, the never seen Carl Thomas Dean, keeps himself so far out of the limelight as to be invisible. Instead drag queen Dolly fills the screen. She was asked recently what her drag queen name might have been, if she were one, that is. "P. Titty, Like P. Diddy," was Dolly's reply.

The Parton state of permanent musical glory reaches its apogee in Sevier County. This is a place pretty near where the first lady of backwoods diamanté was born. Here, where Tennessee bangs up against North Carolina, Parton has established a kingdom created in her own likeness. Dollywood. A place of myths and wish fulfilment, like Dolly herself.

Dolly Parton is respected here. It's where she came from. It's also where she began her charitable giving and, in particular, her Imagination Library. This enterprise donates a book each month to all Sevier County children under five. From someone whose father was illiterate it's an inspired offer, a generous backlash against the pervading electronic tide. I hope it makes a difference.

The car parks at Dollywood itself are a mile long, huge open spaces at this time of the morning. I've driven us here in the oversized auto the hirecar lot managed to rent me. I've no idea where this vehicle's outer reaches are but I've not hit anything yet. We are charged $10 and directed to the far and distant reaches. From here a trolley train takes us five stops back up to the entrance gates.

There's a feeling of end of season here, a vaguely down at heel touch, a lack of ultimate Parton brightness to the signboards, chips in the paintwork, dust in the corners of the displays. The park is advertised as closing tomorrow for two days to prepare itself for Dollywood's forthcoming Gospel Season. God's centrality to Tennessee is never far away from anything. Entrance costs $60 but you get a whole day for that and access to all shows, exhibitions and, should you want to go on them, the countless hurl you around, rocket you, pull your stomach into the air and wave it about rides.

Dollywood is a theme park that combines high-excitement space-age ride experiences with a sort of schmaltzy craft-persons dollop of candle making, wood carving and straw plaiting. It's all set out in full Thomas Kincaid Appalachian mountain hillbilly style. It shouldn't work, but it does. Prices for goods that are still chargeable (consumables and gifts) have been pushed as high as they can go. Refreshments are unamericanly small, over sugared, fried and in the Gordon Ramsey price-range. There are restrooms everywhere. I don't think I've ever been to an operation where there are so many opportunities to pee. Weak bladders are not a thing to fear in Dollywood. Most of the customers appear old. It's end of season in both ways. There are few children and hardly a young person anywhere. It's a land of the overweight and the stumbling, the slow and the slug who move by osmosis if they move at all. Dollywood hires out strollers, electric convenience vehicles, carts with sun shades, carriers and trailers. There's a special service animal relief area and a comprehensive range of family assisted rest rooms. Try not to fear the reaper, if he's coming soon you'll be well catered for here.

We've come here to see how the music of these mountains has been adapted to work for a branch of the vacation industry. Dollywood publicity promises live music at a host of venues throughout the park. Given the backdrop it'll be country for sure. Approved tunes and authorised costume, just the right amount of saccharine sound and melodies the audience stand a chance of knowing. The mountains themselves have become a brand, a national product, a marketable entity right across the new world.

The site on which Dollywood sits was first developed back in the sixties by the Robins Brothers. This pair of entrepreneurs used it for their Rebel Railroad Ride. In its day this was a quite adventurous steam train entertainment aimed at the increasing numbers of visitors to fast developing Pigeon Forge. In 1986, and with her country wealth increasing, Parton became co-owner and renamed the park. Dollywood. The name has just right combination of spunk and slush. It now covers almost 300 acres and operates to the side of Parton's 35 further acre Splash Country water theme park and the presently being developed 100 acre DreamMore Resort next door. Life here increasingly resembles science fiction's sybaritic future. Otherness prevails, reality retreats. You need for nothing, for a price all is permanently supplied.

The park is wound round with not so much UK-style health and safety but with American hands-on almost suffocating care. There are warning signs telling of slopes that are mere rises in the path. There are cautions against peanuts, gluten, and the heat of coffee. There are long waits before you are allowed to get off or on anything. Movement will have ceased and the atoms stopped spinning before any aged American foot can be allowed to again touch the floor. "Hold on there folks until you see the green light. Won't be a moment and then the driver will tell us all that we can safely demount." The Dolly world makes sure you survive the experience.

The original Rebel Railroad has survived and been much extended. It is now the Dollywood Express. This is a three foot gauge genuine steam railway. The engine is a huge fire and smoke breather, like something out of Disney. Number 192, a 2-8-2 built in 1943, once a US military loco from White Pass. The journey, in open sided carriages and sitting on a painted wooden seat, is enlivened by constant train whistle hoots, gouts of steam and air filled with genuine smuts. It's all riddled with non-stop tannoy-delivered rubbish talking up the entertaining sights available each side of the rattling train. It's a good five miles of track. In the Dollywood brochure the journey is described as a "moderate thrill attraction – may contain unanticipated thrills". A thrill I had not anticipated is what I need right now. An announcement warns us to keep our body parts inside the carriages at all times. Rock on.

At Back Porch Theatre we find The Smoky Mountain String Band playing. This is a bluegrass trio with a bearded and guitar-playing lead in the mould of Noel Edmonds. The music is mainstream string band but at least the trio have their CDs on sale. Three for $20. Best offer all week.

At the Valley Theatre Country Cross Roads, a country and western karaoke and dance troupe, are in operation. It's glib and all-embracing and during its half an hour run encompasses all the country hits. The performers are caked in lip gloss and blusher and dance as much as they sing. It's as slick an operation as the gift store or the concession selling fries and burgers. Not a step out of place and, pretty much like the rest of Dollywood, everything to time.

Inside the much larger Celebration Theatre Dolly's Great American Country Show rattles on in subdued light. This features a Stetsoned lead in a wheelchair, a full electric band, and a set of denim-wearing male and female singers enthusing with gusto. The offer is new country, things you don't recognise, but which sound vaguely familiar. They have a guest, the ambling and overweight Marty Raybon, who does the good old country boy routine, sentiment and tuneful slosh, with his guitar pushed out on the top of his belly.

Up beyond the theatres the rides on offer increase in intensity. The River Battle Ride. The Sky Zip. The Lumberjack Lifts. The Thunderhead Coaster. The Mountain Slidewinder. The Smoky Mountain River Rampage. There are places where you can get doused with water, step through sprayed mists, be splashed by cars thundering down shoots, be poured upon by overhead spouts. If the humidity was up all would great. But it's not.

We choose the Fire Chaser which has a zig-zag entrance path normally full of punters and bearing signs that read "Your Ride is One Hour Away At This Point." Except today on this season fag end we march straight on in. It's described as a moderate thrill attraction but in its sky high climbing and diving rock and roll has me clinging to the safety rail with my eyes firmly closed. The journey feels like a good ten minutes of churn and whirl but it's actually only just over two. You get off. You get your bags and camera back from the locker and then stagger slightly as the world continues to tilt and spin.

Near the exit and beyond the wheelchair hire facility is Dolly's best attraction, The Southern Gospel Music Association Hall of Fame. This is another American music memorabilia as tourist attraction in the style of Nashville's Johnny Cash celebration. This one, though, is far more moderate in size. An animatronic quartet of white men in sombre old fashioned grey suits stand just inside the entrance singing *Give The World A Smile*. These are Spitting Image figurines at life size. In the sombre light they look frighteningly like versions of Prince Charles.

Centrepiece is a bus, it's always a bus. This one once belonging to The Blackwood Brothers. This Bible-pushing quartet plus piano were pioneers of Christian Music. Emerging from the Holiness Movement Churches they began in the great depression turning secular music round to the service of the Lord. The Blackwoods still sing today although their membership has changed totally. In their day they were pioneers. Their bus was one of the first to be used by touring bands in the States. Elvis is reputed to have ordered his after seeing the Blackwoods in theirs. According to the literature the vehicle here in Dollywood is a replica. Around me reality shimmers and fades.

Next to the vehicle is a side hall full of hundreds of bronze plaques, one for each Southern Gospel singer inducted. Beyond are the expected cases showing stage costume, instruments, lyric sheets, music and Bibles. At the exit is a vinyl dump. It holds what has to be several thousand 12-inch lps of holy music. They are offered for sale now at $5 a time. This slice of history has now been abandoned. God's work done and the world moved on.

Outside the expansive reaches of the Dollywood car parks remain largely unfilled. There are clouds now, up there above the mountains. As Dolly has it, as inspirational as ever, "The way I see it, if you want the rainbow, you gotta put up with the rain!"

In the new millennium Dolly has reinvented herself, lost weight and returned to her roots. In the wake of the bluegrass success of the film *O Brother* she has recorded three albums of genuine mountain music – *The Grass Is Blue, Little Sparrow* and *Halos & Horns* (which includes a bluegrass version of Led Zeppelin's *Stairway to Heaven*). By anyone's standards they are great music. She has also returned to mainstream country with recordings made with Billy Ray Cyrus and her straight ahead Nashville album *Backwoods Barbie* (2007).

She'll endure as long as the facelifts, nips and tucks and false everything else allow her. To date her music shows little sign of fading. She's composed more than 3000 songs and had 114 hits. Would that make her bigger than Elvis? Back out among the hills it is actually raining.

26 • It's All Made Of Wood

Appalachia, the land I've been zig-zagging through for most of this book, is a land of wood. Quite how much I'm only just realising. I don't mean the greenness of the trees nor the knowledge that the logging of this place provided much of economic drive for the emergence of early America as an independent nation and a power with which the world would soon have to contend. The Manifest Destiny it certainly became. But wood, was more than the backbone. For a time it was the entirety.

The Appalachian range, the great blue wall that held back European explorers for centuries, runs north right to Canada. But it's these southern stretches, the Blue Ridge and the Smoky Mountains, the hills that held out the longest against exploration that have held and fascinated me. This is Daniel Boone territory. It was he, the frontiersman and great American folk hero who fought in the Indian and the Revolutionary Wars, who forged the Cumberland Gap. This was a route through the impenetrable wilderness where Virginia, Kentucky and Tennessee meet. Cumberland Gap, the route through the mountains that opened up the territories beyond. *Cumberland Gap*, sung about by Lonnie Donegan in the British hit parade of 1957 and cemented in the race memory, well mine anyway.

Boone wasn't born here nor did he die here but that hasn't stopped towns and counties getting named after him. Folk heroes have this done to them. They lose reality as their fame rises like warm air. Boone was only one of the early explorers, the men who opened up these dense southern reaches of the then distant Appalachians. Alexander Spottiswood, the Governor of Virginia, led colonists through the Blue

Ridge in 1716. The ranges themselves were mapped by Arnold Guyot in 1849 but their highest peaks[92] were not climbed until Elisha Mitchell went up them in 1857. As testament to their difficulty he fell to his death in the process.

That there is a preponderance of wood here is self-evident. Remote, hard to get into and even harder to get out, with no obvious routes to the cities and towns, no easy pathways down to productive farmland, scant resources beyond water, bears and the trees themselves. No milk, no honey. Live in these hills and you'll need to adapt. If you need something then you do without or you make it yourself. You use what you have to hand. You make everything out of wood.

Back in 2013 an Appalachian mountain singer had found her way to Cardiff and stood on the stage with the stained glass backdrop on level three of municipal St David's Hall. This was Diana Jones. Her name makes her sound Welsh but she's not. She's not wholly Appalachian either but has adopted the tradition well enough for it to inform her singing. Her songs sound old time enough with their sawing fiddle and picked guitar to have come right out of the hills. For her new album Jones sought authenticity and had looked for a place where singers sat in a circle and played for themselves. The old way. Everyone watching and listening to everyone else.

In Clinton Tennessee, out on the Andersonville Highway she found her answer. The Museum of Appalachia. Here, in Peter's all-wood Homestead House, a large long cabin complete with working fireplace, she pulled her chosen musicians together and sucking up the spirit of the Appalachians concentrated in this place laid down a dozen songs. No banjo breaks, no histrionics, new age Appalachia without the tie-die. Good tunes, tunes you could recall hours later, the ultimate test. *The Museum of Appalachia Recordings*[93] were the result.

The Museum of Appalachia was the invention of collector and suit wearing backwoodsman John Rice Irwin. By its nature the past crumbles and sinks into the soil on which it stands. Irwin decided to preserve a little, to make an attempt. He was from Oak Ridge, East Tennessee at the edge of the mountains, right next to a place called Rocky Top and with roads called Hickory Trail and Chestnut Drive all around. If Appalachia hadn't already been in his blood then it would have seeped in from outside.

His family were all farmers and, as a young boy, Rice took an interest in some of the hand tools that lay about the farm. If they were discarded then he kept them. His grandfather suggested that maybe he should keep all these old things that "belonged to our people and start a museum someday"[94]. The seed was sown. Over the years Rice's concern with the old world of Appalachia around him, the one that was getting thrown away or sold on to unscrupulous antique hunters, turned from mild interest to complete obsession.

Rice "travelled into hollows and valleys, up narrow dirt roads and along mountain creeks, knocking on doors, seeking items that people didn't use anymore that they might wish to sell to him: objects connected with log cabin building, butter churning, soap making, cooking, hunting, trapping, herbal healing, quilting, blacksmithing, spinning, weaving, fiddles, banjos, guitars, wagon making, hog dressing, moonshining, beekeeping, tanning, coal mining, revivals, general stores, and so on". He stored them at home and then, sensing that build-it-yourself wooden structures might turn out to be just as interesting as homemade, handmade, largely wooden objects, he acquired his first building.

This was an old log cabin, The General Bunch House, that a local coal company had on their land and wanted rid. In 1964 they donated it to Irwin. He re-erected it on the farm and stored his collection of old tools and other artefacts inside. Next thing he knew people wanted to come round and see so he began charging them admission.

Today that small start has developed into the Museum of Appalachia, sixty-three acres and thirty-six rebuilt salvaged structures. Wooden Appalachia preserved. Rice's diligent and, it has to said, civilized collecting has occupied a lifetime. His approach was not to attend auctions but to knock on doors. To turn up wearing a suit and a tie and ask straight if he could buy old items they might have. He didn't want their fiddles, their furniture, their weird and wonderful hand built banjos to sell in the cities and profit by. He wanted to preserve them and if they had a story then he'd preserve that too.

On the brochure it says that the Museum is a Smithsonian Affiliate, incorporated, and with a formal board of directors. St Fagans' style, I imagined, a folk museum in the formal tradition. I needn't have worried. Rice's Appalachian make do and mend approach remains all pervading.

Signs are hand painted and interpretation boards hand written, mostly by Rice Irwin himself. They range from the fascinating to the naive, from the folksy to the surreal, from the profound to the amazing. In addition to the buildings there are four exhibition halls. The range and extent of the collections on show give Oxford's Pitt Rivers[95] a feeling that if it wanted to compete then it would need to drop acid.

Highlight is the Kentucky coal miner turned Bible-pusher Harrison Mayes' collection of evangelical extravaganzas. These include concrete crosses, a bike covered in urgings to convert to Christianity, and inspirational Christian messages prepared for use on the moon. Mayes believed that his tracts, if suitably placed, would eventually be visible throughout the Solar System. There's a photo of him and his wife, craggy, withered, and smiling. He wears a badly pressed, ill-fitting suit, topped with a trilby hat. In his hand he holds the Good Book. He could be coming out of the Gospel Hall in Minster Road, Cardiff.

Elsewhere are collections of Indian arrow heads, rocks, wood carvings, a whittling exhibition, wooden toys, furniture, tools, a complete general store and rural post office, naïve paintings, cases containing examples of the sort of trading goods white men used to bribe local Native Americans. Beads, pins, watches, hats. The halls do not seem to end. Rice Irwin collected anything and everything. He labelled it all, and went to huge lengths to be complete. There's not a single aspect of hillbilly mountain life that isn't covered. Everything individually made and at least eighty per cent of it from wood.

Here's a note attached to a rocking chair: "Rowe Martin, a bachelor, used this chair to sit in with any women visitors. In his 80s he sold me the chair because he was 'getting too damn old to be interested.'" And another next to a bottle: "Jep Mackey lives far back in the mountains of Hancock, Co., and likely never saw a ship so he made a 'chair in a bottle'."

In the little wooden chapel there's a book entitled *We Welcome Your Prayer Requests For Reverend Brock*. Included in it is a handwritten list of requests for intercession on behalf of the sick and needy including one that asks we "pray that mam finds her way back to simplicity". Just to ensure we are still in the real world on the opposite page Kristina writes that if you want a good time she's the best. She leaves a mobile number.

Music, the thing that interests me the most, I find last. In the bowels of the Appalachian Hall of Fame, down beyond the folk art and the coopering and the fully-furnished Appalachian Port Office counter, is a whole exhibition hall devoted to Appalachian music.

Rice Irwin could have ignored everything else and just left his acquisitions to the musical. If he'd done that then he'd still have managed to assemble a collection that was worth coming half way round the world to see. Rice's thinking was direct. He'd visited a hundred distant cabins set in hollows and on the sides of mountains. Most of them would be shy of furniture but they would all have one, two, maybe three musical instruments. Nothing bought mail order, everything created by the occupant from whatever it was that came to hand.

To begin with there are displays that relate to the musical pioneers. Bill Monroe's summer hat and whole host of photos. The Carter Family in sepia glory plus their hand saw, plough point, and possum board. There's a case devoted to the Solemn Old Judge George D. Hay who founded the Opry. There are cowboy hats, neck-ties and shorts that belonged to a whole raft of local singers and musicians. There are features on Roy Acuff, Hugh Ballad Cross (who was the first to record *Wabash Cannonball*), Horney Rodgers, Fiddlin' Bob Seivers and Chet Atkins.

Horney Rodgers, who was Irwin's cousin, was asked how he rated himself as a fiddler. He took his time thinking and then he replied "I'm the only man that I ever heard that played the fiddle jest exactly the way I wanted to hear it played[96]".

Finally there's the centrepiece – John Rice Irwin's unrivalled and gargantuan collection of hand-built musical devices. Here are banjos made from ham tins, lard cans, bed warmers, kettles, cooking pots, gourds, cardboard and metal boxes. They have tops of wood, and of home-cured groundhog hide and resonators made from metal hub caps. They are round. They are square. They are octagonal. They have frets and they are fretless. Some look like the real thing. Others look like creations out of *The Clangers*.

In each case Irwin has tried to detail ownership and geographic origin. Uncle Tim Tinch's banjo. The Hiram Sharp fiddles from Scott County. The Dora Mullins bowed dulcimer (which looks like a small submarine) from Lee County, Virginia. Hiram Sharp's mouth bow from Norma, TN. There's a shot of Lawrence Warwick of Dark Hollow playing it. It reminds me of an overlarge tooth flosser. You look at it all and try to imagine how all these things sounded, on dark nights in the electricity-less hills.

There are hand carved approximations of what a guitar might be like. A sort of dobro made from an ironing board, and cases containing scores of harmonicas, mouth bows, Jew's harp and other things you blow and thump and pluck. It's a total wonderland.

Next to Tommy Cline's banjo, from Ball Play, Monroe County, the foot of the Great Smoky Mountains, is a sign where Irwin tells us how he found it. "'Now ain't that something,' Tommy said when I pulled the banjo from under a pile of old boxes and discarded clothing. 'I ain't tried to play him for years – never did play much. They's a feller named Kenneth Williams that made that fer me. He kilt a groundhog and tanned his hide to make the head with. It ain't doing me no good; so I reckon I'll jest sell him to you fer the Museum so people can see how poor folks had to do.'"

In the café out front locals gather. This is Sunday and they've all just come from church. With everyone in their ironed Sunday best it's a living exhibit. The café serves only Appalachian food of the kind you might have eaten when the roads were dirt and the secessionists were still in charge. Devilled eggs, sweet potato casserole, grits. Pay for a coffee and then get several Appalachian fill-ups for free. We drive on feeling that this is still as much the frontier as it used to be.

I recall once, years ago, sitting at the back of the London Musician's Collective in the ragged scruff of a building it occupied in Chalk Farm. I was there for a Bob Cobbing-organised day of sound poetry bewilderment, about as far from bluegrass as you can get. Clive Fencott had already been on wearing a sort of broadcasting radio receiver round his neck and we'd watched Paul Burwell manipulate his "new and discovered musical instruments" – wasp trap buzz phones and Aeolian things that whistled and clanged when you swung them round. Hand built, all of them. For all the world they resembled the kind of thing I've just been looking at in Rice Irwin's museum. Bill Griffiths was explaining to me about how roads that go west have a golden quality. For him it was something to do with the way the leys ran and how the world's alignment made it so. For him the west was an experience filled with cloud castles and horse-mounted armies wearing diamond vests. For me the west could only ever contain cowboys and men with gnarled faces playing harmonicas and fiddles. Hear that sound and you knew the land of the button down shirt and the spreadsheet had been left behind.

A little north of the museum but west of the mountains is Dumplin Valley, a place where the back of your neck gets red from the bending over the plough and the Confederates failed for lack of cannon, ammunition and shoes[97]. The Valley is one of those like the Dulais in South Wales, where there are no apparent valley sides, no discernible notch in the landscape and no sense of enclosure. There is simply a watercourse bubbling and land that slides slowly down. We've come here for the Dumplin Valley Bluegrass Festival which advertises itself via a homemade web site that makes it sound pretty much like the one we experienced back at Cherokee.

The festival is run by Joe and Mitzi Soward. Joe is "in construction". Mitzi takes care of their camping ground rental and the family. The farm they live on is a real one with four silver grain storage elevators standing next to it like ivy-covered spaceships.

Parking is in a field. Already a great cluster of RVs and Winnebago-style motorhomes rings the performance space. Some have set out tubbed plants, satellite dishes and hammered name boards into the grass next to their step-up entrances. "Rudy & Deola's Bar and Grill. Joe's Homestead." It's reassuringly warm.

The set-up is pretty much as it usually is for these affairs: covered stage, bring your own chair, food stalls and merch surrounding. It costs $30 each to get in. Everyone is welcoming and super friendly. Our accents still cut it.

Writers before me have already worked out that bluegrass is often an enjoyment of the middle-aged and the elderly. It's like that again today. Bluegrass has added value as music with mystique. It's an ancient-sounding new magic with banjo that kills and voices that can scrape lines of mist across the skies. Its festivals dot the mountains. Camping ground to camping ground, farm field to barn to empty space. There are festivals, it seems, running anywhere where there's a highway and a place to park your SUV. But unlike the old folk celebrated back at the Museum of Appalachia today's music's practitioners are young. They are bright sparks with supple hands and soaring voices, kids who can play the hell out of fiddle and use a banjo to stop charging bears. Their audiences sit. Dungareed, overweight, baseball-hatted. Wrong side of forty. Still.

Mitzy, whom I meet at the gate, tells me that a decade or more ago she and her husband saw a concert in a field somewhere in North Carolina, up near Boone. On stage was the amazing Doc Watson. Man, voice, technique, range and guitar. Joe and Mitzi were entranced. They decided then that they could do that. Not play like Doc but set up a festival to which he could come. They had the land, the farm, the already concreted spaces. What things would make a difference? Rain cover, hardcore floor, a proper toilet block. They laid these things on and invited a few bands round to their farm to play. The idea worked. The Dumplin Bluegrass Festival is now in its fifteenth year

Around the field are leaflets advertising future shows – Racoon Mountain, Chattanooga; Bluegrass on the Plains at Auburn, Alabama: Cherokee Bluegrass at the Happy Holiday RV Village and dozens more. The names of the performers permutate. You want to hear Rhonda Vincent? She's at Dumplin on Saturday and again next week at both Cherokee and Auburn. Little Roy and Lizzy are here and show up again soon at Cherokee. Marty Raybon will be there too. Last seen at Dollywood. A field in West Virginia next. It's work, wolves need to be kept at bay.

Dumplin's afternoon programme, performed in front of a goodly crowd of still and largely silent locals, repeats in the evening. Same bands, different order. The show finishes with stars Cordle, Jackson and Sally who do a sort of strong on harmony Eagles-take on mainstream country. Three mature guitar players, weather-beaten, bronzed, check-shirted men. Each sitting on a stool. More California than old time but they go down well.

The evening slots are stronger than the afternoons warm-ups. As ever there are frequent praise the Lords and gospel numbers performed by everyone. At one point, during Jimbo Whaley's Greenbrier slot – we are all actually asked to pray. Most do. "I've let the Lord into my heart, you do too." The bands are all slick and highly professional. They stay in tune and know how to keep their public onside. They barely draw breath between numbers. Adkins and Loudermilk are followed by Junior Silk and Ramblers Choice. The Little Roy and Lizzy Show featuring a still pretty spritely seventy-odd year old Roy Lewis adds humour and breakneck banjo.

Out on the merch stall Jimbo, the largest personality present by a long chalk, is keen to demonstrate the app he has on his phone that will process credit cards. I oblige. On stage earlier he told the tale of how the Knoxville Girl got herself beaten to death for using up her lover's iPhone minutes. We talk about the song's origins. He prefers The Osborne Brothers' version to The Louvins'. In his second set he undergoes the ice bucket challenge to raise money for a cancer victim and then invites his father up on stage to sing bass on a Christian number.

It's great. Despite the frequency of the presentational clichés and the hillbilly flavour to bluegrass itself. That's its joy. The high speed meshing of fiddle and banjo that make such a spiralling sound.

Mitzi wants to visit the UK. She asks American questions about distance and the weather. Word gets around that we've come here all the way from distant Wales. Home always appears further when people tell you that they don't know where your home is. "Right there," I say, "between England and Ireland. Not so far." They all want to know about the Queen. Where we stand on Scottish devolution and what will happen to HMQ? Does she have Scots's blood? Does she actually own Buckingham Palace? Might she like Jimbo showing up at St George's Chapel to liven up the hymn singing? And does it actually rain all the time?

27 • The Big Bang

The road skirts Newport and then rolls down towards Bristol. The topography of river valley, farm and conifer begins gently to remind me of home. I look for a Cardiff or a Swansea but amid the green only find Rogersville, Jonesville, and Jefferson City. Bristol is right on the border line where Tennessee turns into Virginia. Both states are putting themselves up as mother lodes for Americana. Virginia has The Crooked Road, which makes it sound like Ireland. Tennessee settles for the more prosaic blues to bluegrass. Whichever one you choose you are going to experience music.

Bristol itself manages to owe allegiance to the two States simultaneously. The Tennessee half and the Virginia half each have their own mayor, government, local ordinances and police force. Administrative schizophrenia you'd imagine but despite variations in local taxes and totally different police uniforms it seems to work. The State line, marked by brass plates in the centre of the road, runs right along State Street. Visitors puzzle at it, locals rarely do. Bristol was named after its west of England predecessor. Totally inappropriately. It's not on the coast, has no suspension bridge and has never been big in the wine trade.

It turns out to be a small and knowable town, well laid out, with parks, a war memorial and a fire station. A watercourse called Little Creek flows right through it. John Updike could have set a novel here. He didn't. Instead Stephen Hunter used this part of Tennessee for one of his Bob Lee Swagger fictions, *The Night of the Hunter*, filling the region with southern fried conspiracy, murdering hillbillies and a preponderance of meth labs. Didn't see any of those although I didn't really look.

Bristol is currently billing itself as the home to what it calls country music's big bang, the place where the music was first recorded. This was a totally different sort of country from the kind of thing that emerged later back in Nashville with its steel guitars and its radio-friendly songs and singers. Bristol's version was a mix of hillbilly scratch and Christian boondock gospel. At the start of the twentieth century, the dawn of recording, what we now call country music meant fiddles and banjos playing tunes that had been around for a lifetime. Opinion divides over just who it was who made the first country record. Much in the same way that argument rolls over where the blues came from and who actually recorded the first number. Best verifiable claimant is Texan Eck Robertson who, with his collaborator fiddle player Henry Gilliland, travelled to New York City in 1922 and recorded four fiddle duets for the Victor Talking Machine Company. The following day he returned and recorded a further six numbers on his own. Victor were slow to realise what they had and didn't imagine many would be interested in recordings of old fashioned jigs and scratchy dances. They didn't rush to take anything to market. Soon, though, things began to change. Radio, then a new and exciting medium, was carrying music into the hills and out to the farms. Hard to imagine this, steam radio being new. It feels to me as if it has always been there, rolling its non-stop chattering voices out into the ether. The farmers and the lumberjacks and the hillbillies didn't want to hear grand opera or great orchestras. They wanted their own music. Melodies they knew, tunes that had been handed down through the generations. *Ragtime Annie. Sally Gooden. Done Gone. There's a Brownskin Gal Down the Road. Turkey in the Straw.* Just like those recorded by Eck.

On record Eck was soon joined by others. In 1923/4 Henry Whittier, a Virginia mill worker who played guitar, recorded for Okeh. *The Wreck of the Southern Old 97* and *Lonesome Road Blues* were both released in the early twenties. But it was with Fiddlin' John Carson, a garrulous old-time fiddle convention winner, that country music finally broke through. Carson had broadcast on the brand new WSB radio station in Atlanta. His fame spread and Okeh president Ralph Peer was persuaded to come to the Georgian capital in 1923 to record him. In a vacant building on Nassau Street Carson cut two sides. *Little*

Old Log Cabin In The Lane and *The Old Hen Cackled and the Rooster's Going to Crow*. Peer thought the recordings "pluperful awful" but, so as not to waste the session completely, produced 500 blank label copies for Carson himself to sell. They went like lightening. Peer then formally released the tracks on Okeh and sold them into the new and emerging backwoods market. Rural country music as a commercial proposition was born.

The Big Bang that Bristol claims was Peer's attempt to capitalise on his discovery. Rural music could make money, as he'd proved. But you needed product. In New York City there were not many country fiddle players nor backwoods banjo men singing in nasal harmony. Uncle Dave Macon, Vernon Dalhart, Ernest Stoneman and others had made recordings but they hardly constituted an industry. Peer, who had now left Okeh for Victor, set out to find what he needed at source.

He used the newly invented electronic recording equipment. Unlike its acoustic predecessors (of the kind employed by Eck, Whittier and Carson) this kit was both portable and able to pick up the sounds of softer instruments such as guitars, dulcimers, and Jew's harps. On the advice of his friend and collaborator, the autoharp, harmonica and guitar player Ernest Stoneman, he travelled right through southern Appalachia looking for talent. He recorded what he found, paying artists on the spot. But the hunt was random and results were slow to arrive. He needed to consolidate. He decided to set up someplace and have the performers come to him. Like Henry Ford he'd create his own production line.

In 1927, again at Stoneman's urging, he settled on Bristol as a likely centre and advertised his needs in the local paper. "Don't deny yourself the sheer joy of Orthophonic music" ran an advert in the *Herald Courier* for Clark-Jones-Sheely and Company's Victrola retailing operation on State Street. In a square below a drawing of a woman sitting on a sofa in front of her new (and huge) gramophone was a note asking for likely players to enquire in store about Peer's forthcoming recording sessions. Word got around. Between 25th July and 5th August, 1927 Peer captured on record 76 tracks from 19 performers. These included not only old hands Ernest Stoneman and Henry Whittier but also scooped up, among others, The Blue Ridge Corn Shuckers,

Dad Blackard's Mountaineers, The Bull Mountain Moonshiners, Ernst Phipps and His Holiness Quartet, Alfred G Karnes, Mr and Mrs J W Baker and The Alcoa Quartet. In addition he recorded both Jimmie Rodgers and the legendary Carter Family. If anything launched country as both a musical form and a commercial industry then this was it. Bristol's bang was big for sure.

In Bristol's Big Bang country music there are no parts, voices sing together when they sing at all. Diction is crude, the right notes are reached only occasionally. Guitars scrape. Fiddles sound as if they are sawing their way out of a retirement home for ancient tunes. Harmonicas wow and flutter. You could make these sounds yourself with a washboard, a tea chest and a three-chord guitar. You could stand on a street corner and people would put coins in your hat. But that's what the rural world wanted and what they got. Old time. And, as ever, with God pretty high up in the mix.

Kurt Wolff, in his *Country Music – The Rough Guide* (2000) says that it's one of the great dichotomies of the American South that hardcore traditionalism and, as he puts it, "good-ole-boy partying" are equal parts of a single heritage. You fear God and you follow his ways. You also drink corn liquor and sing your head off.

The 1927 Bristol sessions were the first of many. In them Peer sought not simply to record the traditional musics of the hills but to add and amalgamate and create new sounds. Further sessions followed in Bristol again the next year and also in nearby Johnson City. None, however, had quite the ground-breaking impact of his first Bristol recordings. Hillbilly music was proving itself a marketable, and enjoyable product. Country music soared.

Not that the music was actually known as country at the time. During the Twenties and the Thirties record companies and radio stations called the music *old-time, old-fashioned, string-band, old familiar, music from Dixie* or *hillbilly*. The term *country* didn't arrive until the Forties when a new name to encompass cowboy music, western swing along with the original hilly bill sounds of the mountains was needed. Country, rather than town, was the perfect word.

Bristol celebrates its centrality in this musical universe by hosting the annual three-day Bristol Rhythm and Roots Reunion Festival.

This year it has also opened a brand new and literarily sparkling Birthplace of Country Music Museum. They've already renamed the road outside as Birthplace of Country Music Way, a fact not understood by our gps. Not that this matters. For the Festival the whole town is shut to traffic.

Rhythm and Roots centres on Americana which means loads of bluegrass, acoustic, and backwoods music along with anything that scratches and nasally swings. The whole downtown gives itself over to music. "You can't go ten yards," as Festival Director Leah Ross points out, "without hearing something." Walking in the sun among the 55,000 attendees, the twenty-one stages and the countless food and drink concessions you get the sense of a Glastonbury without the mud, a Green Man with a US accent, or an acoustic Sŵn.

It started in 2001 at the suggestion of local councillor David Shumaker. He was standing before the town's country music mural – a great side-of-buildings painting of the Big Bang stars created in 1987 by artist Tim White – and realised that the next step was clearly to bring the music back. As festivals do this one began small and grew. Leah Ross reckons the size is about right now. Scheduling 150 acts might be a nightmare but the results work. Small but perfectly formed.

Motel 6's slogan is officially "We'll leave the lights on for you." On a wall next to reception it says "Why spend money on a hotel when you could spend it on life". Better would be "because you deserve better than the backseat of some car". Rates are up. This is Festival time and there's a Festival shuttle bus stop in the parking lot outside.

Our room has all the joy of a student residence. No carpet, wipable vinyl instead. No doors on the wardrobes. No drawers. Open rails with hangers that fall off when you touch them. No fridge. No coffee maker. A basic bed offering a single foam pillow each. The view is the side of the warehouse next door. You can see the sky if you put your face right by the glass and peer. The air con makes a massive roaring noise as it blows the plastic curtains out horizontally. Bugs crawl on the ceiling. They crunch when you squash them. During the small amount of time we actually spend in this desperate chamber I manage to despatch fourteen. The lift is broken, access is via the fire stairs. A notice suggests that there is free coffee every morning in the lobby. In the three days we are here I never saw a pot.

At the new museum country music is banging big. You'd think it ran the world. Maybe here it does. In the mock recording studio you can perform your own karaoke version of tracks taken from the original sessions. We select *I Am Bound For The Promised Land*, recorded in 1927 and from which the voice of Alfred G. Karnes has been removed. Karnes was a guitar-playing Pentecostal preacher from Bedford, Virginia. His gospel was fervent but his faltering tenor restrained. On our version we let it rock. Out front you can still buy the original. It is included in the multi-disc complete sessions box but you need to be rich to own that.

The actual site of the original Bristol Big Bang recordings was the Taylor-Christian Hat Company Warehouse round the corner on State Street. Naturally, and like so many things of historical value, it's gone. The building burned down in the 1940s. It has been replaced with a parking lot. I take another photograph of historically-relevant empty space.

Downtown is festival full and it buzzes. There are crowds on the streets and sun in the sky. You can buy street food in a hundred flavours and in a bewildering array of tastes. Shaved Ice, Nachos and Cheese, Chocolate Dipped Cheesecake, Spiral Cut Taters, Fried Green Tomatoes, Footlong Corn Dogs, Po Boy Sandwiches, Crawfish Etouffee, Cheddar Jalapeno Hush Puppies, Funnel Cakes, Jerk Chicken, Deep Fried Pickles, Dogs, Dips, Coke, Chips. You can buy scented candles and spiral-dyed tees, jewellery made from guitar picks, books of Bristol short stories. There's a stand which offers you a stool, amplification and a plugged in guitar. You sing the song. There is an atmosphere of Orthophonic joy everywhere.

The stages multiply. They run from the corners at the back of bars to a grand reconditioned 1920s movie house. There are stages set in the parks, on parking lots, at the top of streets, on waste ground, in the main square. There are twenty-one venues and more than one hundred and sixty acts spread over three days. Highlight is the woman who has been at the near centre of alternative country music for decades, Emmylou Harris. She's on with a new band featuring a young Australian, Jed Hughes, on roaring Jimi Hendrix lead. St Paul and The

Broken Bones, soul revivalists from Birmingham, Alabama give her a run for her money. Elsewhere the mix is as eclectic as the word roots will allow. Bluegrass, newgrass, folk, alternative, old time, swamp rock, blues. Red Molly, Love Its, Balsam Range, Flat Lonesome, Town Mountain, Parker Millsap. Dozens of others.

Wandering the Bristol festival streets it's hard not to home in on the tees. Almost everyone has a slogan on their back:

Heartless Bastard
Knoxville Girl
Enjoy Freedom – Thank a Marine
Willie F@$%#n Nelson – That's who
Supercolt Cowboy Land
Hate The Runs
Drink Wisconsibly
If You Ain't The Lead Dog The Scenery Never Changes

A day later and it's Sunday. We walk to the First Southern Baptist Church just up beyond the famous Bristol illuminated sign that tells us all that this is a good place to live.

The church is white in both congregation and structure. It's large and well kept. It's offering a special Rhythm and Roots service featuring local gospel singers Westwend and everyone is so enormously pleased to see us. The pastor, Ronnie Brewer, looks just like an evangelical TV southern pastor would. Tall, fit, bronzed, clean-shaven, grey locks flowing back in waves, crisp slacks, deep navy blue blazer. He shakes our hands, gives us a blessing from the front. We sing a hymn, say a prayer and then listen to what has to be nine whole songs by Westwend, not the most innovative duo I've come across but tuneful and engagingly Christian.

There are around a hundred in the congregation, older mainly. Across the aisle is a man in his seventies with white hair worn long over his collar. He wears a white suit which has faint blue stripes. He has crocodile shoes and no socks. On his wrist is an expensive gold watch. As the service progresses he takes notes.

"If you are a Southern Baptist you don't dance or jig around. My daddy told me that," says Westwend's Wendy Crowe. It's unseemly and

God will frown. My man over the aisle hasn't heard this. When the songs demand it he taps his reptile-skinned foot.

Back in town it's Jerron Blind Boy Paxton, Ancient Cities, The Honey Island Swamp Band, Swear & Shake, The Tumbleweed Wanderers, Motel Rodeo, Billy Joe Shaver and more.

On the far side of the nearby drinkers' enclosure, half under the trees, The Appalachian Highlanders are tuning up. These surreal-looking performers consist of six Scottish pipers and three drummers – one bass and two side. All wear a full Scottish regalia of kilt and socks and sporrans. Before they begin I ask their leader, Pipe Major Randy Stanley from Big Gap, Virginia, where he stands on Scottish Independence. "I'm asking you this simply because of the way you are dressed, you understand". He smiles. "The *Guardian* rang and asked me the same thing. They wanted to get a perspective from here but we don't really have one. The Scots-Irish in these hills are more Irish than they are Scots. I think the Scots should stay." With that he turns and the pipe and drum Highlanders, all wearing the Mackenzie tartan "for the beauty and elegance it brings", break into *Shenandoah*, followed by *Amazing Grace* and then *Scotland the Brave*.

Frank Fairfield, described in the programme as "channelling the spirit of another era", is stranded on a tiny stage under a fire escape in a side street. He appears to have lost his nerve and is asking the mc if he can finish early. The audience seem nonplussed. In desultory fashion Fairfield creaks and plucks at his banjo. The mc nods. Fairfield stands and bows and says he's sorry he's been such an arse. Everyone cheers, either in support or agreement. How can I tell?

Back at the Motel I count up the number of acts I've witnessed over the past three weeks. Seventy-six. Same number as the tracks Peer recorded at the first Bristol sessions. In this hunt for roots I'm leading such a symmetrical life.

28 • Nashville Again

The Tennessee State Fair is rather like the Royal Welsh Show. It has a permanent showground and it features animals. After that comparisons fail. The ground is just south of Nashville's downtown, next to the speedway. I feel rather as if I am in an episode of the Simpsons. As ever the Fahrenheit is high. Ahead is the prospect of garishly decorated rides, massive pumpkin contests and fast food. There'll be a car park so big we'll lose the car and the fair itself will rock with records from my youth.

My knowledge of State Fairs comes almost entirely from the musical film of the same name with a little bit extra picked up from their appearance outside Smallville in Superboy comics. I expect to encounter giant hog contests and all you can eat shows. There will be displays of huge pies, demonstrations of cow branding and open top car racing. When we get there it turns out to be free entry for over 50s day with most of the rides shut. Instead there's a shambles of schoolkids bussed in to see all the agricultural stuff and hordes of oldsters playing bingo and having free lunches provided by the Chamber of Commerce. No huge pies – meat loaf and gravy in their place. At the entrance gate the uniformed ticket taker waves us through without checking anything and tells us that if we're quick we can get a complimentary lunch too.

We've been taken up the slowly rising entrance path by electric buggy as if we were disabled somehow. At the top is a welcome machine. This is outside the dining hall, currently stuffed with furiously eating baseball-capped pensioners. The machine's operator, a spindly woman in her late 50s, thrusts cards into our hands. "Just slide them down that there slot an see if you won a prize." We do and we have. Everyone does. You need to enter your full contact data in order to claim which means they've then got you. The prize, it turns out, is a night at a hotel in the Smokies where you have to buy dinner in order to avoid any charge. Dinner costs $60. "What kind of hotel is this," I ask? "Mid-range," drawls the over-weight salesman inside the booth. "A nice place. Certainly not Motel 6." I know what he means, if the place we stayed in Bristol was anything to go by. "We're not here long enough," I tell him, "sorry." What I should have done was say that I hadn't won and see what reaction that provoked.

The displays in the fair itself consist of the advertised giant pumpkin contest with a sideshow of cakes, tarts, biscuits, waffles and pies. These things are a huge as you imagine them to be. A single Tennessee pumpkin would fill our fireplace. Best is the hay contest where entrants pitch their bales against each other for colour, texture, durability and cost of seed. When it's not singing Tennessee is hay country. There are displays of machinery and booths selling lease deals to help you get your giant crops in. Beyond these agricultural wonders is a gargantuan model railway manned by two oldsters dressed as footplate men. There's a sign alongside advertising meetings of The Happi Hookers of Nashville. I looked them up. They are a sit and stitch crochet group.

Walking through the rides with their silence and stillness feels as if the whole of Porthcawl funfair had been transferred to the moon. Nobody is selling funnel cake, the Spinning Jenny and the Mine Shaft Rock and Rolla are completely at rest. At the bottom, beyond the deserted replica of a real gold mine, there's a corral in which a lone horse is being exercised by someone looking just like Tex Ritter. As we approach he smiles. "Gotta water ma horse," he mumbles and leads the animal into a distant stable. A smell of animals wafts over in the rising heat. In the air conditioned dining hall they have moved on to the advertised Champion Bingo.

At the exit lines of black kids are being loaded onto a bright yellow school bus. They are all talking at once. For them the Fair has worked. Day out. Sight of giant root vegetables and racks of apple tart. No one asking you to add anything up or write anything down. What more could you want. We start the long walk through the parking lot for our car, slotted tidily several miles off. The sun beats. Barry Island without the sea. And the rides come to that.

Despite the heat outside there's now a rainstorm. We are back at the hotel and need to go two or three blocks down towards the Columbia River to visit the new Johnny Cash Museum. Cash is an icon. He's the Sun rock and roll singer who never quite fitted. Looked the part but wasn't. He's also the country star who to my ears rarely ever sounds as if he's singing country. He does the old time tunes. He sings about the flag, the Indians, gambling, fighting, trucks, trains, prisons and rivers. He does it rockabilly. He does it folksong. He does it half spoken and overloaded with mawkish sentiment. He does it with his family encircled, presenting himself as a God-fearing red neck American. He does it as an outlaw, a fighter, a blue-collared gangster just ridden in from the west. He gets nearer to God than most and sings hymns and praises as if he really means them. And he does. He's had a career as long as your arm, made more than 100 albums and worked his way into the long black coated heart of most Americans.

He began in Memphis in the mid-fifties. Like Elvis he walked into Sam Phillips' Sun studios and, after a couple of false starts, recorded *Hey Porter* and *Cry! Cry! Cry!* The songs, despite their clear rockabilly leanings were hits on the country chart. His backing musicians who established his trademark boom-chicka-boom rhythm from the word go were The Tennessee Two. Luther Perkins on guitar and Marshall Grant on bass. They were joined later by drummer WS Holland cleverly rebooting themselves The Tennessee Three.

Cash led a life full of extreme opposites. He slid from meeting presidents to falling apart on narcotics, from landing in jail seven times to winning the National Medal For The Arts, and from setting fire to whole forests to becoming a national treasure with his own Christmas TV shows promoting a fervent Southern Baptist religion. Cash was a regular backslider, a cultivator of his gunfighter outlaw image and a rebel to the end. His career had highs followed by long periods of red neck low. But in his final years Cash once again triumphed. His long series of new millennium *American Recordings* present some of the most enduring songs he ever cut, folk songs still, slices of rockabilly, touches of rootsy pop, gospel, pain, pure Johnny Cash.

He was born in Arkansas but the Cash family home was in Hendersonville. That's about as far up the Cumberland River from Nashville as Pontypridd is up the Taff from Cardiff. Nashville claims him as a native son.

Because of the rain we take a taxi. Three blocks downhill. Our cab has a driver who insists pedantically in putting the museum's address into his sat nav. "Do you have the zip code?" he asks. He's new to the job, recently arrived from Ethiopia. Immigration is still how the USA works. "How do you like America?" I ask. "It's wonderful," he says.

The Johnny Cash Museum in a converted warehouse on Third Avenue South opened last year. It replaces the one lost to fire at the old Hickory Lake site in Hendersonville. Compared to the lavish Elvis displays in Memphis and the glorious industrial-strength reach of the Country Music Hall of Fame round the corner this museum is compact. However, it packs a punch. Cash memorabilia is available in quantity. His guitars, his clothes, his gold discs, his hundreds of 12 inch albums, his air service code books, the amp on which Luther Perkins laid down the infectious two-beat thump of *I Walk The Line*, Johnny Cash on reel to reel, 8-track, 10-inch 78, cassette, 7-inch vinyl. You can listen and compare the quality. The 78 seems to have by far the most power.

The audio-visual content blisters. In front of the John Cash on film display, thankfully with seat provided, I watch slices from the Man in Black's many movie appearances. There are far more than I imagined. In one of the earliest, *Five Minutes To Live*, made in 1961 and starring the singer as Johnny Cabot, a two-bit gangster, Cash comes over as about as accomplished an actor as Elvis. But he does improve. In 1971, opposite Kirk Douglas, he plays a cowboy in *A Gunfight*, making a convincing job. He's a Christian in *The Gospel Road* and the narrator in a film about Gene Autry, *Melody of the West*. His broadcast credits are even more extensive. He guests on *Colombo* and appears as any number of western characters from Jesse James' brother to Davy Crocket in a score of made for TV pictures. If he'd never sung a note he could have made a decent living here.

Beyond the rooms which display Cash costumes, hats and guitars, the Museum opens out into an echoing performance area. This is currently in use to display 'The Legends of Sun Records'. There's a big screen showing a rolling programme of rock and roll film clips – Elvis in action, Jerry Lee beating the hell out of *Whole Lotta Shakin'* and Roy Orbison rocking as ever without moving a muscle. Around the walls are display cases of Sun Records memorabilia and giant photos of the big five: Roy Orbison, Jerry Lee Lewis, Johnny Cash, Elvis Presley and Carl Perkins. There's something spooky about Perkins in his 50s persona. He reminds me, just a little, of Bert Weedon.

There's a case showing shoes – Roy's performance boots in gold and white leather looking like the kind of thing a pantomime princess would wear. Then there are Perkins' original blue suede shoes – the ones that launched a whole era. They are tooled, pale blue suede uppers, black leather heel and sides. Thin leather sole. Slips-ons. Absolutely nothing like the brothel creepers favoured by British teds. Again history has been lost in translation.

Outside we tour Nashville's Lower Broadway which is alive with activity. This is honky tonk street where you drink and listen to music. Most of the bar bands on show this time of the day are not playing country music at all. At Jimmy Buffett's Margaritaville Restaurant Bar (Live Music) Adam Rausche does *Brown Eyed Girl*. Over the road the Lower Broadway band are knocking out a version of Fleetwood Mac's *Rhiannon*.

At Ernest Tubb's Record Shop which has been selling country music for at least sixty years there is the largest collection of country and roots CDs anywhere. It was once the largest collection of country on vinyl but mediums change. Soon digital download will see Tubb fail. The future looks bleak. But it's not here yet. Rear of the store is a stage where they mount weekly concerts. The staff are the experts you'd want them to be (although they can't locate Shawn Camp's *Bluegrass Elvis* which I'm hunting). "Who is the best female country singer around now?" "Well you could try Jewel, Kellie Pickler or Jessica Simpson but much better would be Rhonda Vincent." Amongst all the acres of country space we are pretty much the only customers. That future is arriving fast.

Down the street Paul Lawrence's large Record Shop is also on its last legs. Customers are as scant as free beer, the air feels full of dust.

There are vinyl stacks in a quantities rivalled only by the record dump I found earlier in Asheville. The hunt through this graveyard is so dispiriting. The past flicking through my fingers. Once wonder now dross. Has he got Shawn Camp? He shakes his head.

At Dixieland Delights, branded as a souvenir shop and offering a menagerie of weirdness in the same league as Schwab's Dry Goods in Memphis, the attraction is the Willie Nelson Fortune Telling Machine. Here a glass-cased approximate replica of the great man offers to speak to you in exchange for a dollar. I insert a bill and Willie springs slowly to life. "Your fortune will be good," he tells me, jerking his head a little in his illuminated box, "I can talk for a while but I talk too much. If you want to hear more then give me further money." Then he shuts up and a ticket pops out of a slot down below, where his legs would be, if he had any. "Your flower is a jonquil" this piece of yellow paper informs. "Learn to keep a secret," it advises. "Your golden qualities make up for your talkativeness." Talkativeness, me? I depart the store silent but with all my golden bits glowing.

Outside a collection of half a dozen kids all under 12 have been assembled by their mother. She's on guitar. They play trumpets, cornets and a trombone. They do the most rocking version of *Soul Man* I've heard in a long while. A crowd has gathered blocking the traffic but no one cares. The dollars are going into the collecting basket by the dozen. The band rolls into *Knock On Wood*, the brass roars and young faces squeeze their eyes shut in soul-driven transportation.

We dine at the overfull Demos, the legendary steak and spaghetti house where you queue on a good day but in high season, and this is such a time, the wait can be 60 minutes. We leave our names. You get called over a street-mounted loudspeaker when your table is vacant. "Finch, party of two, your table is ready". Eventually this happens and we squeeze into a highly organised swinging joint full of rich laughter and smiling faces. I have grilled chicken tenderloins with all the usual American additions of plate salads, dips, southern sauces, greens you don't recognise, fried potatoes, and little crispy salt crackers done up in packets. In the washroom I can still hear the street loudspeaker calling the diners in. "Bryant party of two your table is ready, Jones party of twenty-nine your table is ready." We leave as the black Jones extended tribe arrive, all hugeness and glittering smiles. Getting into Demos makes you think you've beaten the world.

Nashville is mounting Live On The Green, a free street music festival with a main stage in the central square and stalls everywhere. After dark lasers light the sky. Half the local population are carrying glow sticks. Some have looped themselves, arms and wrists, waists and thighs. They resemble twenty-first century versions of a hoop decorated African tribe. The Lone Bellow, a young band centred on the trio of Zack Williams, Kanene Donehey Pipkin and Brian Elmquest are on stage. They are also on the de rigeur giant screen behind. This is southern roots rock, an indie-sounding twenty-first century mix of acapella and Jimmy Page guitar solos. In the rush of chant-worthy music which spins across the energy is palpable. It runs from native-sounding Appalachia right into a soul roar in the style of Janis Joplin. The instrumentation tells a lot. Mandolin, electric lead, double bass. Put those in the hands of Elbow, add close harmony and a high female voice and you might get something approximating what we are hearing now.

We miss the diminutive British platinum-seller Jake Bugg, along with the Cyndi Lauper-voiced singer, LP, Laura Pergolizzi, who looks like a 1966-era Bob Dylan. She's out back at the merch stall having her photos taken with a long stream of schoolkids, a queue dotted with the occasional bear-size gent in dungarees. LP dutifully smiles as she's hugged by huge hairy arms. Anything for a sale and everything for the selfie camera.

The following day the clouds are still with us. We roll south under high slate skies. The destination is Woodlawn Memorial, a huge cemetery where many departed country stars are buried. The graveyard is well kept, undulating, and almost completely free of upright memorials. Not one is visible although there are a small number of appropriately solemn statues – angels, obelisks, scrolls unscrolling, pots of fake flowers. The style here is for the memorial to be made of metal and laid flat onto the ground.

Dominating everything is a large, triangular-shaped and fenced-in plot headed by a grand and ornate Arc De Triomphe, a marble arch that radiates tack. This is the last resting place of drunken but enduring country giant George Jones. The acre of land in front offers space for the present generation of country singers. Jones wanted to gather them as they checked out and to pay for their last resting spaces. So far there's one admission – Johnny Paycheck. Flowers, metal marker. 1938-2003. Guitar in relief. Bunch of everlasting flowers.

George Glenn Jones' memorial has angels, vases, and guitars. "Jones – He Stopped Loving Her Today – The Possum". That's how he looked. A Possum. His nose and his ears gave him this unlikely nickname but he was one of country's most involving singers. Waylon Jennings said of him "If we all could sound like we wanted to, we'd all sound like George Jones." We are joined in our admiration for this totally over the top confection by two fellow grave hunters, here from North Carolina. "He wanted to give something back to the culture that sustained him," I'm told. Fair enough.

Inside the mausoleum building that dominates the cemetery a well-powdered elderly receptionist directs us across the plush carpet towards the halls where bodies lie behind marble. They are safe here in their elaborate coffins from the withering deprecation of Tennessee's soil. I am looking for Felice and Diadorius Boudleaux Bryant, composers of some of the most lasting of twentieth century pop songs. The country-edged rock numbers that dominated my youth. The slow and harmoniously aching sentiments that rolled right through the Americana movement. The songs that have been repeated by revivalists again and again. *Love Hurts, All I have To Do Is Dream, Bye Bye Love, Raining In My Heart, Brand New Heartache, Like Strangers, Devoted To You, Wake Up Little Susie, Take A Message To Mary, Rocky Top.*

Born in Georgia the duo had ended up in Tennessee's Smoky Mountain resort of Gatlinburg where they'd bought the Rocky Top Village Inn. Here they composed their best known work, *Rocky Top*, which became a bluegrass standard and was adopted as the state song for Tennessee. Now they are at rest, no longer creating but still singing. I can make *Love Hurts* appear as the soundtrack of my head anytime I want. But I can't find the location of their grave.

A pale wisp of a man in neat check slacks and soft shoes assists. "I'm looking for Boudleaux Bryant. You know where he is?" "Yep. The country songwriter. He's here, right next to my wife." He takes us. The Bryants are central, behind marble, names and dates, no fuss. "My wife, she passed last year. She borrowed a wedding dress from June Carter Cash. We got married with her wearing that. You'd like to see the other stars?" Beyond the unadorned Bryants is Tammy Wynette, 1942-1998, covered in flowers and photographs. Loving you, we do. Together forever. Gordon Stoker from The Jordanaires is here. Liz Anderson. JD Sumner. Otis Blackwell. Little Jimmy Dickens. The future is what you allow for here. Our informant, Ralph Martin (b.1935), has his already labelled up. It's there next to his wife. Closing date waiting to be filled.

Outside, on a slow rise which, according to Woodlawn's hand-out is called Sermon on the Mount, we find the line of Orbison tragedies, all of them, including Claudette. But no Roy. He lies, unmarked, in Westwood, California. Below, in Chapel Garden, lies Richard E Arnold – Eddy Arnold – second only as a country hit scorer to George Jones himself. But unlike Jones there are no after death celebrations here. Just a simple plate marking his spot along with that of his wife Sally. 1918-2008. Country music has now moved on.

Eddy lies pretty near William Owen Bradley, the Nashville patriarch who started the sound (see Chapter 12). Porter Wagoner is in Everlasting Life. Red Sovine is in Good Shepard. Marty Robbins is in Gethsemane. If you didn't know you were in a Christian country then you do now.

We drive south towards Murfreesboro. At the unincorporated township of Triune, where they have models of white horses on their roofs, we stop at an advertised flea market. Such things back home usually indicate bric-a-brac and antiques, clothes, old records, the detritus of society coming round again. This one turns out to be different. There's a $2 entrance charge collected by an weather-beaten cowboy perched on a stool. Apart from the guy running the livestock concession he's pretty much the only white guy on site. This market is an entirely Mexican affair. Stalls have been erected more or less where their owners have parked their cars. No rows, no order, a shambolic sprawl of covered stands selling clothes, brightly-coloured kids toys, slush puppy syrup in great jars, tools, bad denim jeans you wouldn't even see at Makro, Technicolor religious statuary, well rounded Christs and grinning sculls, plates, mugs, coils of wire, sweets by the shed load and then live chickens and ducks in cages. There's a hillbilly with a ZZ Top beard, tall denim dungarees, no shirt and sockless sneakers, running the poultry franchise. He pulls slowly on a pipe. For all the world this could be 1947.

It's rumoured that south of here a photographer has built himself a replica of Castell Coch. The entrance money cowboy knows the location. "Head south towards the interstate and you'll find it. He's been there a time. They built that interstate right across his land. Caused a whole heck of trouble. But I think he survived."

Castell Gwynn, an eight story conical-towered and very white actual castle does indeed stand in the trees a few miles to the south. Mike Freeman, the owner, and his wife Jackie, have done that typically American thing. Self-made and self-determining they've carved their own piece of the dream out of the woodlands of central Tennessee. "We had more land once," Mike tells me pointing south of his front door, "until they came and built that roadway." The original sweeping entrance drive was truncated when State authorities decided that the new I-840 had only one potential route and that was right across Mike's land. "They blasted their way through and we had roars and rocks flying and cracks appearing. There's been quite a bit of litigation. Don't get me started on all that."

Mike is a professional photographer who made his money at the end of the film era by photographing school seniors. "I could go in and take 900 shots and sell pretty much all of them the following day," he tells me. "But then digital photography arrived and the market collapsed." While we're talking I'm snapping as much as I can of the castle's white dazzle. "When they first built them most castles were as white as this," he says. "It made invaders imagine them to be bigger. We're keeping up the tradition."

Mike Freeman, a shambling Tennessean, a poor boy from Flat Rock he calls himself, has roots that go back to the British West Country. He's an eagle scout and a mason. He has an eye for history. As a student in the early sixties he saw Charlton Heston's film *War Lord* in which a single-tower Norman castle made an appearance and he was hooked. He looked up castles in the school library and came up a picture of

Castell Coch. William Burges' nineteenth century gothic adaptation of a Norman original in all its South Wales glory. That was it. He had to have one. Exhibiting great resolve he visited Wales, toured Castell Coch and got access to Burges' original drawings. He determined to adapt Bute's nineteenth century fantasy into a twentieth century one of his own. A dream it all might have been but here we are, fifty years later and, in the southern humidity, magnificently Freeman's vision has arrived.

With its twin white towers, conical roofs, slit windows and with space for a drawbridge out front this could well be how Castell Coch might have looked when it was first built by the invading thirteenth century Normans. Freeman tells me that he has no worries about any of this being considered as excessive (if, indeed, such a thing were possible in America). He's worked 18-hour days for decades and still does, so why shouldn't he now have what he wants?

The castle was begun in 1980. Avoiding professional architects totally the multi-talented Freeman produced sketches of how he imagined the castle to look – an historically accurate four tower edifice – and passed these over to a builder.

As we tour it becomes apparent that Mike is a total medievalist given to collecting anything and everything that might sit gracefully in a fortified residence. He mixes his periods fluidly filling rooms with swords from Viking to Civil War, suits of armour, helmets, face plates, halberds, instruments of torture, daggers, spears, flails and maces. He accumulates big time. Where the item he wants can't be found he signs up onto weapon-making metallurgy courses and creates his own. "That armour." he points to a full twelfth century-style set mounted astride a life-size model of a white horse. "I made that. And this one". He hands me a weighty Viking-style sword. I swing it slowly around myself. It's heavy enough to slice a car in half.

We climb the tight spiral staircase while Sue and Mike's historian friend Joy Marshall who has joined us use the lift. "Smallest elevator in Tennessee," says Mike. Inside the shaft the floor is about the size of a breadboard. The upper floors of Castell Gwynn are reserved as Mike and Jackie's private apartments. There are galleries of helmets (including one that looks just like Darth Vader), walls covered in lances and knives. The views out are always superb – miles of forest as far as the eye can go, cut, it has to be noted, by the unwanted snake of I-840. "They can see us when they drive west," says Mike. "Some of them come visiting. It's not an activity that we encourage. This is not a public facility."

In the bedrooms Mike has installed beautifully crafted wood panelling, much of it again made by his own hand. The panels twist and slide to reveal cupboards, shelves and in one case a secret passage. The castle is as castles should be. Except that this one has electricity, running water and insulated cavity walls.

Walking around Castell Gwynn's many floors there's a pervading sense of work in progress. While the bedroom and the bathroom are complete and offer the height of style and luxury other areas have still to be painted. There's a conventional Victorian-style conservatory half built on the sun facing side. Next will come a great hall with five car garage below. After that two more towers. Mike is telling me this while we relax on a plush leather sofa surrounded by Elizabethan portraits. We are drinking Coke, his wife Jackie's obsession. I've already been shown her collection of Coca-Cola memorabilia and marketing aids stacked out in the vast photographic studio Mike has built just down the hill. Entering this tribute to the real thing is like walking into a Disney-style fantasy. Coke cars, Coke glasses, Coke figurines, Coke clothes, Coke furniture, Coke bottles, Coke counters, Coke posters, Coke teapots, Coke trays, Coke life.

Jackie is enlivening proceedings with a string of anecdotes from her time at the Ryman. She collected tickets, managed the dressing rooms, showed the public in. "Dolly would sit with us and eat her sandwiches. Country singers are just folk."

So far capitalising on their Tennessean Celtic Border Castle has been restricted to one video shot for Taylor Swift (2009's *Love Story*) and the Freeman's own annual Tennessee Renaissance Festival. The Festival puts into play most of Mike's interests. There are horse-mounted jousting matches, medieval food, jesters, equestrian games, magic, displays of armour and heraldry, falcons, singing, and craftworks. Robin Hood puts in an appearance as does Queen Elizabeth. The programme for a recent Festival lists some unmissable attractions: bump a monk, knackerball, camel rides, mud slides, Oops! knife throwing, a human chess match, the Washing Well Wenches, the Da Vinci Brothers comic opera and Sloanwolf who entertain with bagpipes. Like the castle around which it is centred this is a grand affair. Seven stages and more than eighty stalls. "You'll have to come," suggests Mike. We must.

29 • The Stetson and Other Signs You Are In The Country

I'm outside the twin-domed front of the Gaiety cinema on City Road. I've got a mackintosh over my back like a western cape and a stick for a gun shoved inside my elastic s-buckle belt. Near as I can get to a fifties cowboy. I've got friends with me, a whole gang of them. It's Saturday mid-day and we've just emerged from a few hours of bliss watching episodes of Flash Gordon, Laurel and Hardy and a full B-movie western. Today it was Cody of the Pony Express in his buckskin jacket riding the range and vanquishing all foes with a brace of six-shooters. The mail, even out there in the arrow-filled desert wilds, just had to get through.

Back at Peter Hughes' house the only television in the entire district sat like a religious relic. It was encased in walnut and revered by all. Before it we clustered. On the black and white 405-line screen Hopalong flickered. Black Stetson, silver studded belt. There were others too. Gene Autry, the singing cowboy, unexpectedly breaking into *Back in the Saddle Again* while wearing an embroidered shirt with smiling mouth pockets and mother of pearl buttons. Roy Rogers, King of the Cowboys, in a Stetson and red bandana, galloping Trigger to the tune of *Happy Trails* or *Cool Water*. There was something here, subliminally, about gun smoke and western songs, about the rhythm of horses hoofs and the thrumming of guitars, about Stetsons and country music.

As kids we didn't know if we should become singers or marshals, Indian hunters or steel guitar pluckers, sharp shooters in white broad-brimmed hats or weary cow punchers squatting before camp fires playing *Home Home on the Range* on a Larry Adler harmonica. It got into the blood. On TV by far the most authentic-looking and stylish rustler hunter was the one with no name, The Range Rider[98]. Revered for his six shooting, his fairness and his unerring ability to always get his man the Rider was the perfect role model. He wore a yellow suede shirt with a big collar completely drenched in fringes long enough to fly out horizontally in the Texas breeze. There was nobody I knew who didn't want to be him.

Western dress, de rigueur in the actual west, rarely surfaced in British fashion. There were moments when cowboy boots, in particular cowboy boots for women, would be acceptable, even sexily racy. For a time they were a feature on London's Kings Road. But these moments were not many. Elements of western dress, in particular the bolo or shoe-string tie, moved as if by osmosis into the dress of Teddy Boys. There were also times when fringes hanging down from the arms of your massively round-collared leather jacket in the hippie seventies recalled the kind of thing Indians habitually wore, or so the films said. But if you wanted to see what cowboys dressed in then you needed to visit the places where they roamed.

The Stetson hat, which would make you look a little like Crocodile Dundee if you wore one on the streets of New York is common throughout the south. It's the big signal of western wear, this large, broad-brimmed, and certainly not inexpensive headpiece. Once thought to have been the hat of choice throughout the west during its wilder days, study of old photographs shows this to be entirely untrue. If you were on the frontier as a pioneer in the first part of the nineteenth century then you were far more likely to be seen wearing a black derby bowler hat of the kind regularly seen on the streets of London than you were some wide-brimmed sombrero. Despite Frederick Remmington, populariser of the image of the wild west in paintings and a whole host of Hollywood films, the Stetson did not make an appearance until around 1870.

Its creator, John Batterson Stetson, himself the son of a hat maker, came up with the design for the first "boss of the plains" hat in 1865. This had a wide brim to keep off the rain and sun, a high crown to hold in a pocket of insulating air and could, at a push, be used to carry water. They were great for fanning recalcitrant trail-side camp fires. A version was adopted by the US Cavalry and the hat style took off right across the whole cowboy west.

Sharp shooters adopted it. So did sheriffs and just about everybody else with business attended to from the back of a horse. When the movies finally arrived they depicted a western population where the Stetson, in both its black and its white incarnation, was what you had on your head. Some stars adopted wilder styles, innovating with the super-large ten gallon version, fine on celluloid, impractical on the plains. There's a photo out there of Tom Mix wearing one that's taller than his face. There's another showing Gene Autry plus police escort leaving the Cardiff Capitol Cinema in 1939. He has on his head a white ten gallon. He looks more of a cowpoke than Cowboy Copas. Copas stuck to a flat topped Stetson. But he did go for enormously wide brims.

So, too, did most of the other singers in the emerging country and western style of music. Didn't matter if you were a steel guitar player with a western swing band, a mainstream Nashville country singer in the style of Eddy Arnold, an outlaw like Waylon, a man in black or a Dwight Yokham Americana purveyor you wore a hat. Alan Jackson, George Strait, Clint Black, Brad Paisley, Garth Brooks and other mainline Eighties and Nineties singers all did and became known as hat acts. Man, guitar, and Stetson. The style of dress persists.

Turning the supermarket aisle corner in Food City in 2014 Dandridge, Tennessee, a sleepy tiny town on the edges of Douglas Lake, I bump into an oldster coming the other way. He's pushing a trolley loaded with pensioners' goods – cheap meat cuts, packets of grits, large cans of beans. He's wearing cowboy boots, western jeans, a shirt with smiling pockets and black piping. On his head he has a white Stetson hat.

Country music, or at least its stage and TV appearance component, was the driver behind much of present-day western apparel. Right across America there are stores that specialise in retailing hats, massively expensive tooled leather cowboy boots, embroidered shirts, ranch buckle belts, string ties and the rest of the regalia.

The original cowboys dressed as they did for practical reasons. Their hats kept off the sun. They were tied to their chins with strips of leather or ripped-off hat bands. Their brims were decorated with Indian beads, woven horsehair or rattlesnake hides. Their boots could slide easily into the stirrup. The high Cuban heel prevented them from slipping out. The tall laceless style of the boot protected the leg. Shorter versions with cut-down walking heels came later. The cowboy's denim shirts, derived from the sort worn by Confederate soldiers, lasted well in a difficult climate. They wore leather chaps to keep off the cactus spines or woollen ones as a hedge against cold wind. Round their neck they wore a bandana to stave off dust.

Early cinema cowboys and country singers took the style and elaborated it. Boots became increasingly ostentatious and were manufactured from alligator and rattlesnake skin or coloured highly decorated leather. Shirts were tailored with contrasting yokes often outlined in piping and began to be embroidered with cattle insignia, stars and entwining roses. Colour, which the real cowboys avoided for fear it might spook the cattle, rolled like a rash of rainbows. Stripes, plaids, garish checks, bright greens, blues and reds. John Wayne, as the Ringo Kid in the film *Stagecoach* (1939), wore a bib fronted Western shirt in a style adapted from those worn in the Civil War. Casey Tibbs, the bronco rider, did the same. In 1938 Denver shirt maker Jack A Weil replaced standard buttons with a metal ring gripper snap made by Scovill of Connecticut. The C&W shirt popper button. The style caught on.

Ties were reduced to bootlaces held together with elaborate silver clasps. You need only check a few country museums to see what happened to the jackets of the famous. Diamanté covered they were (and are) a mass of light reflecting colour. Have a look at the garb of Dolly Parton's early duettist and the man who launched her, Porter Wagoner. His elaborate, highly decorated suits, manufactured by famous western apparel creators Nudie Cohn[99] and Manuel Cuevas, are the kind you would not wear down the pub and expect a quiet drink. Today they sit in museum display cases in Nashville and Memphis showing you from just where the idea of the Rhinestone Cowboy came and proving, as an aside, that Wagoner was no Charles Atlas either.

Western wear for women was pretty much the same but with maybe more rhinestone, fancier waistcoats and a preponderance of long, rose-covered dresses. Sometimes on the country stage it's hard to tell the difference between male and female urban cowboy apparel. Although maybe not every male would want to dress up daily in a version of Dolly Parton's diamanté rich, crotch necklaced stage trousers.

For many outside country music's heartlands western apparel meant nothing until the advent of country rock and the arrival of The Byrd's *Sweetheart of the Rodeo* (1968) and, in particular, The Flying Burrito Brothers' album, *Gilded Palace of Sin* (1969). Here, on the album cover of the Gram Parsons and Chris Hillman show-stopper, the band sport lavishly embroidered Nudie suits. These show roses intertwined with marijuana leaves which added a whole new dimension to the style of alt country that this album was to launch. There might not have been an immediate rush to appear on the streets of cities across the world dressed as country stars but the style of dress did become socially more acceptable. Just a little.

Today western dress does duty in many parts of America's Southern States as formal wear. You dress in your alligator boots and your bolo tie to worship at church, sell insurance, go for a job interview, attend a funeral. The style is so common no one notices.

I track the outfit I'm going to buy down in a store in Pigeon Forge. Boots, shirt, jacket. There's a range of footwear that runs two entire fifty metre walls. Boots in just about every colour and style possible so long as they're cowboy. Levi jeans, tooled leather belts with elaborate decorated silver buckles. Chaps seem to be missing which is understandable. Urban cowboys do not look cool turning up wearing what look like giant fleece waders on their lower limbs.

I try on a hat, a black wide-brimmed outlaw headpiece with a deep red hatband of the kind I imagine law breakers might sport in their desert hideaways in New Mexico. It fits but I look ridiculous, even here in the heartland. A Welsh-accented cowpoke with a face that lacks both beard and weather-beaten gnarls. How it would be walking down St Mary Street back home I just can't imagine. I settle for a shirt with green and red roses intertwining across the yoke and those famous metal popper buttons. It's heavy, tailored, and perfect for strolling down Nashville's Broadway. I love it. It's on a hanger now in the back bedroom wardrobe. Preserved in a plastic bag. Never worn it once.

30 • What's The Bluegrass Scene Like Where You Come From?

Not as prevalent as many of us would like. I knew this and Chris Tweed confirms it. Out there in the world of British live music bluegrass provision is poor. There *is* a UK bluegrass scene, of course. It has festivals and a raft of fans. The British Bluegrass Music Association list twenty active UK bluegrass bands and a similar number of festival get-togethers. There's one at Kemble Airfield, Gloucester, one in Tamworth, Staffordshire, and another at Newquay in Cornwall. But that's all small beer compared to the one hundred and sixty or so UK folk clubs currently operating or the even larger number of British jazz venues available to retired men who still blow trumpets and slide trombones.

"The problem," Chris tells me, "is that there's no common repertoire. They've got one in both Scotland and in Ireland where there is a shared canon of songs. If you are, say, a fiddle player, then you can turn up and ask to join in. The other musicians will almost certainly be playing something you recognise. Same thing happens in Appalachia. But in England and Wales it's not like that. In the States you are always welcome to jam. Here it's much more cliquey."

Chris plays a resonator guitar or dobro with The Garth Mountain Boys. He's originally from Ballymoney, Co Antrim, has a solid hard rock guitar background and is full of tales of seeing Commander Cody, Canned Heat, Greg Allman and even The Flying Burrito Brothers at the Cardiff Students Union. His turning point was hearing an album featuring dobro player Jerry Douglas who later joined Alison Krauss's band. Douglas is a master of speed and melodic invention who has played on thousands of bluegrass and country recordings and when he isn't on tour with Krauss's Union Station plays with Shawn Camp's Earls of Leicester. I'd originally suggested to Chris that, in the spirit of things, we might have best carried out our chat while actually walking up over Garth Mountain. The Garth is small for a mountain. It's barely a hill really and is only a few miles north of where we are sitting. But time is not on our side. Chris has been playing with The Mountain Boys from about a year after they formed in 2007. He first came across them trying things out in a pub in Llantwit Fadre. With an eye on changing the world he joined.

'Dobro' is actually a brand name for a resonator guitar. As a name it has become generic much as Hoover has in the world of vacuums. Dobros are metal fronted instruments and are loud. The original Dobros were made by the Dopyera Brothers in the nineteen-twenties. The brand has since been acquired by Gibson. The version Chris uses hangs from his neck horizontally and is played with a metal bar much in the manner of a steel guitar. "When I was in my teens, I always wanted a pedal steel guitar," Chris says, "but they have ten strings controlled by pedals and levers, are hellish expensive, are difficult to move about and need electricity. A dobro you can pack up and carry with one hand, which is why I started there. I have both now."

The dobro adds breadth to The Garth Mountain Boys sound, even if, as some argue, it isn't actually a traditional bluegrass instrument. The problem for Chris now is more the nature of the Mountain Boys repertoire. The band gets most of its gigs in pubs where the audience want to hear things they know. *Randy Lynn Rag* won't hack it. Numbers by Coldplay will. The Mountain Boys, whom I last heard at the Llantristant Folk Club[100] in Pontyclun, have a tendency to mix the real stuff with driving versions of *Norwegian Wood*, *Copperhead Road*, The Eagles' *Midnight Flyer* and, in times of desperation, a banjo-led *Route Sixty-Six*.

They are hardly high lonesome, six Welsh men dressed in western gear and with a stand-up harmonica player often taking melodic lead. But they are fun. *Roll In My Sweet Baby's Arms, Sitting On Top Of the World, Man of Constant Sorrow* mix with band-written numbers about love, loss and South Wales trains.

The folk club atmosphere is, of course, supportive. The audience may not be hard core old time and mountain music fans but they recognise good acoustic renditions when they hear them. The room in a pub atmosphere, all mismatched tables, gloss painted woodwork, beer mats and carpeted floors is redolent of how it has always been. Folk clubs are no longer anywhere near the cutting edge, at least not in this South Wales incarnation. On the wall are a few framed posters advertising past and future club events, a black and white photo of New York skyscrapers I must have seen a dozen times and then the inevitable giant Ikea red rose. Around me are acres of white hair and beards, beards are de rigeur, if you don't have one yet then you don't shave. This is a people's movement. There are former hippies. There are others who look like they might have done something once but have long ago forgotten what the world of work was about. What you get, though, is warmth. Former front man with the bands Calennig and Swansea Jack, Mick Tems, sings *A Miner's Life,* "Keep your hands on your wages and your eye upon the scales, Union miners stand together, do not heed the coal board's tale[101]". The audience join in with the chorus. It's 2013 although hearing this lyric on everyone's lips you wouldn't know. Then we all do *Will the Circle Be Unbroken,* lyric sheets have been provided to every table. There was a time when you wouldn't have needed that.

We go round the room and there are solo contributions from the most unlikely of singers. Greg does *Sailing to Philadelphia.* A woman ensconced behind a full bottle of red sings *Who'll be the lady, Who'll be the lucky lord* from where she sits. One of the organisers, Pat Smith, spiritedly contributes a Welsh-medium song about the killed at Passchendaele posthumous bardic chair winner, Hedd Wyn. Then the Garthies come on and, apart from a break for the drawing of the raffle, entertain us for the rest of the night. Old fashioned but live. Social, familiar, soft edged.

The antithesis of all this down home folksiness was the club John Williams and his late wife Charlotte Greig ran for most of the noughties. Alt Cardiff. Alternative Cardiff. A place where the roots music that challenged prevailing commercial norms could be presented. This was the kind of material I'd experienced at the Bluebird Café and in east Nashville. Alt country is a grab-all term. It's a music that emerged in the 1990s and was played by musicians working outside the mainstream of country music and who often eschewed Nashville's slick production values, manicured instrumentation and smooth vocals. It was and is a music of middle America, aligned with the storytelling and political and social agitation of Woody Guthrie and the whole Fifties American folk revival. The difference being that alt country bands do their stuff on electric instruments often adding in a raucous slice of rock and roll. The movement began with The Long Ryders, The Jayhawks, and Uncle Tupelo as well as the bands that sprang from those sources – Wilco, Son Volt and The Bottle Rockets. Young America. Roots post punk. Where country might have gone if it had been the indigenous music of north London pubs or Beatles-era provincial beat clubs.

By the time John and Charlotte started putting on shows in the Welsh capital alt country had grown to encompass any number of solo singer-songwriters of engagingly non-mainstream talent. These were singers who were working the patch once ploughed by bluesmen, Bob Dylan clones and the jumbo guitar end of traditional folk. Charlotte herself had emerged as an alt folk singer playing self-written numbers and understated guitar accompanied reworkings of traditional folk tunes to superb effect. The pair wanted to showcase music that was neither the gnarled veteran rock often on display at pubs like the Royal Oak nor the indie rock scene prevalent in places like Clwb Ifor in Womanby Street. Their first guest was Oh Susanna, the Canadian-American alt singer Suzie Ungerleider, whose guitar-backed songs of personal experience hit the spot. The club grew. They brought in Fred Eaglesmith, Dolly Varden, The Sadies, Chip Taylor, who'd written The Troggs' *Wild Thing*, and now toured in the company of southern sounding electric fiddle player Carrie Rodriguez, former Jayhawks frontman Mark Olson, Victoria Williams, Richmond Fontaine and Neal Casal.

There were guests from Britain, including The Fence Collective, Alastair Roberts, Cardiff alt country pioneer Chris Rees, and local country rockers Lone Pine, but this was mainly an American populated experience. Support acts were occasionally Charlotte herself but more likely to be the youthful acoustic guitar wizard Ed Mugford playing instrumentals taken from the *Angi* cannon of forty years back. Music runs in circles.

Amy Allison was an early Alt Cardiff performer. She is the singer songwriter daughter of the pianist Mose Allison. Mose had been there at the sixties start providing models – *Eyesight to the Blind, The Seventh Son, Parchman Farm* – for the likes of John Mayall and Georgie Fame. Fame in particular could sound just like Mose. Amy was totally different. She'd appeared on John Peel singing Laura Cantrell's *The Whiskey Makes You Sweeter* and Alt Cardiff's mainly blue-collar autodidact audience knew who she was. The rarefied obscurities of this American overtly non-mainstream music had found a welcome home in west Cardiff.

Alt Cardiff ran out of steam around 2007 as festivals such as Green Man began to take up the British alt music slack. The music was no longer quite so different. Williams and Greig needed to move on to other things[102].

Back at Llantristant again in 2015 I'm listening to bluegrass-powered acoustic music sung by Chris and Wendy Moreton. This is the pub-ready end of Americana. Chris, a first class guitarist who switches readily between Doc Watson-style rags and slices of Frederick Handel rendered for six unamplified strings, presents a roots show to which virtually no audience could object. In the mix are banjo tunes from the Clinch Mountains rendered on Chris's 1926 Clifford Essex-built instrument, skiffle numbers like *Freight Train*, takes on Jimmy Rodgers and Johnny Cash and then, allowing the whole pretence of authenticity and alt everything to slip, tuneful renditions of The Kinks' *Sunny Afternoon* and Simon and Garfunkel's *The Boxer*, complete with foot-operated cymbal.

Something has happened here in the years that have intervened between the arrival of Bill Haley and the appearance at Cardiff's Chapter Arts Centre of scratchy-voiced but addictive alt country auteur Amy Allison. The roots have spread. Acoustic music can include anything the musicians want to play. Traditions are living things, dynamic, unthinking. Cecil Sharp and Ewan MacColl would hate it all.

31 • Shake It And Break It

It's no great hardship, sitting on a French Mediterranean beach looking out to sea. Here the tide is a gentle lap rather than the thunderous half a mile deep onslaught I'm used to back home. Across the bay are the lights of Cannes, the Croisette, and the Musée de la Castre. There lies a whole stylised world of diamond-collared lapdogs, mincing madams and film starlets in profusion. The Cannes inheritance as epicentre of the Côte d'Azur.

I'm in Théoule sur Mer at the southern edge of the red Alpes-Maritimes. To my left a moules frites restaurant juts out into the water. There's music coming from this eatery's speakers, the synthesised Gallic chill-out that is Air. It's rootless artifice. If there's tradition behind Air's music then it has little to do with France. Twirling atoms. Electro Euro. Anonymous dance that's pulled out of the sky. Not that this stops it being as French as a baguette. Why? Because France says so. If the band, a duo, have any antecedents then they include Walter Carlos, Jean Michel Jarre, Tangerine Dream and Kraftwerk. To a man these are people who have never listened to Big Bill Broonzy. They have never thrilled to nasal high harmonies. If they wanted the sound of the violin, then it would be created by the keyboards of their twenty-first century machines. They would never have it delivered live by a fiddle player with a face that's seen better days. Tradition – what's that?

Nicolas Godin and Jean-Benoît Dunckel, the duo who make up Air, went to French universities where the tide almost permanently flowed away from Anglo-Americana. The blues, if not anathema, were certainly a faded thing. Europe instead was endless. It was filled with other things.

But in Fnac, on the Rue d'Antibes, a branch of the great French multi-media chain, I pick up a two-CD set that has on it just about everything of significance ever recorded by Charley Patton. Amid the French oldies I might have expected Gallic rock and roller Johnny Halliday or 60s chanteuse Françoise Hardy but that's not what I got. Patton's tracks are selected from his four major recording sessions, 1929-1934, all I'd thought lost back in the depths of time.

Patton was a blues pioneer, a delta music maker with a facility for the slide guitar, able to sing blues as authentically as minstrel songs. He was there when the blues arrived. He knew already what made an audience dance. He was as popular in his day as it was possible for such a singer to be. He was a great early influence on both John Lee Hooker and Howlin' Wolf. He played with The Mississippi Sheiks and wrote some of the world's seminal blues numbers: *Pony Blues, Jesus is a Dying Bed Maker,* and *High Water Everywhere.* With its monied Mediterranean culture the south of France is far from Patton's Dockery plantation, sawmill and cotton farm. Yet here he is, done up in a French boxed set with a French biography attached. "Le chanteur-guitariste Charley Patton, né au coeur du Mississippi dans les années 1880, est l'un des plus anciens blues-men connus." – The singer-guitarist Charley Patton, born in the heart of the Mississippi in the 1880s, is one of the oldest known bluesmen.

In the car, I slide one of the CDs into the player and from the speakers Patton's worn rasp emerges, his guitar driving, his slide sounding out its second voice. Patton was a street corner singer well used to making himself heard. You don't get soulful refection here, you get rhythmic foot stomping. *Shake It and Break It (But Don't Let It Fall Mama).* As if any Mama worth her salt would.

What conclusions can I draw about these musics that I've been chasing? I thought that at least here where the old world blossoms its charms I could get beyond their reach and have time to think. But I had not counted on the blues filling the racks on main street Cannes. Nor, for that matter, for the existence of the European Blues Union with a French president, Jean Guillermo, and its star performers the French band, Les Trophées France Blues, and Bordeaux blues picker Cisco Herzhaft. Just a small amount of hunting among the local French directories throws all this data up. The new world delta blues have certainly won over the old.

Roots music is ancient. Everyone knows that. Except from what I've discovered it almost uniformly is not. The blues was not an early African music, brought to the States by slaves and then spun into prominence on guitars with bent fretboards and banjos made from gourds and groundhog hides. It was an Afro-American fad of the twenties, a largely commercial music played in juke joints, street corners and dance halls. Bluegrass did not come over with the Scotch-Irish. It was not a slow outgrowth from ancient Appalachian mountain music. It was the commercial invention of Bill Monroe, taken up by The Stanley Brothers, popularised by Flatt and Scruggs. It was mountain banjo jazz welded onto reinvented up-tempo hillbilly music. It did not seep. It was sold.

Country music, the country and western of my youth, sung by cowboys and played right across the wild west did not reach America on the *Mayflower*. It was, it turned out, largely a Nashville invention. A music honed and smoothed to sell as many records as possible, an industry created under the large and open skies of a rapidly developing America.

And where there were roots, genuine folk origins, traditions that led in some convoluted timeless way up to the present, the music always turned out to be peopled by great re-inventors. Individuals who took the past and made it massively the present and then spun it on into the future. Blind Lemon did it. So, too, did Big Bill. Captain Beefheart and The Grateful Dead made Broonzy's blues transcend themselves. Big Bill himself had abandoned his small band sophisticated origins to play the part of the poor boy delta singer.

On the country music stage, with Eddy Arnold and Roy Acuff already offering a pretence at long history, The Byrds and The Flying Burrito Brothers added electricity to create a whole new 'traditional' music: country rock. Steeleye Span and Fairport Convention did the same thing for English folk. The Pogues and Moving Hearts repeated the process in Ireland.

Further back the great folk music collector, Cecil Sharp, as we've heard, had meddled severely with reality. Sharp bowdlerised what he found. He then scored it for piano and communal voices and reintroduced it, turning his folk music into a 'tradition' that it had never actually been.

What does hold these roots musics together, however, is a pervading sense that they come from the people rather than the commercial song machine. This might not be entirely accurate, in fact it almost certainly is not, but that hasn't stopped countless individuals with access to a guitar, a squeeze box, a harmonica, a piano or simply their own unaccompanied voice from joining in. On occasions roots music does occupy the concert stage. John Hammond put it there with *Spirituals to Swing*. So did Seán Ó Riada when he presented ancient Irish jigs as material for well-dressed and sophisticated urban concertgoers. But mostly it doesn't. It is performed where you can get at it, touch it, in backrooms and pubs and clubs and small halls where it feels as if it belongs.

Roots music's strands have become interchangeable. Elvis took Bill Monroe's *Blue Moon of Kentucky* and made it up-tempo rock. Monroe listened and then re-recorded his own roots rock version. The Chieftains, masters of traditional Irish music, have spent the past two decades touring the world and making albums in the company of non-Irish musicians. The Chieftains in Nashville. The Chieftains in Spanish Galicia. The Chieftains and Willie Nelson. The Chieftains and The Nitty Gritty Dirt Band. The Chieftains in China. The Chieftains in South America. The Chieftains play the world. They recorded *Will The Circle Be Unbroken*, a song famously first laid down in the Bristol Big Bang sessions. Steeleye Span, core British folkies, made an acapella version of Buddy Holly's *Rave On*. Deep delta bluesman Mississippi John Hurt moved seamlessly from the folk tale of *Stagalee* to the civil rights protest of *I Shall Not Be Moved* to end up making a tuneful version of *Keep a Knocking*. That song was later made core rock and roll by Little Richard. Richard, with his six inch stacked hair and thunderous piano playing, America's most unlikely traditional musician.

I walk on up the French beach. That Charley Patton set was a catch. But it's one of the last I'll make. I can see it now – the vinyl dumps and second-hand stacks that once gave me so much expectation and excitement with their thrill of the chase, finding that lost album, that rare artist, those songs I always wanted, heard of in rumour but never in fact. Those dumps will go. On the evidence of my American travels they are already almost gone. They'll be replaced by CD mountains, the silver twinkle and somehow unattractive slide of plastic slipcase in boxes and racks and heaps on shelves. And then they too will vanish, relegated to museums and the collections of antique hunters. Their value as repositories of wonder faded into nothing.

For now we are at the end of it. The push of lost, pre-1962 now out of copyright material along with record companies getting the last rush out of their early signings have given us as many bargains in recorded music as the mind is able to imagine. I've bought complete boxed sets of almost everything ever released by Ewan MacColl, Conway Twitty, Duane Eddy and The Stanley Brothers. These things come in slip cases at less than the price of a good meal for 185 tracks. Did you know your heroes recorded such lost and unlovely first singles? Have you heard their early compilations? Do you own their greatest? You do now. Frank Sinatra's entire fifties album output was recently seen on offer for fifteen quid. Johnny Cash the same. Elvis, hell Elvis, he's been bargain basement now for at least a decade.

If such things had been available in my youth then my future music trails might well have been so different. Back then there was rumour of rareness, whispers about great albums where those you loved had recorded songs you just couldn't imagine. You wanted such things but they were vague, unavailable, too expensive, unfindable, unplayable, unobtainable.

On my phone, with the plugs tight in my ears, I press and up they come. The entire output of music of the western and eastern worlds combined. Almost. If not in entirety just yet then completeness cannot be long in coming. The mp3s and mp4s and the rest of the compressed sound files trickle out their sounds. I can hear anything I want. I just click and flick and there it is. Tracks not albums. Songs and more songs. How many versions are there in the world of that most famous of dopers blues, *Candy Man?* The extreme variety is terrific. Roy Orbison, Wanda Jackson, Dale Hawkins, and other mainline rock and rollers have all made versions which show the songs rock and roll roots. Fred Neil has done it with Dylan–like harmonica up front and the

Great White Wonder himself made it sound like the most ancient and authentic of blues. Don Partridge played it as a one-man band. John Fahey made it a psychedelic misaligned acoustic guitar extravaganza. While Mississippi John Hurt, him again, whose song this actually is, brought up the rear with the song as a melodically picked hymn to pot heads the world over. It took me ten minutes, sitting here in the sun, and now I know more about this song and its variants than a decade ago would have been possible. *Candy Man*. The mystery is stripped, the compressed file is biteless, the lights have all gone out. Do I feel a sense of wonder? All I feel is loss.

But then tonight there's live music at the Cotton Club on Rue St Antoine. It's sort of roots. Gallic crooners doing American big band blues. But real enough. You've had a good run, recorded music, almost a hundred years, but now we are back to spit and vibrancy, immediacy and excitement, breath and passion. Live roots, keep them so, that's the future.

Timeline

1685	Murder of Anne Nichols in Shropshire, basis for the *Knoxville Girl* song
1868	Stephen Foster composes *Oh! Susanna*
1871	Nashville's Fisk Jubilee Singers founded in Nashville, TN
1873	Fisk Singers perform *Go Down Moses* and others in front of Queen Victoria
1877	Thomas Edison invents the wax cylinder phonograph
1893	Formation of the Gaelic League in Ireland
1899	Sleepy John Estes born
1901	Victor Talking Machine Company issues its first shellac 10" record
1903	WC Handy hears a blues slide guitarist at Tutweiler rail station in Mississippi
	Birth of Big Bill Broonzy
1906	Founding of Cymdeithas Alawon Gwerin Cymru / Welsh Folk Song Society
1910	Song collector John Lomax publishes *Cowboy Songs and Other Frontier Ballads*
1912	WC Handy's *Memphis Blues* published as sheet music
1916	WC Handy writes *Beale Street Blues*
	Cecil Sharp collects ballads in Appalachia
1920	Blues queen Mammie Smith records *Crazy Blues*
1922	First country record, by Eck Robertson, recorded in NYC
1923	Bessie Smith and Ma Rainey make their first recordings
	Country guitarist Henry Whittier records for Okeh
1925	Electrical recording replaces acoustic recording
	Blind Lemon Jefferson makes his first record
	Pre-war folk blues era begins
	WSM radio first broadcasts from Nashville. WSM Barn Dance begins.
1926	Radio station 2RN, the forerunner to RTÉ 1, begins to broadcast folk music in Ireland

1926	WSM Barn Dance rebranded as the Grand Ol Opry
1927	Great Mississippi flood
	Country Music Big Bang recorded by Ralph Peer in Bristol, VA
1929-34	Charley Patton's four major recording sessions
1930	Bob Wills forms The Light Crust Doughboys
1930s	Singing cowboys popular
1931	George Jones born
1932-38	Robert Johnson on the road
1932	*English Folk Songs of the Southern Appalachians* published
1933	Radio Luxembourg founded
	John and Alan Lomax, song collectors, meet Lead Belly
1934	Bob Wills forms The Texas Playboys – Western Swing becomes popular
1935	Elvis Presley born in Tupelo, Mississippi
1937	The Blue Sky Boys record *Knoxville Girl*
1938	John Hammond puts on *From Spirituals To Swing* at Carnegie Hall
1939	Bill Monroe forms The Blue Grass Boys
1941	Alan Lomax records Muddy Waters for the Library of Congress
	Karl Davis writes and records *Kentucky*
1942	T-Bone Walker records *Mean Old World*
1943	The Opry moves to the Ryman
1946-48	Bill Monroe's band featuring Earl Scruggs create the bluegrass sound
1945	Muddy Waters gets his first electric guitar
1946	Arthur Big Boy Crudup records *That's Alright Mama* in Chicago
1947	Ernest Tubb Record Store founded in Nashville, Honky Tonk music popular
1948	Columbia begin issuing microgroove 12" LPs
	John Lee Hooker records *Boogie Chillen*
	Muddy Waters records *I Can't Be Satisfied* for Aristocrat
	Pete Seeger forms The Weavers. American Folk Music Revival begins

	Stanley Brothers record their first bluegrass record, *Molly and Tenbrooks*
1949	RCA Victor issues the first vinyl 45 rpm record
	Foggy Mountain Breakdown recorded by Flatt and Scruggs
1950	Song collector Alan Lomax visits Britain
	Muddy Waters records *Rollin' Stone* for Chess
1951	Jackie Brenston records *Rocket 88*
1952	Big Bill Broonzy tours UK
	Sun Records founded by Sam Phillips
	Ray Charles signs with Atlantic Records and begins adding jazz and gospel elements to his music
1954	Elvis records *Blue Moon of Kentucky* and *That's Alright Mama* at Sun
	Lonnie Donegan records *Rock Island Line*. Skiffle craze begins
	Bill Haley records *Crazy Man Crazy*
	Meredydd Evans records *Welsh Folk Songs* for Folkways
	Bradley brothers build their Quonset hut studio on Nashville's Music Row
	Country music's countrypolitan Chet Atkins sound begins
	Doris Day's *Secret Love* is best seller of the year in the UK
1955	Haley's *Rock Around The Clock* becomes a huge hit. Rock and roll is branded as a threat to society
	Johnny Cash records *Hey Porter* for Sam Phillips' Sun label
1955-58	British skiffle boom
	Rockabilly emerges as a sub-genre of country music
1956	Howlin' Wolf records *Smokestack Lightning*
	Tommy Steele records *Rock With The Caveman*
	Elvis leaves Sun and records *Heartbreak Hotel* in Nashville for RCA
	Chet Atkins and Steve Sholes open RCA's Studio B
1956-61	Trad Jazz boom in Britain
1957	Bill Haley arrives in Cardiff as part of his first UK tour
	Elvis buys Graceland
	Lonnie Donegan records *Cumberland Gap*
	Sister Rosetta Tharpe tours UK

1958	Cliff Richard records *Move It*
	The Everly Brothers record *Songs Our Daddy Taught Us*
	Elvis drafted into US Army
1958-66	Folk boom in Greenwich Village, USA, Ireland, UK and elsewhere
	Emergence of 'protest' singers Phil Ochs, Tom Paxton, and others
1960	Roy Harris founds the Cardiff Folk Song Club
	Elvis demobbed from US Army
	Fame studios established in Muscle Shoals
1961	Sonny Terry records an album of Jew's harp music
	Columbia issue Robert Johnson's *King of the Delta Blues Singers* album
	British blues boom begins
	Jimmy Cotton tours UK with Chris Barber
	Stax Records established. Soul boom begins
1962	The Twist dominates the dance floors
	John Lee Hooker tours Europe with the Folk Blues Festival
	Cyril Davies records *Country Line Special*
	Booker T. and the MG's record *Green Onions*
	Bob Dylan guests at Ewan MacColl's Singers Club in London
	Bob Dylan issues his first album on Columbia
	Sleepy John Estes 'rediscovered' by Sam Charters
1963	Audio cassette makes a commercial appearance
1964	Granada broadcast *The Little Richard Spectacular*
	The Rolling Stones release *5x5*
	Folk Blues Tour with Wolf, Estes, Sonny Boy & others visits UK
	British Invasion of America begins
	Bob Dylan issues *The Times They Are a-Changin'*
	Prototype for Museum of Appalachia opens
1965	First weekend bluegrass festival held at Fincastle, VA
1966	Bob Dylan goes electric
1967	Aretha Franklin records at Fame
	Muscle Shoals Sound Studios open

1968	Bonzo Dogs ask *Can Blue Men Sing The Whites?*
	The Byrds issue country rock boom classic, *Sweetheart of the Rodeo*
	David Ackles issues *Road To Cairo*
	Cream record *Crossroads*
1969	Elvis makes his American Recordings
1971	Alan Stivell records *Renaissance of the Celtic Harp*
	Led Zeppelin record *When the Levee Breaks*
1972	Outlaw Country begins
1973	Dolly Parton's *Jolene* a hit
1974	Opry moves from the Ryman to Opry Mills
1975	Robert Altman makes the film *Nashville*
	Stax Records goes bankrupt
1975-79	Punk era
1977	Death of Elvis in Nashville
1978	Root Boy Slim and The Sex Change Band active
1980s	Era of country pop, Kenny Rogers, Alabama and Ronnie Milsap
1982	Compact discs first issued
	Bluebird Café in Nashville opens
1986	Dollywood opens
1990s	Stadium country era – Garth Brooks, Shania Twain, Faith Hill
	Americana and alt country emerge
1994	Ryman refurbished
1995	First digital MP3 file appears
2000	Coen Brothers release the film *O Brother, Where Art Thou?*
	Stax Studios, Memphis, rebuilt as a museum
	Dumplin ValleyBluegrass Festival founded
	Country music draws new breath
2001	The Steep Canyon Rangers formed in Brevard, NC
	Rhythm and Roots Reunion Festival begins
2003	Y Bechgen Drwg visit upstate New York
	First Annual Elvis Festival in Porthcawl, South Wales
2006	Taylor Swift issues her first album
2008	The Cherryholmes play the Muni in Pontypridd

2009	Leonard Cohen concert in Dublin
2010	Steve Martin's annual prize for Excellence in Banjo and Bluegrass announced
2011	Cherryholmes disband
2014	Dolly Parton headlines Glastonbury
2015	Taylor Swift mounts *1989* world tour. Her country roots to pop crossover is complete

Thanks and Acknowledgements

M ost of this book would not have been possible without the encouragement and selfless assistance of my wife Sue who, against all ticketing odds, persistently gets us into places like Motorpoint and the Albert Hall, and, come to think of it, was instrumental in turning the rented car off that bluetop highway in Cherokee way back and getting us our first live full-frontal experience of bluegrass. Without that it's doubtful if there would have been a book at all.

I also need to thank Mick Felton at Seren whose early enthusiasm turned my notes into a fully-fledged project and to all those other fellow music enthusiasts who've talked to me, listened to me, advised me and opened doors beyond which new musics play. John Williams who with his late wife the singer and author Charlotte Greig, put so many ear-opening acts on live at Alt Cardiff; the man who started an interest in real rock and roll for me, Ian Thomas; the late Dave Reid who spent almost as much of his money on new sounds as I did; Philip Jenkins who turned me onto John Cage, Terry Riley, Captain Beefheart and a whole new way of doing it; Pete Morgan who showed me that Robert Johnson was much more than a piece of scratchy-sounding history; Chris Tweed who explained just how it was with bluegrass this side of the water; and all those other fellow travellers who have shared their passions with me and got just as excited as I did when a man on the corner of St John's Square started selling bootleg copies of *The Great White Wonder* or Chuck Berry appeared, duck walking, guitar flashing, at the Cardiff Capitol. Thank you all.

Works Consulted

Music

Bean, J.P. *Singing From The Floor – A History of British Folk Clubs*, Faber, 2014

Boyes, Georgina, *The Imagined Village – Culture, Ideology and the English Folk Revival*, No Masters Co-Operative, 2010

Cahill, Marie (ed), *I Am Elvis – A Guide To Elvis Impersonators*, Pocket Books, 1991

Cardwell, Bruce, *The Harp in Wales*, Seren, 2013

Cohen, Ronald, (editor), *Alan Lomax: Selected Writings, 1934-1997*, Routledge, 2005

Dewe, Mike, *The Skiffle Craze*, Planet, 1998

Dylan, Bob, *Chronicles Volume One*, Pocket Books, 2005

Ellis, Royston, *The Big Beat Scene*, Music Mentor Books, 1961 reprinted 2010

Elvis Presley Enterprises, *Elvis Presley's Graceland – Official Guidebook*, Elvis Presley Enterprises Inc., 2009

Frame, Pete, *The Restless Generation: How Rock Music Changed The Face of 1950s Britain*, Rogon House, 2007

Fussell, Fred C, with Kruger, Steve, *Blue Ridge Music Trails of North Carolina A Guide to Music Sites, Artists, and Traditions of the Mountains and Foothills*, UNC Press, 2013

Gordon, Robert, Respect Yourself – *Stax Records and the Soul Explosion*, Bloomsbury, 2014

Gracey PE, Michael T and Atchison, Sammy Stone, *My Life As An Elvis*, CreateSpace, 2011

Guralnick, Peter, *Last Train To Memphis – The Rise of Elvis Presley*, Little, Brown, 1994

Guralnick, Peter, *Careless Love – The Unmaking of Elvis Presley*, Little, Brown, 1999

Guralnick, Peter, *Sweet Soul Music. Rhythm and Blues and the Southern Dream of Freedom*, Penguin 1991

Harper, Colin, *Dazzling Stranger – Bert Jansch and the British Folk and Blues Revival*, Bloomsbury, 2000

Harrington, Beth, *The Winding Stream: An Oral History of the Carter and Cash family*, PFP Publishing, 2014

Hast, Dorothea E., and Scott, Stanley, *Music In Ireland – Experiencing Music, Expressing Culture*, OUP, 2004

Heckstall-Smith, Dick & Grant, Pete, *Blowing the Blues – Fifty Years Playing the British Blues*, Clear Books, 2004

Hodgkinson, Will, *The Ballad of Britain: How Music Captured The Soul of a Nation*, Portico, 2009

Houghton, Mick, *Becoming Electra – The True Story of Jac Holzman's Visionary Record Label*, Jawbone Press, 2010

Irwin, John Rice, *Musical Instruments of The Southern Appalachian Mountains*, Schiffer Publishing, 1979

Kosser, Michael, *How Nashville Became Music City USA – 50 Years of Music Row*, Hal Leonard Corp, 2006.

Lott, Eric, *All The King's Men: Elvis Impersonators and White Working-Class Masculinity*. In Stecopoulos, Harry and Uebel, Michael, (editors), *Race and the Subject of Masculinities*, Duke University Press, 1997

Mansfield, Brian, *Grand Ole Opry Picture History Book*, Gaylord Entertainment Company, 2008

Mazor, Barry, *Ralph Peer and the Making of Popular Roots Music*, Chicago Review Press, 2014

McColl, Ewan, *Journeyman*, Manchester University Press, 2009

McLean, Duncan, *Lone Star Swing – On the Trail of Bob Wills and his Texas Playboys*, Vintage, 1998

Milner, Greg, *Perfecting Sound Forever – The Story of Recorded Music*, Granta, 2009

Minhinnick, Robert, *Island of Lightning*, Seren, 2013

Newman, Richard, *John Mayall Blues Breaker*, Castle Communications, 1995

O hAllmhurain, Gearoid, *O'Brien Pocket History of Irish Traditional Music*, The O'Brien Press, 1998

Palao, Alec, Rounce, Tony, & Rudland, Dean – *The Fame Studios Story – 1961 1973*, Kentbox 12, Ace Records, 2011 (3 CD set with illustrated 84 page book)

Ritchie, Fiona, and Orr, Doug, *Wayfaring Strangers – The Musical Voyage from Scotland and Ulster to Appalachia*, University of North Carolina Press, 2014

Rubinkowski, Leslie, *Impersonating Elvis*, Faber & Faber, 1997

Rosenberg, Neil V., *Bluegrass A History*, University of Illinois Press, 2005

Shapiro, Harry, *Alexis Korner - The Biography*, Bloomsbury, 1996

Smith, Richard D., *Can't You Hear Me Callin' – The Life of Bill Monroe, Father of Bluegrass*, Da Capo Press, 2001

Stanley, Bob, *Yeah Yeah Yeah – The Story of Modern Pop*, Faber, 2013

Szwed, John, *The Man Who Recorded The World- A Biography of Alan Lomax*, Arrow Books, 2011

Turner, Alwyn W., *Halfway to Paradise – The Birth of British Rock – Photographs by Harry Hammond from the V&A Collection*,V&A Publishing, 2008

Tosches, Nick, *Hellfire*, Penguin, 2007

Van Ronk, Dave, *The Mayor of MacDougal Street* – A Memoir, Da Capo Press, 2005

Wald, Elijah, *Escaping The Delta* – *Robert Johnson and the Invention of the Blues*, Amistad, 2004

Wallis, Ian, *American Rock'n'Roll* – *The UK Tours 1956-72*, Music Mentor Books, 2003

Williams, Hugo, *No Particular Place To Go*, Cape, 1080

Wolf, Charles K and Olson, Ted (editors), *The Bristol Sessions* – *Writings About The Big Bang Of Country Music*, McFarland & Co., Inc., 2005

Wolff, Kurt, *Country Music: The Rough Guide*, Penguin, 2000

Other

Bond, Dr Beverly G., & Sherman, Dr Janann, *Images of America* – *Beale Street*, Arcadia Publishing, 2006

Bryson, Bill, *A Walk In The Woods*, Black Swan, 1998

Douglas, Mason, *Now You Know Nashville* – *The Ultimate Guide to the Pop Culture Sights And Sounds That Made Music City*, Wild Cataclysm Press, 2013

Gove, Doris, *Exploring The Appalachian Trail* – *Hikes In The Southern Appalachians,* Stackpole Books, 1998

Greenlaw, M. Jean, *Ranch Dressing* – *The Story of Western Wear*, Lodestar Books, 1993

Holmes, J.S., *Common Forest Trees Of North Carolina- How To Know Them*, North Carolina Forest Service, 2012

Irwin, John Rice, *The Museum of Appalachia Story,* Schiffer Publishing, 1987

O'Neal, Catherine, *Hidden Carolina*, Ulysses Press, 2003

Plemmons, Jan C., *Ticket To Toxaway*, Jan Plemmons, 2004

Raban, Jonathan, *Old Glory* – *An American Voyage*, William Collins, 1981

Risk Management Solutions, *The 1927 Great Mississippi Flood: 80-year Retrospective*, RMS 2007

White, Jon Manchip, *Rawlins White* – *Patriot to Heaven*, Iris Press, 2011

Discography

There was a time when discographies would be simple affairs. The author would list details of significant and appropriate long playing albums which would illustrate and illuminate the text. The albums would be those in print and available at the time of writing. If the artist concerned had produced a *Best of* then this would be enthusiastically listed as a bonus. But that old world of vinyl lps and, indeed, of the album itself, is fast disappearing. It might indeed have actually vanished by the time you come to read this. As discussed in the final chapter of this book record companies are not just furiously reissuing selected *Best ofs* but complete back catalogues, boxed, slip cased, and offered for prices that are so reasonable that the buyer imagines that something has to be wrong. You can buy, for example, the first thirteen albums recorded by the British folk rock band Steeleye Span for about £40. There's a pre-War blues selection running to 200 tracks on sale for around £11. You can get complete album sets by both Johnny Cash and Bob Dylan for less than a hundred.

Music copyright, itself a sprawling mire depending just where you live, has given the world access to pretty much everything before 1962 without the need to make royalty payment. Reissue companies such as Real Gone and Proper have risen to take huge advantage. Available now are multi-disc sets of a given artist's complete early albums, seven, eight, twenty-four at a time, plus singles and rare broadcasts. To save cash these come in a single jewel case box with no notes and just the simplest of track listings. They are regularly offered for the bargain basement price of less than £10.

The lists of recommend listening that follow offer a mix of both the classic albums referred to in the text along with a selection of bargain compilations of an artist's early albums. Where appropriate I have also included a number of first class and often extensive overview compilation sets that will give the listener all they need to hear on a given avenue of interest, sub-form or speciality.

Selections are listed by chapter and where an artist is referred to in more than one chapter so too may my recommended listening selections.

The future of recorded music, however, is no longer here. The keeping by collectors of examples of relevant albums in vinyl and CD form is on the cusp of being over. In the twenty-first century ownership of physical copies of recordings has ceased to be a viable practice. In its place is the digital music file.

These tiny arrangements of binary information were at first actually owned and stored locally on iPods, iPads, digital jukeboxes, mp3 players, smartphones, tablets and desktop computers. Increasingly, though, they are being stored off site in the digital cloud or, music's ultimate fate, made available by providers online anywhere and everywhere. Music which you don't own but simply rent or borrow is streamed to your local device. That can be your computer speaker system, your in-car entertainment centre, digital watch, TV or Sonos-style home Wi-Fi music system. Wave your hand and it's there.

Everything that has ever been recorded, anywhere in the world, is now instantly available. It is playable at a press or a click. It is often free, supported by advertising, but where that doesn't hold then it is always inexpensive. The future is not the album either, but the track. The single returns. Stripped of its long player context the solo song has once more become dominant.

There are debates in progress about sound quality, about the frequencies lost when a music file is compressed, about the warmth of vinyl that digital music cannot replicate, about the slippery ease of selecting things this way. But these will in time be resolved or, at worst, accommodated.

The bridge could well be the playlist. Log onto Spotify, Apple Music, Deezer, Amazon Prime, Google Play or one of the other leading online music streamers, for example, and you can find selections of an artists' best made by fans, fanatics, insiders and even the artists themselves. Following the chapter selections below I offer my own *The Roots Of Rock* playlist of 60 must-hear tracks. Try those. Then hunt around for the albums those tracks came from. It's all out there. Just listen.

Chapter 1 • Howlin' Wolf In City Road
Howlin' Wolf • *The Complete RPM & Chess Singles As & Bs 1951-62* (3CD), Acrobat
Howlin' Wolf • *The Real Folk Blues / More Real Folk Blues,* Import Music Services
Various Artists • *Land of a Thousand Dances* • All Twisting Edition, Ace
Big Bill Broonzy • *Four Classic Albums Plus (Big Bill's Blues / Big Bill Broonzy Sings The Blues / Folk Blues / The Blues),* Avid Roots
Big Bill Broonzy • *The Big Bill Story* (3CD), Verve

Champion Jack Dupree • *Two Classic Albums Plus 40s & 50s Singles (Blues From The Gutter / Natural & Soulful Blues* (2CD), Avid Roots
Champion Jack Dupree • *Champion Jack Dupree of New Orleans*, Storyville
John Lee Hooker • *Eight Classic Albums* (4CD), Real Gone Music
John Lee Hooker • *Blues From The Motor City*, Sagablues
John Lee Hooker • *The Complete '50s Chess Recordings* (2CD), Chess

Chapter 2 • Back In The 1950s UK
Kingston Trio • *Close Up and Sold Out* (2CD), Jasmine Records
Kingston Trio• *Leaders of the 60's Folk Revolution* (2CD), Jasmine Records
Various Artists • *The Best of British Rock and Roll* (3CD), Odeon
Various Artists • *Rock 'n' Skiffle* • *Brit Beat Beginnings* (4CD), Proper Records
Various Artists • *The First Rock and Roll Record* (3CD), Famous Flames
Various Artists• *British Stars of the 50s,* Xtra
Tommy Steele • *Rock With The Caveman* (2CD), Decca
Various Artists • *Mum and Dad Bought Their Records At Woollies* (2CD), (Embassy Records) Cedar
Various Artists • *The Embassy Records Story* • various volumes, Embassy

Chapter 3 • Bill Haley Reaches Cardiff General
Bill Haley • *The Early Years 1947-1954* (2CD), JSP
Bill Haley and the Comets • *Seven Classic Albums plus Bonus Singles* (4CD), Real Gone Music
Bill Haley & Friends • *The Story of Rock Around The Clock* (2CD), Hydra Records
Elvis Presley • *The King of Rock and Roll – The Complete 50s Masters* (5CD), Sony
Gene Vincent • *The Absolutely Essential 3 CD Collection* (3CD), Big 3
Cliff Richard • *The Rock and Roll Years* (2CD), Go Entertain
Little Richard • *The Original British Hit Singles*, Ace
Various Artists • *Fifty Rock and Roll Originals* (2 CD), Performance

Chapter 4 • The Down and Out Blues?
Chris Barber • *Just About As Good As It Gets! The Original Jazz Recordings 1951-1957* (2CD), Smith & Co
Chris Barber • *Just About As Good As It Gets! The Original Jazz Recordings 1954-1962 Vol 2* (2CD), Smith & Co
Ken Colyer • *The Original Jazz Recordings 1950-1956* (2CD), Smith & Co
Cyril Davies • *Preachin' The Blues* • *The Cyril Davies Memorial Album* (2CD), GVC

Alexis Korner's Blues Incorporated • *R&B from the Marquee*, Radioactive
Downliners Sect • *The Sect*, Repertoire
John Lee Hooker • *Don't Turn Me From Your Door*, Rhino
Sonny Boy Williamson • *The Best of Sonny Boy Williamson* (Rice Miller), Spectrum Audio
Various Artists• *Hoochie Coochie Men, A History of British Blues & R&*(4CD), Indigo. Includes just about everyone including Cyril Davies and his R&B Allstars.

Chapter 5 • Trying To Play A Stringed Instrument
Sonny Terry • *Sonny Terry's New Sound: Jawharp in Blues & Folk Music*, Folkways
Various Artists• *The Singer Songwriter Project*, Elektra
Various Artists • *Vigilante Man: Gems From The Topic Vaults 1954-1962* (2CD), One Day Music
Graham Bond Organisation • *Wade In The Water* (4CD), Repertoire
Bob Dylan • *Bob Dylan*, Columbia/Sony
Davy Graham • *Folk, Blues & Beyond* (Extra Tracks), Les Cousins

Chapter 6 • How The Blues Made It To The UK
The Rolling Stones • *12 x 5*, Decca
The Four Pennies • *The Very Best of the Four Pennies*, Spectrum Audio
Various Artists • *201 Blues Hits* (10CD) 201 Hits – a bargain set of post-war electric blues
Various Artists • *Before The Blues – the Early American Black Music Scene*, Yazoo
Various Artists • *Essential Delta Blues* (2CD), Not Now Music
Various Artists • *Definitive Delta Blues* (3CD), Not Now Music
WC Handy • *WC Handy's Memphis Blues Band*, Memphis Archives
Various Artists • *The Great Women Blues Singers* (2CD), Retro
Various Artists • *I Can't Be Satisfied – Early American Women Blues Singers Vol I* – Country, Yazoo
Various Artists • *I Can't Be Satisfied – Early American Women Blues Singers Vol 2* – Town, Yazoo
Various Artists • *The History Of Rhythm & Blues Volume 1 – The Pre-War Years 1925-1942* (4CD), Rhythm & Blues Records
Various Artists • *The History of Rhythm and Blues Volume 2 – 1942-1952* (3CD), Rhythm & Blues Records
Various Artists • *History Of Rhythm & Blues Volume 3 – Rocknroll Years 1952-1957* (4CD), Rhythm & Blues Records
Various Artists • *Chicago Blues: The Absolutely Essential 3CD Collection* (3CD), Big 3
Various Artists • *American Folk Blues Festival '62-'65:* Highlights, Evidence
Howlin' Wolf • *The Complete RPM & Chess Singles As & Bs 1951-62* (3CD),

Acrobat
Elvis Presley • *Elvis Blues*, RCA
Willie Dixon • *The Chess Box* (2CD), Chess
The Bonzo Dog Band • *The Doughnut In Granny's Greenhouse*, EMI

Chapter 7 • Getting To The USA
Various Artists • *British Invasion Gold* (2CD), Hip-O
Sue Foley • *Where The Action Is*, Shanachie
Wynton Marsalis • Majesty of the Blues, Sony
Various Artists • *Bob Dylan's Greenwich Village* (2CD), Chrome Dreams
Various Artists • *The Greenwich Village Folk Scene – 60 Songs From The American Folk Revival* (3CD), Not CD
Fred Neil • *Tear Down the Walls / Bleecker & MacDougal*, Elektra
Dave Van Ronk • *Down In Washington Square, The Smithsonian Folkways Collection* (3CD), Smithsonian Folkways
Bob Dylan • *Bob Dylan*, Columbia/Sony
Harry Belafonte • *The Midnight Special*, Wounded Bird

Chapter 8 • Bluegrass Number One
The Byrds • *Sweethearts of the Rodeo* (extra tracks), Columbia/Legacy
Various Artists • *25 Greatest Bluegrass Hits* (not the same as my cassette tape but still pretty good), CMH Records
Various Artists • *Absolutely Bluegrass – Over Eighty Classic Bluegrass Tracks* (3CD), Delta Leisure
Bill Monroe • *The Music of Bill Monroe 1936-1994* (4CD), MCA Nashville
Earl Flatt & Lester Scruggs • *16 Biggest Hits*, Columbia/Legacy
The Everly Brothers • *Songs Our Daddy Taught Us*, Ace
The Everly Brothers • *The Definitive Everly Brothers* (2CD), WSM
The Everly Brothers • *Walk Right Back, The Everly Brothers On Warner Bros. 1960 to 1969* (2CD), Warner Archives
The Louvin Brothers • *20 All-Time Greatest Hits*, Tee Vee Records
Various Artists • O *Brother, Where Art Thou?* (soundtrack), Mercury/Lost Highway
Doyle Lawson & Quicksilver • *Gospel Parade,* Sugar Hill Records
Doyle Lawson & Quicksilver • *The Hard Game of Love*, Sugar Hill Records
Charlie Waller and the Country Gentlemen • *Crying In The Chapel*, Freeland Records
The Osborne Brothers • *Once More Vols 1 and 2,* Sugar Hill Records
The Primitive Quartet • *The Best of the Primitive Quartet*, Mountain Heritage
Doc Watson • *Best of the Sugar Hill Years,* Americana Master Series, Sugar Hill Records
Dr Ralph Stanley & The Clinch Mountain Boys • *Live at McCabe's Guitar Shop,* DCN

Chapter 9 • Bluegrass Number Two

Raymond Fairchild and the Frosty Mountain Boys • *Mama Likes Bluegrass Music*, Rural Rhythm

Frank Buchanan, Raymond Fairchild with the Crowe Brothers • *Picking and Singing in Maggie Valley*, Fairchild

Roscoe Holcomb • *An Untamed Sense of Control*, Smithsonian Folkways Recordings

Chapter 10 • Bluegrass In Pontypridd

The Cherryholmes • *Cherryholmes*, Skaggs Family Records

The Cherryholmes• *Cherryholmes II* • *Black and White*, Skaggs Family Records

The Cherryholmes • *Cherryholmes III – Don't Believe,* Skaggs Family Records

The Cherryholmes • *Cherryholmes IV – Common Threads*, Skaggs Family Records

Various Artists • *Celtic Folk From Wales*, Arc Music

Various Artists • *Gwlad Y Delyn*, Sain

Robin Huw Bowen • *Harp Music of Wales*, Saydisc

Nansi Richards • *Brenhines Y Delyn*, Sain

Meredydd Evans • *Welsh Folk Songs*, Folkways

Gorky's Zygotic Mynci • *Spanish Dance Troupe,* Mantra

Chapter 11 • The Irish Connection

Leonard Cohen • *Live In London*, (2CD), Sony Music

Georgia Ruth • *Week Of Pines*, Gwymon Records

Seán Ó Riada • *Seoda an Riadaigh – The Essential Collection* (3CD). Gael Linn features Ó Riada film music, a selection from Ceoltóirí Chualann (the predecessors of The Chieftains) and the music score of The Playboy of the Western World.

Various Artists • *Music In Ireland – Experiencing Music, Expressing Culture*, The CD from the book and CD set. Oxford University Press.

The Chieftains • *Further Down The Old Plank Road*, RCA

Dessie O'Halloran • *The Pound Road*, IML

Sharon Shannon • *Diamond Mountain Sessions*, Grapevine

Alan Stivell • *Renaissance of the Celtic Harp*, Import Music Services

Johnny Cash • *American IV, The Man Comes Around*, UMC

Chapter 12 • Flying to Nashville • Country Music's Heart

Bob Dylan • *Nashville Skyline*, Columbia/Sony

Chet Atkins • *8 Classic Albums* (4CD), Real Gone

George Jones • *The Essential George Jones: The Spirit of Country* (2CD), Sony

Various Artists • *The Music of Nashville – Original Soundtrack,* Decca / Big Machine

Taylor Swift • *Taylor Swift*, Virgin / EMI

The Fisk Jubilee Singers • *The Gold and Blue Album*, Folkways
Various Artists • *Grand Ole Opry 75th Anniversary*, MCA
The Byrds • *Sweetheart Of The Rodeo – Remastered* (2CD), Columbia Legacy
Charlie Worsham • *Rubberband*, Warner Brothers
Sara Haze • *My Personal Sky*, Strategic Alliance Records America
Del McCoury Band • *The Streets of Baltimore*, McCoury Music
Connie Smith • *The Essential Connie Smith*, RCA
John Conlee • *Harmony and American Faces*, Tbird Americana
Moe Bandy • *Best of the Best*, Starday
The Willis Clan • *Chapter Two – Boots*, The Willis Clan Records
Scotty McCreery • *See You Tonight,* Wrasse Records
Various Artists • *Live At The Bluebird Café* (Steve Earle, Townes Van Zandt,
    Guy Clark), Snapper Classics
Various Artists • *The Nashville Sound – Country Music's Golden Era* (4CD),
    Proper Records
Various Artists • *Historic RCA Studio B*, RCA
Various Artists • *Country Outlaws* (3CD), Not Now Music
Garth Brooks • *Ultimate Hits* (2CD & IDVD), Sony
Various Artists• *The Rough Guide to Americana*, RGNet
Various Artists • *Alt Country*, Simitar

Chapter 13 • Memphis • Only Just Tennessee
David Ackles • *The Road To Cairo,* Elektra
Various Artists • *The Memphis Jukebox Vol 1*, Vee-Tone Records
Various Artists • *The Memphis Jukebox Vol 2*, Vee-Tone Records
Various Artists • *It Came from Memphis – The Legendary Sounds of Memphis*,
    (2CD), Manteca
Elvis Presley • *Elvis At Sun*, Sony
Sleepy John Estes • *Complete Works Vol 1*, Document
Sleepy John Estes • *Complete Works Vol 2*, Document
Sleepy John Estes• *Goin' To Brownsville*, Testament
Various Artists • *Stax 50th Anniversary Celebration* (2CD), Stax
Jerry Lee Lewis • *A Whole Lotta…The Definitive Retrospective* (4CD), Salvo
Cream • *The very best of Cream*, Polygram
Booker T. & The MG's • *Green Onions,* Atlantic
Booker T. & The MG's • *McLemore Avenue*, Stax
Various Artists • *Sun Rockabilly – The Essential Recordings¸* Continental
The Rolling Stones • *Singles Collection – The London Years* (3CD), London
Memphis Slim • *Rockin' The House – The Best of the R&B Years* (2CD), Fantastic
    Voyage

Chapter 14 • Memphis • Where Sun Shines Everyday
Elvis Presley • *The King of Rock and Roll – The Complete 50s Masters* (5CD),

Sony
Bill Black's Combo • *Smokin* (2CD), Jasmine
Various Artists • *Sun Records – The Essential Collection* (3CD), Union
    Square
Various Artists • *The Sun Blues Story* (3CD), One Day Music
Various Artists • *The Roots of Presley,* Catfish
Various Artists • *Sun Record Company – Good Rockin' Tonight. The Legacy of
    Sun Records*, Sire
Paul Simon • *Graceland*, Sony
Mark Cohn • *Mark Cohn*, Atlantic
Merle Haggard • *My Farewell To Elvis*, MCA
No More Kings • *NMK III*, Deaf Eye Music
Richard Thomson • *Watching The Dark* (3CD), Hannibal
Elvis Presley • *From Elvis Presley Boulevard, Memphis, Tennessee*, RCA

Chapter 15 • Clarksdale
Jimmy Cotton • *Dealing With The Devil's Music – Bluesmen in Britain,* Lake
    (includes music by others including Memphis Slim and Speckled Red but
    also Jimmy Cotton's two Chris Barber Eps)
James Cotton • *Best of the Verve Years*, Verve
Jimmy Page and Robert Plant • *Walking Into Clarksdale*, Virgin
Peetie Wheatstraw • *The Complete Recorded Works in Chronological Order, Vol 2,
    1934-1935*, Document
Sleepy John Estes • *Broke and Hungry*, Delmark
Muddy Waters • *You Shook Me – The Chess Masters Vol 3, 1958-1963* (3CD),
    Chess
Robert Johnson • *King of the Delta Blues Singers*, RCA
Peter Green Splinter Group • *Me & The Devi,* (3CD), Snapper – contains 2
    CDs of Green's take on Johnson and then a CD of Robert Johnson
    originals
Eric Clapton • *Me and Mr Johnson*, Reprise
John Hammond Jnr • *At The Crossroads – The Blues of Robert Johnson*,
    Vanguard
Muddy Waters • *Down On Stovall's Plantation*, Doxy
Davis Coen • *Jukebox Classic*, Soundview

Chapter 16 • Tupelo
John Lee Hooker • *Country Blues of John Lee Hooker*, Concord
Gene Simmons • *I Done Told You*, Charly
Ray Harris • *Ray Harris and Friends – Mississippi Rockers*, El Toro
Elvis Presley • *Elvis At Sun*, Sony
Elvis Presley • *The Complete '68 Comeback Special* (4CD), RCA
Elvis Presley, *From Elvis In Memphis* (2CD) The American Recordings.

RCA Legacy
Johnny Cash • *American Recordings,* American Recordings
Neil Diamond • *12 Songs*, Sony
Neil Diamond • *Home Before Dark*, Columbia

Chapter 17 • The Death of Elvis in Wales

Joan Baez • *Farewell Angelina: Remastered,* Vanguard
Elvis Presley • *Forty Greatest Hits,* Greatest Hits
Fabian • *I'm A Man. 5 Albums. 1959-1961* (2CD), Jasmine Records
Cliff Richard • *Hot Hundred* (4CD) Import
Conway Twitty • *Six Classic Albums plus Singles* (4CD), Real Gone
Ral Donner • *The Complete Ral Donner* (2CD), Sequel
Phil Ochs • *Rehearsals for Retirement / Gunfight at Carnegie Hall* (2CD), Collectors Choice
Various Artists • *Tribute To Elvis Presley,* (includes El Vez & others) (3CD), Doppelganger
Various Artists • *Welcome to Fabulous Porthcawl,* The Elvis Festival CD
Bukka White • *Fixin' To Die*, Complete Blues

Chapter 18 • The Alabama Music Hall Of Fame

Linda Russell, Ridley Enslow, Steve Schneider, & Julianne Baird • *Stephen Foster Songs,* Albany
Michael Jackson • *Thriller*, Epic
Alabama • *Original Album Classics* (5CD), Sony
The Eagles • *The Studio Albums* (6CD), Rhino
Lynyrd Skynyrd • *Greatest Hits*, Island
Lynyrd Skynyrd • *Live In Cardiff 1975*, Plastic Soho
The Doobie Brothers • *The Very Best of the Doobie Brothers*, Rhino
Dion and the Belmonts • *Six Classic Albums Plus Bonus Singles* (4CD), Real Gone
Various Artists • *This Is 80s Hair Metal* (3CD), Cleopatra
Various Artists • *Country and West Coast – The Birth of Country Rock*, Big Beat
Bob Dylan • Nashville Skyline, Columbia

Chapter 19 • The Shoals

The Rolling Stones • *December's Children (and Everybody's)*, Decca
The Beatles • *Please Please Me,* EMI
Various Artists • *The Fame Studios Story – 1961-1973* (3CD plus book), Kent
Various Artists• *Muscle Shoals – Original Motion Picture Soundtrack*, Republic, 2013

Chapter 20 • I'm in Love With A Knoxville Girl

The Cherryholmes • *Cherryholmes II – Black and White*, Skaggs Family

Records

Various Artists • *Paramount Old Time Recordings*, (contains Arthur Tanner's Knoxville Girl) JSP

The Blue Sky Boys • *Legends of Country Music* (3CD), Proper

Charlie Feathers • *Legend of Rockabilly*, Bringin Music

Nick Cave and the Bad Seeds & PJ Harvey • *Henry Lee,* Mute

Billy Bob Thornton and the Boxmasters • *The Boxmasters*, Edsel

Louvin Brothers • *Tragic Songs of Life*, Righteous

Charlie Louvin • *Charlie Louvin*, Tompkins Square

The Everly Brothers • *Songs Our Daddy Taught Us*, Ace

Bob Dylan • *The Times They Are A-Changing*, Columbia / Sony

Norma Waterson & Martin Carthy • *Fishes and Fine Yellow Sand,* Topic

Almeda Riddle • *Granny Riddle's Songs and Ballads*, Minstrel Records

Various Artists • *Inside Llewyn Davis* (soundtrack), Nonesuch

Chapter 21 • Asheville

Hot Club of Cowtown • *What Makes Bob Holler*, Proper Records

Bob Wills & His Texas Playboys • *Take Me back To Tulsa* (4CD), Properbox

Milton Brown and his Musical Brownies • *Daddy of Western Swing* (4CD), Delko

Root Boy Slim and The Sex Change Band • *Root Boy Slim and the Sex Change Band*, Warner

Chapter 22 • The Blue Ridge Mountains

Various Artists • *An Hour With Cecil Sharp and Ashley Hutchings*, Music By Mail

Various Artists • *An Anthology of American Folk Music* edited by Harry Smith (6CD), Smithsonian

Chapter 23 • Pigeon Forge

Various Artists • *Country Gospel*, Dynamic

Ray Charles • *Pure Genius: The Complete Atlantic Recordings* (7CD), Warner Classics

Gary Davis • *The Rev Gary Davis At Home & Church (1962-1967)* (3CD), Guitar Workshop

Gary Davis • *The Sun Of Our Life – Solos, Songs, a Sermon 1955-1957,* World Arbiter

Shawn Camp • *Fireball¸* Emergent

Shawn Camp & Billy Burnett • *The Bluegrass Elvises*, Emergent

The Tennessee Mafia Jug Band • *Poor Leroy's Almanack*, Spring Fed

Chapter 24 • Slick Fisher Road

Various Artists • *Cold Mountain – Music From The Miramax Motion Picture*, Sony

The Steep Canyon Rangers • *Steep Canyon Rangers*, Rebel
The Steep Canyon Rangers • *Lovin' Pretty Women*, Rebel
The Steep Canyon Rangers • *Mr Taylor's New Home*, Rebel
The Steep Canyon Rangers• *One Dime At A Time*, Rebel
The Steep Canyon Rangers • *Deep In The Shade*, Rebel
The Steep Canyon Rangers • *Nobody Knows You*, Rounder
The Steep Canyon Rangers• *Tell The Ones I Love*, Rounder
Steve Martin and the Steep Canyon Rangers featuring Edie Brickell • *Live* (2CD), PBS
Steve Martin and The Steep Canyon Rangers • *Rare Bird Alert*, Decca

Chapter 25 • Dollywood
Dolly Parton • *Blue Smoke* • *The Best Of* (2CD), Sony
Dolly Parton • *The Bluegrass Collection*, Camden
Marty Raybon • *Southern Roots & Branches*, Rural Rhythm
The Blackwood Brothers • *Gospel Heritage Series*, Varese Fontana
Various Artists • *Southern Gospel Jubilee*, Crossroads Records
Various Artists • *Saving Grace* • *A Southern Gospel Collection*, Day

Chapter 26 • It's All Made of Wood
Diana Jones • *Museum of Appalachia Recordings*, Proper Records
Roy Acuff • *Four Classic Albums Plus Singles* (4CD), Real Gone Music
The Osborne Brothers • *Osborne Brothers 2* (1968-1974), Bear Family Records
Greenbrier • *Smoky Mountain Memories – The Tradition Continues*, Greenbrier Records
Greenbrier • *Preaching The Fire Down*, Greenbrier
Dave Adkins • *Nothing To Lose*, Mountain Fever Records
Edgar Loudermilk • *My Big Chance Tomorrow*, Mountain Fever Records
The Little Roy & Lizzy Show • *Pop! Goes The Banjo*, Vine

Chapter 27 • The Big Bang
Eck Robertson • *Old Time Texas Fiddler 1922-1929*, County
Fiddlin' John Carson • *Complete Recorded Works Vol 1, 1923-1924*, Document
Ernest V Stoneman • *The Unsung Father of Country Music 1925-1934* (3CD), 5 String
Various Artists • *Bristol Sessions, Historic Recordings From Bristol*, Tennessee (2CD), CMHF – contains Jimmie Rodgers and Carter Family
Various Artists • *The Bristol Sessions 1927/1928, Country Music's Big Bang* (4CD), JSP – everything else
Emmylou Harris • *Wrecking Ball*, Nonesuch
St. Paul & The Broken Bones • *Half The City*, Single Lock
Red Molly • *The Red Album*, Red Molly

Loves It • *All We Are*, Loves It
Balsam Range • *Five*, Mountain Home
Flat Lonesome • *Too*, Mountain Homes
Town Mountain • *Leave The Bottle*, Pinecastle
Parker Millsap • *Parker Millsap*, Okrahoma
Westwend • *Linger For A While*, Ante Flow Records
Frank Fairfield • *Out On The Open West*, Tompkins Square

Chapter 28 • Nashville Again
Johnny Cash • *The Man In Black, The Definitive Collection*, Sony
Johnny Cash • *Twenty Original Albums*, Columbia/Sony
Johnny Cash • *American Recordings*, American Recordings
Rhonda Vincent • *Only Me* (2CD) Vincent
Willie Nelson • *Legend* • *The Best Of*, Sony
The Lone Bellow • *The Lone Bellow*, Red UK
LP • *Forever For Now*, Warner
George Jones • *The Essential George Jones* (2CD), Sony
Various Artists • *The Quiller Memorandum Vol 1 – 22 Songs from the Pens of Felice & Boudleaux Bryant*, Fantastic Voyage
Eddy Arnold • *America's Most Successful Country & Western Star* (10CD), Documents

Chapter 29 • The Stetson and the Country Singer's Clothes
Gene Autry • *The Essential Recordings* (2CD), Primo
Roy Rodgers • *The Best Of*, Music Digital
Cowboy Copas • *Songs That Made Him Famous*, Righteous
Dwight Yokham • *The Platinum Collection*, Rhino
Alan Jackson • *The Greatest Hits Collection*, Sony
George Strait • *50 Numbers Ones* (2CD), Import
Clint Black • *Greatest Hits*, Sony
Brad Paisley • *This Is Country Music*, Sony
Garth Brooks • *Ultimate Hits* (2CD & IDVD), Sony
Porter Waggoner • *Green Green Grass Of Home – A Singles Collection 1961-1980* (2CD) SPV Yellow
Porter Waggoner & Dolly Parton • *Essential Porter & Dolly*, SBME
The Byrds • *Sweetheart Of The Rodeo – Remastered* (2CD), Columbia Legacy
The Flying Burrito Brothers • *The Gilded Palace of Sin*, 4menwithbeards

Chapter 30 • What's The Bluegrass Scene Like Where You Come From?
Jerry Douglas • *The Best Kept Secret*, Koch
Charlotte Greig • *At Llangennith*, Harmonium
Amy Allison • *The Maudlin Years*, Koch

Chris Moreton • *Not Strictly Bluegrass*, Moreton

Chapter 31 • Shake It And Break It
Air • *Moon Safari*, EMI
Charley Patton • *Complete Recordings, 1929-1934* (4CD), JSP
Captain Beefheart • *Safe As Milk*, Sony
Captain Beefheart • *Strictly Personal*, Liberty/EMI
Grateful Dead • *Grateful Dead*, WB/Rhino
Big Bill Broonzy • *Four Classic Albums Plus* (*Big Bill's Blues / Big Bill Broonzy
Sings The Blues / Folk Blues / The Blues*), Avid Roots
Big Bill Broonzy • *The Big Bill Story* (3 CD), Verve
The Byrds • *Sweethearts of the Rodeo* (extra tracks), Columbia/Legacy
The Flying Burrito Brothers • *The Gilded Palace of Sin*, 4menwithbeards
Steeleye Span • *The Lark In The Morning* • *The Early Years* (2CD), Castle Music
Fairport Convention • *Liege And Leif*, Island
Pogues • *The Best Of The Pogues*, Rhino
Moving Hearts • *Moving Hearts*, Warner
The Chieftains • *The Wide World Over*, Sony
Mississippi John Hurt • *Complete Studio Recordings Remastered* (3CD), Vanguard

The Roots of Rock Playlist. 61 Tracks You Have To Hear
The Shadows • *Apache*
Howlin' Wolf • *Down In The Bottom*
Big Bill Broonzy • *Joe Turner's Blues*
John Lee Hooker • *Boogie Chillen*
Kingston Trio • *O Ken Karanga*
Lonnie Donegan • *Rock Island Line*
Bill Haley and the Comets • *Rock Around The Clock*
Cliff Richard • *Move It*
Cyril Davies and his Rhythm & Blues All Stars • *Country Line Special*
Sonny Boy Williamson • *Help Me*
Bob Dylan • *In My Time Of Dyin'*
Davy Graham • *Angi*
The Rolling Stones • *2120 South Michigan Avenue*
T-Bone Walker • *Mean Old World*
Wynton Marsalis • *The Majesty of the Blues*
Fred Neil • *Bleecker and McDougal*
Bill Monroe • *Blue Moon of Kentucky*
Stanley Brothers • *A Man of Constant Sorrow*
Raymond Fairchild • *Orange Blossom Special*
Roscoe Holcomb • *I Am A Man of Constant Sorrow*
The Cherryholmes • *Don't Give Your Heart to a Knoxville Girl*
Meredydd Evans • *Bugeilio'r Gwenith Gwyn*

Doc Watson • *The Fisherman's Hornpipe*
Dessie O'Halloran • *Say Way You Love Me*
Patsy Cline • *Crazy*
George Jones • *He Stopped Loving Her Today*
David Ackles • *The Road To Cairo*
Sleepy John Estes • *Milk Cow Blues*
Booker T. & the MG's • *Green Onions*
Bill Black Combo • *Smokey Part Two*
Elvis Presley • *Mystery Train*
Jimmy Cotton • *Polly Put The Kettle On*
Robert Johnson • *Ramblin On My Mind*
John Lee Hooker• *Tupelo*
Ray Harris • *Come On Little Mama*
Ral Donner • *You Don't Know What You've Got*
Bukka White • *Fixin' To Die*
Alabama • *Mountain Music*
Dion • (I Was) *Born To Cry*
Arthur Alexander • *You Better Move On*
Aretha Franklin • *I Never Loved A Man (The Way I Love You)*
The Louvin Brothers • *Knoxville Girl*
The Everly Brothers • *Down In The Willow Garden*
Bob Wills and his Texas Playboys • *The Waltz You Saved For Me*
Root Boy Slim and The Sex Change Band • *I'm Not Too Old For You*
Uncle Dave Macon and The Fruit Jar Drnkers • *Wreck of the Tennessee Gravy Train*
Shawn Camp • *Fireball*
Rev Gary Davis • *Candy Man*
The Steep Canyon Rangers • *The Road To Knoxville*
Steve Martin & The Steep Canyon Rangers • *Rare Bird Alert*
Dolly Parton • *Jolene*
Diana Jones • *O Sinner*
Greenbrier • *I'm In Love With A Knoxville Girl*
Eck Robertson • *Sally Goodin*
Carter Family • *The Wandering Boy*
Johnny Cash • *Cry Cry Cry*
Gram Parsons • *Love Hurts*
The Byrds • *Hickory Wind*
Flying Burrito Brothers • *Do Right Woman*
Charley Patton • *Jesus is A Dying Bed Maker*
The Chieftains • *Did You Ever Go-A-Courtin' / Will The Circle Be Unbroken*

Notes

1. *Apache Mania* Magic Records 3930412 (2004) compiled by Jean Bachèlerie.
2. See The Penarth Con Club in *Real Cardiff Three – The Changing City* by Peter Finch. Seren (2009).
3. Today the dominant feature is the kebab shop supplemented by multi-cultural restaurants, fast food outlets and men's hairdressers.
4. A 'woodie' was a car with its rear panels infilled with wood. Examples include the Buick Roadmaster and the Ford Country Squire. Such vehicles were popular with Beach Boy era surfers.
5. In 2013 the Britain amended the law on copyright in respect of sound recordings. It extended the period of protection from 50 to 70 years. This meant that the practise of recorded material entering the public domain now ended at 31.12.1962. This practise had effectively removed any payment to artist obligation from companies wanting to reissue pre-31.12.1962 material as a commercial product. However the new law meant that the hits of, 1963 would not become copyright free until 2034. The Beatles were safe. Elvis, however, at least in his rock and roll splendour, was not. Much depends on how you look at it. *The Complete 50s Studio Releases* in a boxed set of 4 CDs for £10 sounds good deal to me. As does Duane Eddy's *6 Classic Albums Plus Bonus Singles and Session Tracks* – "digitally remastered and enhanced for superior quality" – all for around £6. Shift forward twelve months to 1963 and the price of reissues more than doubles.
6. For a great sample of just how the station came across the airwaves try *The Sound of Fury: Billy Fury with The Tornados. The Radio Luxembourg Sessions.* These were captured by an obsessive with a tape machine recording the original broadcast under typical British reception conditions. How it all used to be is here again, wavering, fading, swaying back. *Halfway to Paradise, Wondrous Place, Last Night was Made For Love.* 1962 all over again. Castle Music double CD CMQDD1170.
7. In Szwed, John, *The Man Who Recorded The World – A Biography of Alan Lomax*, Arrow, 2010.
8 This is a line in Tom Russell's song *Haley's Comet:* "'Do you know who I am?' said Bill Haley, In a pancake house down near the Rio Grande, Well the waitress said, 'I don't know you from diddley....To me you look like one more tired old man'." *The Wounded Heart of America*, HighTone Records 2007.
9. Denmark Street in London, the British Tin Pan Alley and centre of the traditional music trade.
10. D.A. – lit duck's arse, a term which describes the Fifties practice of combing the hair on the back of the head to resemble a duck's rear.
11. PrinzSound products were imported from the Far East but branded with what Dixon's management thought as a German-sounding name. The products of

Japan had yet to prove their worth. They soon would.

12. A rock and roll send-up record made by the Goons in 1956. On the other side was *The Ying Tong Song*.

13. CP Lee, *Ewan MacColl: The People's Friend?* North West Labour History (www.workershistory.org).

14. As quoted by Ian Inglis in *Popular Music: History, Place and Time*, Ashgate Publishing, 2006.

15. Russel Ward (editor), *the Penguin Book of Australia Ballads*, 1964.

16. Young, Neil, *A Letter Home*, Warner Brothers 2014.

17. This is what he told me he'd been during the War. I was to learn later that the Poles, the ones I came into contact with, had a propensity for exaggeration. They were nearly all former cavalry officers, fighter aces or émigré members of the lost Polish aristocracy. Their country had been treated like a football. If I'd been Polish I'm sure I would have claimed similar things for self.

18. With Anne Hemmingway, Graham Hemmingway would later form one half of the now highly regarded psychedelic folk duo Sun Also Rises.

19. Brian Lee, 'The Pub where the old boys would gather for their scrumpy', Media Wales, 2013.

20. Performed by The Rolling Stones in the studio on that one occasion and never performed again.

21. A single-stringed primitive instrument used in the rural South, initially by children. It consisted of a single string of bailing twine nailed to a piece of wood with an empty bottle acting as a bridge.

22. Jelly Roll Morton hotly disputes this claiming that it was he, Morton, who first wrote down and copyrighted the blues.

23. There is only one surviving photograph of Blind Lemon Jefferson. In it he looks as neat as possible but his tie has been painted in by hand.

24. *second aeon*, an international literary magazine, edited by Peter Finch. It published 21 issues between 1966 and 1974.

25. http://dlib.nyu.edu/findingaids/html/fales/second_aeon/

26. The corduroy road was a variation on the plank road where highways were built of wood covered with sand. The corduroy variant used logs.

27. Sue Foley's 2002 album, on launch that night, was *Where the action is …..*, Shanachie SH8038. I had my photo taken standing next to her, all middle-aged smiles, but the Ixus flash failed to pop.

28. Richard D Smith in his *Can't You Hear Me Callin'* 2000 biography of Bill Monroe (Da Capo Press) suggests that the five-string banjo, an instrument "developed primarily in the United States" was originally called the merry-wang.

29. Strictly speaking pecks and bushels are measures of volume rather than weight. They are in the same range as dry pints, imperial fluid ounces, firlots, lippies, forpets and other designators of size and shape that are now long forgotten.

30. Bill Monroe, 1939, as quoted in *Can't You Hear Me Callin'*, Richard D Smith, Da Capo Press, 2000.

31. The practice derives from Mark: "And these signs shall follow them that believe: In my name shall they cast out devils; they shall speak with new tongues. They shall take up serpents; and if they drink any deadly thing, it shall not hurt them; they shall lay hands on the sick, and they shall recover." Most serpent handling pastors appear to die from snakebites (although this is often explained away as a heart attack or similar). Despite this inbuilt weakness to expansion the tradition appears to be holding its own.

32. Opened in 1983 by Dafydd Iwan and named after the same pont (Welsh for *bridge*) as Ponty itself.

33. Jones, Edward, *Musical and Poetical Relicks of the Welsh Bards*, 1808. https://archive.org/details/MusocalAndPoeticalRelicksOfTheWelshBards

34. Where do they start their imagining? They imagine what sounds the Romans had, they read the extant literature, they scrutinise woodcarvings and ancient relics. They listen to what might have happened in parallel ancient musics. They make educated Welsh guesses.

35. The Brian Boru or Trinity College Harp is one of only three medieval Gaelic harps in existence and the only one kept in Ireland.

36. *Further Down the Old Plank Road*, The Chieftains. Sony, 2003.

37. An academic division of Celtic language into two groups – the P Celts and the Q Celts.

38. Da Capo Press, 2001.

39. *Nashville*, directed by Robert Altman in 1975. The action is set over five days and involves around two dozen characters all following their own plot lines. The mix is a satire on the country music business and a creative triumph.

40. Edmund Havel. *Jubilee Singers at the Court of Queen Victoria*, 1873. Painting currently housed at Fisk University, Nashville.

41. Julie Driscoll, Brian Auger and the Trinity, *The Road to Cairo, 1968*.

42. *Element Man* was created by employees of Haywood Element, at the Brownsville division of the Glenn Electric Heater Corp, as an entry for the 1997 Brownsville Scarecrow competition. According to a sign the heating elements employed for the banjo were originally used locally by Tripp Country Ham to slow-cure their meat.

43. Gordon, Robert, *Respect Yourself – Stax records and the Soul Explosion*, Bloomsbury, 2014.

44. *Sitting On Top of the World* first recorded by The Mississippi Sheiks in the 1930s, rendered electric by Howlin' Wolf and then turned psychedelic by Cream in 1968 (*Wheels of Fire*). *Land of a Thousand Dances* – Wilson Pickett, a huge hit in 1966. It was actually recorded at the Fame Studios in Alabama rather than at Stax in Memphis. In the Stax studios Pickett was regarded as a difficult man.

45. As explained in Robert Gordon's *Respect Yourself – Stax Records and the Soul*

explosion, Bloomsbury, 2013.

46. Cleveland – site of WJW DJ Alan Freed's first rock and roll concert, the Moondog Coronation Ball, held at the Cleveland Arena in 1952.

47. Birthplace of Chuck Berry (1926).

48. Where Bill Haley and The Comets recorded *Rock Around The Clock* at the Pythian Temple Studios in 1954 and where, in 1922, Trixie Smith recorded *My Man Rocks me (With One Steady Roll)*, a commercial success that mentions both 'rock' and 'roll' in the same sentence. Trixie's innuendo-filled disc was not, however, the earliest to use the phrase. That honour goes to a five-inch recording of unknown singers at a religious camp meeting harmonising their love of the Lord with the line "We've been rockin' an'rolling in your arms".

49. Birthplace (1928) and home of Fats Domino who in 1952 recorded *The Fat Man*, the first number to actually sound like rock and roll.

50. Where in the 1950s there were more Teddy Boys than any other valley town and Ian Thomas was born. In the early Sixties Thomas loaned me his record collection of 7-inch rock and roll singles. These came in plastic-cased bundles of around twenty discs a time. Thomas was a fanatic with a huge collection that included, even at that early date, dozens of albums by Jerry Lee Lewis, everything Elvis had ever done plus a comprehensive range of British imitations. He introduced me not so much to Duane Eddy, Carl Perkins and Gene Vincent (whose music I'd already heard) but to the wonders of Chris Kenner (*I Like It Like That*), LaVern Baker (*Tweedle Dee*), Hardrock Gunter (*Gonna Dance All Night*) and that first and earliest *The Fat Man* by Mr Domino.

51. The Overton Park Levitt Shell was built by the US depression-era department of works as one of ywenty-seven outdoor concert stages across America. The Memphis example is one of the few still standing. There have been many attempts to demolish it, mostly to create space for car parks but through diligence, public subscription, municipal intervention and the assistance of rich benefactors these have, to date, all been repelled. The present restoration provides the base for at least fifty free concerts a year.

52. Billy Swann (b. 1942) was a songwriter who worked with Bill Black in Memphis before Black's death in 1965. He had a Billboard number one hit with *I Can Help* in 1974, moved to Nashville to become a songwriter and after some initial success faded. As I write (2014) Amazon lists nothing as available beyond a Dutch vinyl 7-inch of his #1 hit.

53. Sam Phillips called his contrived Sun echo 'slapback'.

54. So too, it seems, did his father. Jerry Lee was there, pissed and violent, outside Graceland at 2.50 am. At 4.00 am the wrecker arrived to tow away Jerry Lee's now abandoned car. Just after that Elmo Lewis, 78 years old and accompanied by a drunken friend recently released from Hernando jail, showed up, intoxicated and complaining. He was arrested later at 7.30 am for speeding and driving while under the influence. He spent two nights in jail and then failed to show for his court case. Given his surname the family should have a Welsh

connection and if you go back far enough you can find that they do. They drink more than the lads in Merthyr, however, and if the Graceland incident is anything to go by certainly do it with more style. Nick Tosches' excellent Lewis biography, *Hellfire* (Penguin, 2007) tells a while lot more.

55. "We'll just put some bleachers out in the sun" – from Bob Dylan's *Highway 61 Revisited*.

56. Lansdowne Jazz Series, *Chris Barber Presents Jimmy Cotton, Volume One and Volume Two*. Recorded 1961, released 1962. Mono. Some trombone on voumel one.

57. Gary Miller died of a heart attack in December, 2011.

58. I have to wait until 2012 for Chess to release *You Shook Me – The Chess Masters Vol 3 (1958 to 63)* to hear again Muddy at what I think is his pulsing, intense best.

59. There are at least four other intersections in Mississippi and in Tennessee that lay claim to being the Johnson crossroads. There's a story that it wasn't a road crossing but a meeting of railtracks and another that it wasn't a road at all but a graveyard. The devil, as most Christians know, sure gets around.

60. http://www.ultimate-elvis.net/ElvisHomes.html offers full details.

61. Old Saltillo Road has been renamed Elvis Presley Drive.

62. The Natchez Trace Parkway is managed by the US Federal Park Service and runs the 444 miles from Natchez, Ms to Nashville, TN. The road loosely follows the ancient bison and Native American walking routes across this part of north America. If you've ever been chicaned, blocked, tailgated and bumped on a US Interstate then you'll appreciate the cool and calm of this national park for the automobile.

63. Schumacher, Michael, *There But for Fortune: The Life of Phil Ochs*. Hyperion, 1966.

64. Ochs issued his *Gunfight At Carnegie Hall* in 1975. It contained both *A Fool Such As I* and a medley containing *My Baby Left Me, Ready Teddy, Heartbreak Hotel, All Shook Up, Are You Lonesome Tonight* and *My Baby Left Me*. As Elvis impersonation it was dire but as a performance supporting Ochs' position that the protest song no longer worked it was perfect. Ochs took his own life in Far Rockaway, New York in 1976.

65. *All The King's Men* by Eric Lott, from *Race and the Subject Of Masculinities*, Harry Stecopoulos and Michael Uebel (eds), Duke University Press, 1997.

66. *Are You Lonesome Tonight* in *Island of Lightning*, Minhinnick, Robert, Seren, 2013.

67. In his book, *The A-Z of Wales and the Welsh* (Christopher Davies, 2000) Terry Breverton makes the claim that the Presley family came from the Preseli mountains in west Wales and were in fact Welsh-speaking themselves.

68. Actually there are: OutKast's black hip hop *Decatur Psalm,* Patti LaBelle and the Bluebells' Mod-era Cameo Parkway *Decatur Street*, and even Jabbo Smith and His Rhythm Aces 1929 jazz-era *Decatur Street Tutti*.

69. Uncle Mac was Derek Ivor Breashur McCulloch (1897-1967) who played records on the BBC's *Children's Hour* on Saturday mornings for a decade from 1954.
70. Recalled by Geoff Bradford in Richard Newman's *John Mayall Blues Breaker*, Castle Communications, 1995.
71. Legitimacy totally trumped by Neil Young and Crazy Horse's barnstorming reworking on his 2012 album *Americana*.
72. America is not alone in allowing its cultural history to be replicated wherever a dollar can be turned. In Wales at Dylan Thomas's Laugharne Boathouse the reading hut doors might have been refurbished but they remain the very ones that Dylan himself used. A sign informs us of this. Down the road at the Dylan Thomas Centre in Swansea another set of genuine, original, as touched by the great poet writing hut doors stand on display in their repainted greenness. You can't get too much originality in the cultural world.
73. Wolf, Kurt, *Country Music: The Rough Guide*, Penguin, 2000.
74. http://www.planetslade.com/murder.html
75. For example: Dylan's *With God On Our Side* lifts the melody of the Irish ballad *The Merry Month of May* (via Dominic Behan's own reworking of the tune as *The Patriot Game*). *Bob Dylan's Dream* reworks the melody of the nineteenth century ballad, *Lord Franklin*.
76. Check out Bob Wills' version of *Big Beaver* an instrumental recorded in 1940 with vigorous rhythm guitar and beefy swing trumpet led choruses. Big Beaver was a dance hall where the band played in Oklahoma.
77. The A470 is a set of Welsh A-Roads joined together to form a rambling, twisting highway that connects the north with the south of the country.
78. Compendium Books traded on Camden High Street in London between 1968 and 2000. In its sixties and seventies heyday it was the centre for the literary avant garde, the British poetry revival, music, politics and alternative publications. Nick Kimberley was the manager.
79. Check Kerouac, Jack, *Book of Haikus*, Enitharmon, 2004.
80. Hot Springs website: http://hotspringsnc.org/play/relaxation/hot-mineral-springs/
81. The Warm Springs Baths are recommended in the treatment of the following diseases, and in most cases of chronic complaint will be found effectual: Rheumatism, Gout, Stiff Joints, Spinal Diseases, Sciatica, Lumbago, Paralysis, St. Vitus' Dance, and all Neuralgias and Nervous Affections; Bright's Disease, Diabetes, Goitre, Specific Locomotor Ataxy; Spurious Vaccinations, and all Blood Poisons, Alcoholism, and the use and abuse of Opiates; all diseases of the Kidneys and bladder; Uterine Diseases, as a class, especially Sterility and Climacteric ills; all Cutaneous Diseases, Scrofula, Ulcerations and Enlargements of the Glands, Catarrh or Ozaena, in all forms; General Physical Debility and mental Exhaustion; Malarial Poison, and every form of Liver Complaint; Syphilis, Mercurial Syphilis, and all types of Mercurial ills, together

with such chronic diseases where alternant and eliminative agency affords relief – from an 1880 advertisement.

82. http://www.mustrad.org.uk/articles/sharp.htm

83. In the book Bryson follows the Gatlinburg cop out with a book tour and then, feeling guilty that he hasn't done enough to satisfy his self-set task, returns to the trail again, this time several hundred miles to the north.

84. The Mandan Indians were the legendary white and Welsh-speaking tribe, supposedly descended from the Welsh Prince Madoc ab Owain Gwynedd who discovered America way before Columbus in 1170.

85. As claimed by Turkish President Recep Tayyip Erdogan in November, 2014.

86. Randall Stephens at http://www.scienceandreligiontoday.com/

87. Rosenberg, Neil V, *Bluegrass – A History*, University of Illinois Press, 2005.

88. *The Bluegrass Elvises Vol One*, Shawn Camp and Billy Burnette. Thirty Tigers, 2007.

89. The Earls of Leicester feature Jerry Douglas, Shawn Camp, Johnny Warren, Charlie Cushman, Barry Bales and Tim O'Brien.

90. *Ain't No Way of Knowin'* on The Steep Canyon Rangers: *Lovin' Pretty Women*, Rebel, 2007.

91. Not until 1992 when Witney Houston recorded the song for the film *The Bodyguard* and it went on to become the best-selling single by a woman in music history. It made Parton a lot of money, something of which she is very proud.

92. The highest peak in the Appalachians, Mount Mitchell at 6684 feet, was named after Elisha Mitchell. In 1835 he determined the mountain's height and died in a climbing accident in 1857 when he returned to verify his measurements.

93. Jones, Diana, *Museum of Appalachia Recordings*, Proper Records, 2013.

94. The HistoryAccess.com Interview: John Rice Irwin By Bob Frost. *HistoryAccess.com*, 2008.

95. The 1884 museum founded by Lt-General Augustus Pitt Rivers which displays its large archaeological and anthropological collections thematically.

96. Irwin, John Rice, *Musical Instruments of the Southern Appalachian Mountains*, Schiffer Publishing Ltd., 1979.

97. Battle of Dandridge, 1864.

98. *The Range Rider*, played in all 79 black and white 30 minute episodes by Jock Mahoney.

99. Nudie Cohn (1902-1984) was a Russian-born tailor who rose to fame making custom stage costume for Lefty Frizzell, Roy Rogers, and Dale Evans. He made the famous Elvis costumes for the singer's Las Vegas shows. His list of clients expanded rapidly to include John Wayne, Gene Autry, Cher, John Lennon, Ronald Reagan, Elton John, Robert Mitchum, Pat Buttram, Tony Curtis, Michael Landon, Glenn Campbell, Hank Snow, and Hank Williams Sr. Manuel Cuevas (b1933) began as a shirt maker and then went to work at

Nudie's making one-off country suits. He set up his own business, Manuel Couture, in 1975 and made stage clothes for Johnny Cash, Neil Young, Ernest Tubb, Marlon Brando and a hundred others. He currently operates as Manuel American Designs at 800 Broadway in Nashville.

100. Llantristant Folk Club which has been in existence for more than 35 years is one of the best programmed and lively clubs in South Wales. It runs weekly at the Pontyclun Institute and Athletic Club.

101. *A Miner's Life* as sung by Dick Gaughan and adapted by him for the 1984 miner's strike. From *True and Bold*, CM Distribution, 1986.

102. Notably In Chapters – a monthly series of performed literature and music blends and the Laugharne Festival which presents cult writing and alt music annually at the seaside town that Dylan Thomas made his own.

Index